# SCENES AND PORTRAITS

VAN WYCK BROOKS *has written:*

Published by E. P. DUTTON & Co., INC.

VAN WYCK BROOKS

*Pastel Sketch, 1909*

*by John Butler Yeats*

# SCENES AND PORTRAITS

*Memories of Childhood and Youth*

By Van Wyck Brooks

E. P. DUTTON & COMPANY, INC.

NEW YORK, 1954

Library of Congress Catalog Card Number: 54-5050

PRINTED IN THE UNITED STATES OF AMERICA
AMERICAN BOOK–STRATFORD PRESS, INC., NEW YORK

For
GLADYS,
CHARLES, KENYON
and
PETER BOUDINOT BROOKS

# CONTENTS

# SCENES AND PORTRAITS

CHAPTER I

# A WALL STREET SUBURB

MY EARLIEST friend Maxwell Perkins, my lifelong friend, used to say that every man has a novel in him. The idea was not originally his,—it was, in fact, a commonplace,— but, being a man of character, he made it his; and I always felt that he might have written a first-rate novel himself if he had ranged over his own life. He was in his way a novelist born, but instead of developing this bent in himself he devoted his intuitive powers to the development of others, leaving his mark, as everyone knows, on the fiction of his time and the work of some of its best writers. As for myself, I have never wished to write a novel. But the scenes and characters of my younger days have come to seem to me like a novel that I read long ago, and I have often thought of reviving that novel.

I was born in February, 1886, in the unloved state of New Jersey. That, like all other states, this had its lovers, I only became aware in later days; for the "old Jersey element," as I heard it called when I was a boy, was remote from the little world in which I grew up. Our families were in it but not of it,—they were inveterate New Yorkers whose local affections and pride were invested elsewhere and who lived for genera-tions there without becoming naturalized, any more than the inveterate Philadelphians across the state. The old Jersey ele-

ment had fixed immemorial ways of its own that were thought
of as generally narrow, provincial and dull, while the new-
comers had brought with them not only a current of world life
but a mind that was more complex and more aggressive. The
suburbs were all theirs and the fullness thereof; and, as their
interests and loyalties were otherwise engaged, the state had
become a prey to all manner of abuses. Yet its history had been
honourable in the days of the Boudinots and Captain Lawrence, the young man who said, "Don't give up the ship."
There lived John Woolman and Philip Freneau, there Fenimore Cooper was born, like Stephen Crane and Randolph
Bourne still later; and various eighteenth-century New Yorkers
had sent their sons to school there to learn to speak pure English undefiled. Alexander Hamilton and Aaron Burr had
studied as boys in Elizabeth, and the poet Shelley's grandfather had been a merchant in Newark where Sir Bysshe Shelley, the merchant's son, was born. But the two great cities that
flanked the state on east and west had as it were depolarized
the New Jersey mind.

My native town was Plainfield, a name that used to mortify
me in my hyperæsthetic youth, for it struck me as naive; and
I was greatly relieved when I found that the name of Tolstoy's
place, Yasnaya Polyana, meant the same thing in Russian. My
grandfather Ames had gone out there in 1869, to be near his
office in New York, building the brown stucco house with
spreading verandahs and a mansard roof in which I spent the
first years of my childhood. For my father and mother soon
abandoned the smaller house with the mansard roof in which
they had set up housekeeping after their marriage and lived
with my mother's parents from that time forward, moving after
my grandfather died into a new house on the edge of the town
that was not without some slight architectural pretensions.

This was the largish yellow brick house in which my formative years were passed and which was later characterized as "colonial outside, baronial inside" by one of the friends of our circle who passed for a wit. For the house fell at last into more affluent hands, and the new owners doubled its size and plastered it with the panels and doors of an ancient English manor-house they had bought from the Duveens. By that time too the old picket fences had been stripped away on all the streets, with the beds of canna lilies and the cast-iron fountains, the monumental urns and painted deer-hounds, and the quiet Quaker village where Woolman had preached in the meeting-house had become a full-blown Wall Street suburb. Even the name of Peace Street had vanished forever.

I little realized as a child the dramatic events that were taking place in the outwardly tranquil dwellings of our friends and neighbours so many of whom were involved in the operations of that savage and lawless epoch of American finance. The trusts were in those days being formed, oil was spouting from Western lands and the country seemed to be drunk with a passion for riches, but, as money was never spoken of, it could scarcely have occurred to us that some of these neighbours were financial buccaneers and brigands. Nor did we ever think to ask why their wives, our mothers' friends, spent so much of their time in darkened rooms, seated in Bath chairs, attended by nurses, the victims of "nervous prostration," the secrets of which the Freudians had not yet exposed. I was always instructed to walk on tiptoe through the dim corridors of one such house with which my mother was often in communication, delivering my messages to the nurse without whom this friend of our household never thought of stirring out of doors. That this was a kind of strategic protest against her husband's double life I did not become aware for many years, and I even doubt if the lady in question knew quite *how* double this life was, though she certainly knew it was far from straight or simple. Everyone was aware in time that he had escaped a prison term only because his brother had become a bondsman for him, while he had an unauthorized family somewhere else; but this was after his big steam-yacht had been swept away, as he had swept away the savings of his coachman and his servants. For years a professional "capitalist," as he called himself in *Who's Who*, he had sat in the seats of the mighty, with a whole floor at the Waldorf, and when my mother went with his family to Cuba they were received at Havana like travelling princes. For the capitalist had financed the new water-works there, and the cardinal in person showed them the ashes of Columbus, which had not yet been transferred to Santo Domingo. But when the blow fell one could only admire the code of sporting ethics with which both he and his wife played the game, reduced as they were to living in three or four rented rooms with a few remnants of silver and one good old portrait. *He* found a small clerical job in the town,—the *ne plus ultra* of humiliation,—and walked home at the day's end with a leg of mutton under his arm and a fresh carnation still in his buttonhole. *She,* moreover, after spending years fanned, like the Pope, in her invalid's chair, rose with zest and cooked the leg of mutton. Both had an air of happiness and confidence at last.

One could tell many another tale of what a French writer might have described as the grandeurs and miseries of Wall Street in this age of buccaneering, the story of another friend, for instance, a much more famous financier who had been known as one of the "Big Four." Ruined by underestimating the cost of a great municipal enterprise which he had financed in New York, he was finally obliged to retire to a Harlem

hall-bedroom, but, with a small pension from Pierpont Morgan
and a membership in his college club, he cheerfully played
the game in reminiscence. He liked to recall his old battles on
the Exchange in Broad Street and how, on a certain afternoon, between two and four o'clock, he had conjured out of
E. H. Harriman three quarters of a million. At another time he
had put together all the locomotive plants and organized the
Locomotive Trust. It was his office in which my father had a
small post towards the end of his life, after vainly endeavouring
to survive as an independent broker, a work for which he was
as ill-equipped as I would be myself, for he had no competitive
instinct whatsoever. How many other ups and downs, not to
say scandals, we heard of, muffled as they were in the reports
that reached our ears,—for one, the descent, like an empire
falling, of a certain conspicuous family we knew when the
head of the house was convicted as an embezzler and ab-
sconder. Then there was the neighbour with the cherry orchard,
a lover of children,—and we all loved him,—who vanished, as
we gathered, into prison; and another family that blossomed
out with governess-carts, tandems, grooms, liveried footmen
and a tally-ho that also vanished—whither? Vast red sandstone
houses rose, like so many Kenilworth castles, with turrets, verandahs, balconies and porte-cochères, with arches, fountains,
coach-houses, kennels and stables and with sons who had an
air of owning all creation and whose thoughts and talk were
entirely about yachting and coaching. Pathetic these boys were
destined to be, how often, when they grew up, for almost invariably their worlds collapsed about them. Some of their fathers ended like George Francis Train, who sat on a park
bench in New York, feeding the squirrels, and who, after owning steamship lines and building street railways in England,
lived in a charitable retreat for down-and-outs.

But beside the "wildcat speculators," as people used to call them, there were the quiet solid men of money, unobtrusive often to the point of being mousy, whose dwellings lined the streets in our corner of the town. No one would have supposed that they were presidents of New York banks, or perhaps of the Cotton Exchange or Western railroads, heads of large mining companies and corporations, for, millionaires almost to a man,—the town had more than a hundred of these,—they seemed to be governed by motives of protective coloration. When, later, I read the American novelists, of whom I knew nothing as a boy, I found that in the case of every character who was a big business man I could replace the original with a name from Plainfield. There was not one type whom I had not somehow known, from Howells's Silas Lapham to Tarkington's Tinker, the "plutocrat," and from Sinclair Lewis's Dodsworth to the Cowperwood of Dreiser. But, looking back, I am still convinced that Henry Adams was quite right when he said that Americans really cared little for money,—less, at least, than various other peoples,—that they pursued it only for want of other interests; for money-getting, with these neighbours of ours, while often a pursuit of power, was even more what it seemed to be, a game. It was the great sport of that epoch, as hunting grizzlies might have been, a sport not always lovely but dangerous and amusing; and the manner in which these friends accepted their losses was sometimes in the best tradition and spirit of sport. I remember the force of utter disgust with which my mother exclaimed "What's *money!*" at a certain juncture in our own family life, as if, in fact, money were too contemptible even to be thought of in comparison with some menaced human value. Yet we, at least, never had money, as our neighbours understood the word; we were sup-

posed to be poor, more or less. I believe this feeling underlay
our whole small world.

In any case, with its ups and downs, it seemed to be a stable
world, permanently supported by cast-iron customs, by a ritual of
living that was immemorial, or assumed to be, and that extended
into every corner of existence. There was even a ritual of smoking, as I remember, looking back at the complex paraphernalia
in my father's den, the only room in which he was encouraged,
behind the plush curtains that veiled his door, to perform the
elaborate mysteries of this masculine rite. Those were the days
of smoking jackets and smoking caps with buttons on top, and
my father's den was a small museum of implements for smoking, candles for lighting cigars, brass trays and pipe-racks. It
was a fixed note of my father's life that I should pick in the
garden for him a flower to stick in his buttonhole at the breakfast-table, while he had a maxim for every occasion, such as
"doing as the Romans do" or never being "the first by whom
the new is tried." When, later, he saw me wearing my trousers,
like Prufrock, with the bottoms rolled, he always said, "I see
it's raining in London"; and a code for everything accompanied
the maxims, how you should tip your soup-plate and what sort
of hat was right for an ocean voyage. He uttered his maxims
humorously and lightly but never with any real doubt that life
was based on laws and there they were, another of them being
that one might wear threadbare clothes, if need were, so long
as one's linen was utterly and immaculately fresh. Those were
the days when young men, job-hunting, wore frock coats and
top hats to make an impression even in a newspaper office; and,
while my father could never have rivalled the sartorial mag-
nificence of some of his friends, he dressed in the ceremonial
manner of the time. His idea of undress was a blue reefer or
a black pea-jacket; but he commonly wore a broadcloth coat, a

cutaway with short tails, a square-topped derby hat and striped
worsted trousers. With these went the usual assortment of
seal-rings, scarf-pins, watch-charms and massive sleeve-buttons
that paralleled the brooches and bangles of the feminine sex.
His shirts, starched like steel breastplates, were made for him
with collars that gradually turned into saws about his neck,
and his straw-yellow silk handkerchiefs, exhaling a perpetual
eau-de-Cologne, spread from his pocket as voluminously as
flags or sails. They were like the enormous handkerchiefs from
which we saw parlour magicians extract a brace of rabbits or a
basket of eggs.

My mother was not behind my father in feeling that she was
always right, if only because her feet were on the Rock of
Ages, and her usual reply was "We won't discuss it" if anyone
questioned the laws on which our little world seemed to be
built. Any dissent was "very provoking," and this evolved into
"aggravating" if the dissent was repeated or even prolonged;
and yet she was always ready to laugh if one cornered her and
teased her until one broke down her by no means fortress-like de-
fences. Years later one of her younger friends told me how, in
church, when both were listening to a rather pompous sermon,
my mother whispered, "Marian, what *are* the eternal verities?"
—referring to some generalization which the clergyman had
uttered. Easily amused as she really was, she had to support
the official views,—or felt that she had to support them,—on all
levels of life; and her way of defending any of these was to
say it was "so considered," though the question never arose,
considered by whom? It was not cricket to ask this question,
which might have resulted in a wholesale retreat, nor was it
fair to challenge her statement, regarding churchly matters,
that "all the best minds" agreed about them. We knew, or I
knew, that "all the best minds" meant Phillips Brooks, for my

father and mother were Episcopalians, as all my four grandparents were, and never supposed that they could have been
anything else. To be anything else, from their point of view,
was somewhat quaint or queer, slightly droll in the case of
Methodists or Baptists, and what, save a Presbyterian, could
one otherwise be? I gathered that the Presbyterians, among
whom we had many intimate friends, were prone to a somewhat excessive evangelical zeal, while Roman Catholicism was
a picturesque foreign religion that only one person we knew
visibly practised. This was an old French lady whom everybody knew and who lived in a gambrel-roofed house too near
the railroad. In her house George Washington had spent one
of the nights of his eight migratory years as an old campaigner.

It strikes me that Voltaire's phrase for history, "a fable
agreed upon," applies to the state of mind of the world we
lived in, and of every other society too, for are not all cultures
based on rules of a game that people half-consciously agree to
play? They well know these are "vital lies," or lies at least in
part, shifts that can be defended only in a measure, like the
summary simplifications regarding religions and races that
characterize the tribal point of view. These latter really mean
no more than Benvenuto Cellini meant when he said that the
people of Ferrara were "very avaricious," that "all" of them were
the same in this respect; and the fictions in question are only
maintained because they are felt to be safeguards of security
and tribal order. The young people who discarded them,—
who were constrained to do so, reading *The Way of All Flesh*
and the Freudian writings,—condemned themselves to playing
lone hands against the universe, with no underlying sense of
security whatever. And how safe, with all its fictions, this world
seemed. For us all Democrats were Ferrarese, not avaricious
but somehow base, and I remember my brother and me, at

election time, when I was six, burning a stuffed pillow that we called "Grover Cleveland." Our automatic Republicanism made for the sense of security that sprang from the regularity of everything around us, the winding of the clocks on Sunday mornings, the universal parade to church and the ceremony of "lying down" in the middle of the day. Did not everyone's mother, presumably, go upstairs for this? The grinding sound of the coffee-mill that rose early from the kitchen mingled with the other summer sounds, the mowing of the lawn and the far-away beating of carpets, the whirring of the water-sprinklers, the rocking of hammocks, bespeaking not only security but endless time for everything, long hours for reading and dreaming of other sorts of worlds.

One really lost oneself in these, whether Thackeray's world or Vasari's, or the mediæval scene of *The Cloister and the Hearth,* and no one felt the need of relating these worlds to one's personal "problems," the universal need of a later epoch. I remember my mother as always embroidering table-cloths, napkins and doilies, which she covered with forget-me-nots, pansies and sprays of wild roses,—in the end I inherited a trunkful of this work of her hands,—or reading with a friend the French that she often spoke with my father at table or playing Mozart, Beethoven, Schumann or Chopin. She had been a pupil of Richard Hoffman, Malvina Hoffman's father, and played, I am quite sure, exceptionally well, and her piano had belonged to Paderewski, who had used it on one of his tours and whose name often greeted my infant ears. Chopin was always her favourite, and if, as Tennessee Williams says, "in memory everything seems to happen to music," I would say that with me it happened especially to Chopin. "Everything" seems to have happened to the notes of the nocturnes and études that I remember as accompanying my earliest child-

hood, floating through open windows on summer afternoons,
accompanied in turn by the buzzing of an occasional fly. To
this day I always associate Chopin with ladies in white or-
gandie dresses and the gentle flapping of curtains in a languid
breeze.

My mother, for the rest, was conscientious, however it
bored her so to be, for, like my father's in earlier days when
youth and pleasure met, her natural taste was all for the
frivolous and gay. I still have a handbook about cotillions with
my father's name in it, a relic of his blazer-wearing tennis-
playing twenties before ill-health and misfortune crippled him.
But he was conscientious too, and he invariably spent his holi-
day afternoons reading out loud at the hospital to the men in
the wards. He usually read Dickens or Mr. Dooley, whom he
really revelled in, partly because he had himself a quarter-
infusion of Irish blood and liked the flavour of the brogue
when he was in good spirits. My mother took my brother and
me on "nature walks" on Sundays, although I am sure she felt
far from at home in the woods, with the pungent skunk-cab-
bages and the salamanders under the rocks; nor can I believe
that she greatly enjoyed some of the books she read to us, even
the *Pilgrim's Progress,* one that I remember. For no more than
my grandmother could she go too far along the attenuated
path of the supposedly improving. My grandmother tried to
read aloud *Rollo at Work* on one occasion, but she was so
overcome with laughing over its priggish absurdities that she
stopped somewhere in the second chapter. But both took seriously, especially my mother, the rights and wrongs of the
spoken word, enunciation, inflection, good usage and so on,
together with the superiority of Worcester's Dictionary, in all
these delicate matters, over Webster.

Meanwhile, the domestic arts had been virtually forgotten,

mainly, no doubt, because servants were so cheap and abundant, when households like ours, without any pretensions, could have seven maids with seven mops for less than the wages of one fifty years later. It was supposed that my mother knew how to make a blueberry pie because, in some legendary past, she had really made one, but the only visible demonstration of anything approaching this was my grandmother's annual battle with currant jelly. For two or three days the rear quarters of the house were turned upside down while this tumultuous ceremony was played out to the end, a whole-souled survival of the days of my grandmother's childhood in Plattsburg that suggested the emblematic ploughing of the emperor of China. The great red cheesecloth jelly-teats dripped all over the laundry-tubs, over buckets, pails, caldrons, bowls and soap tureens, while Christine the chambermaid, Ingrid the cook and my nurse Rosie, who ruled us all, were called into constant requisition. Even the gardener was pressed into service, the tender of the currant patch, the earthy odorous Alsatian Floret Wormser, a name that my grandmother felt was too improbable to be entertained, so she said that for us "Floret" meant "Lawrence." From that day forward Lawrence he remained.

I dimly remember the simpler time, the horse-and-buggy age, when Jerry, the baggage-master, was busy at the station and one saw the liveryman Albert Heddon jogging through the streets in the phæton with the tasselled canopy and the buffalo-skin blanket. I can still hear my grandmother saying, "Now, Jerry, be sure the checks are all on the right trunks." The Civil War was still quite close and there were three generals in the town, one of them General Fitz John Porter, the ultimate hero of a *cause célèbre,* whose elder daughter had been one of my mother's bridesmaids. There were colonels and majors on all sides, and even the dentist, Dr. Wells, had been a captain at Bull Run and liked nothing better than to talk about it. Pinning one down and shutting one up with what he called a rubber dam, he discoursed about the fight at the old stone bridge. During the Civil War itself Hawthorne had prophesied that after the war "every country neighbourhood will have its general or two, its three or four colonels, half a dozen majors and captains without end." Our town was in this respect like all the others.

How many odd characters, for the rest, how many queer folk there seemed to be, as many as one found in Russian novels, —even the novels of Tolstoy, which we had in the house,— types that vanished in later days into sanitariums or were smoothed out by psychoanalysts. There were, for instance, the Von Ohls, reputedly well-born Germans who had fallen upon evil days and drove into town, to market, in a ramshackle gypsy trap and who lived in a rotting old house on the edge of a swamp in the woods that always evoked the story of *No Haid Pawn*. For there was a pond near by this breeding-place for ghosts and a gigantic bloodhound that rushed out once at Max Perkins and me when we were searching in the swamp for turtles. We stood back to back, half expecting a horrible death, only to discover that the old hound was toothless. But odder than these were the "old New York" people,—or some of them, at least,—with whom we were more or less connected, Miss Spencer, for one, who lived by herself with a Great Dane called Nero and an orange-tree that spread through the floor of her parlour. Miss Spencer still wore the bonnets and mantles and tippets of the days when she and my grandmother were both young, almost the days of the red-coated portrait of her English grandfather who had settled in New York and married the young French lady in pale yellow satin. A perfect pair of oddities were our cousins Richard and Lottie Brown,

the deaf old bachelor and spinster brother and sister whom I
somehow associated with Charles and Mary Lamb. Their father had been the partner of Philip Hone, the mayor of New
York who kept the Pepysian diary that has often been re-
printed, and I still have a set of Coleridge that Cousin Lottie
gave me, along with her father's letters of travel. For many
years he had been president of the Mercantile Library in New
York and his peregrinations as an old-time merchant had led
him all over the South and the West, and Europe as well, in
the eighteen-twenties and thirties. He had fallen in with
Daniel Webster at St. Louis in 1837 and had raced in a packet-
ship against the "Great Western," finding himself on one occasion, travelling from London to Paris, in the company of the
poet laureate Robert Southey.

One other character who comes back to me, and whom I saw
constantly as a child, bore the delightful name of Cecilia de
Medina, an impersonation of the tragic muse, as she always
seemed to me, with her black lace, her fans and her mantilla.
I felt that only Goya could have done justice to her, while, in
fact, this great friend of my grandmother was neither Spanish
nor of the stage, although she was the daughter of a once-
famous actor. She had married, however, in Morro Castle, in
Havana, the son of the Duke of Medina who was governor of
Cuba, and she always wore a ring, an intaglio surrounded by
diamonds, that Napoleon had given to one of her husband's
forbears. Her father, long dead, like her husband, had been
William E. Burton, the proprietor of *Burton's Gentleman's
Magazine,* which Edgar Allan Poe had edited for a while in
Philadelphia, publishing in it *The Fall of the House of Usher.*
Burton's Theatre in New York had been the most popular of
its time, but the actor himself, an Englishman, convinced that
he was vulgar, had never permitted his daughter to see him on

the stage, and the dark air of grandeur that she retained for me was merely the natural expression of a histrionic epoch. She was tall and marked in every line of her spare pale face with a high distinction. With her sister, Mrs. Massett, she was always "going back," to Dresden or, more often, Vevey,—in any case, Europe,—after two or three years in America that invariably aroused for the European scene the longing that Europe aroused for America soon after.

There were various literary people in the town, among them Julian Hawthorne, who lived in a little pinkish house with tall pointed windows, like a miniature Venetian palace forlornly astray. A daughter of Julia Ward Howe,—Florence Howe Hall,—lived near the Hawthornes on the Scotch Plains road; and, while Edmund Clarence Stedman had spent part of his youth in one old house, Bret Harte's wife and daughters still lived in another. They had been virtually abandoned by the almost-great writer of whom Mark Twain said that his heart was "merely a pump without any other function." But, if the spirit of any author was active in the town, one might perhaps have said it was Washington Irving's, for half the population had old Dutch names that were all to be found in Knickerbocker's history of New York. There were Beekmans, Van Burens, Bogarduses, Van Zandts and Van Boskercks, Van Rensselaers, Laurenses, Brockholsts, Schuylers and Suydams, a fact that apparently interested nobody, for it was very well known that New Yorkers knew nothing and cared nothing about their forbears. It was because they knew nothing about them that Washington Irving had written his book, for which they abused him roundly after he had done so; and Edith Wharton testified that even in her later day "the New Yorker was singularly, inexplicably indifferent to his descent." The history of New York had been a succession of names that were known for a time and vanished to give place to another set, for the city was "permanently in transition," as Henry James put it, and in this way very unlike Boston where the same names remained at the top and even gathered prestige with the generations. Whatever the reasons for this may have been, —and one of them was that Bostonians were cannier investors than New Yorkers and kept their fortunes,—the Knickerbocker families that had once been known were all represented by survivors in the town along with relations of families that were not yet snowed under. For me Washington Irving was still alive, or he came alive, as I should say, when later I was told that my grandmother had met him. This was at a party in her uncle's house where she had spent her vacations as a school-girl in New York. "A very pretty compliment from a very pretty girl," he had said in reply to one of her remarks.

## CHAPTER II

# MAXWELL PERKINS

THE NOTE of Washington Irving survived in the name of the Knickerbocker ranch, a household word during all my boyhood years,—the Texas ranch of our friends the Tweedys, the closest of my family's friends, some of whom, in fact, were our next-door neighbours. Two Tweedy boys with two nephews of Washington Irving had opened this ranch just after the Civil War, and there my brother, who went through Princeton with the older sons of our time, spent several rapturous summers as an amateur cowboy. They all came north for school and college, and José, the younger son, so called by his Mexican nurse, was equally my special friend and the friend of Max Perkins. He was the perfect type of the engaging ranchman, deeply tanned, manly, frank, with the winning smile and drawl of what Owen Wister called the world's greatest playground for young men. With his atmosphere of round-ups and barbecues and pack-trains in the mountains, José was the "Virginian" to the life, the embodiment of the romantic code, as we saw it, of the plains, and I always thought of him when I read of Kit Carson's grave reserve, his distaste for noise and boastfulness and his loyalty and courage. These traits, openly mentioned then, went underground in after days when it became the fashion not to use "words."

I have often wondered how far this friendship with José

prepared Max Perkins to understand Hemingway later. The "aunts," meanwhile, the Tweedy "girls," one of whom lived to be ninety-nine, remained our friends even to the fourth generation. For half a century before she died, "Miss Belle" always suggested to me the somehow electrified mummy of Rameses the Great, as if he had escaped from his funeral wrappings and leaped out of his painted box in a wild wish to know what was happening in the world. For, wrinkled, with her eyes sealed tight and tiny as she was, she all but ran down the stairs like a twelve-year-old child, and, perching on the edge of her chair, alive with intelligence, fresh feeling and wit, she threw herself into the minds of the oldest and the youngest. She had prophesied that her elder nephew, aged ten, would be the banker that he became, in England, later, and she said to my little son, whom I sometimes took to see her, "Charlie, don't miss *anything!*"—she was then ninety-seven. *His* comment was, "Why, Miss Tweedy's a genius!" as I always thought she was, if genius can be defined as the quintessence of concentrated life, and if uncommon mnemonic powers are also a part of this, for her memories went back almost a hundred years. When I became interested in American history, somewhat late in life, she described for me the funeral of John Quincy Adams, which she had actually witnessed in 1848, and she showed me a picture of the checked gingham dress in which, in 1855, she heard Thackeray lecture in New York on the Four Georges. To test the memory of Dexter Tiffany, her old beau of a nephew, who was eighty-four himself, I believe, at the time, she asked him if he could remember the day when Major Anderson lunched with them after the guns had gone off at Fort Sumter. "Deck," as my mother called him, was annoyed by this, for he too was proud of his memory, and, when I was writing about New England, he told me about his grandfather, the old gossip Bela Tiffany, who had lived in Boston. This grandfather, he averred, sitting in taverns on Washington Street, had told Hawthorne several of his own "twice-told" tales.

At no age at all,—thirteen, in fact,—I had become, as I shall explain, both interested in the history of art and informed about it, and since then I have often thought of some of the pictures in the Tweedy house that were unlike the pictures on other walls. In most of our houses there were dusky copies of Raphael madonnas or Ribera monks, Murillo beggar-boys or Caravaggio gamblers, brought back from abroad perhaps by some travelling uncle,—there was often a "Beatrice Cenci" somewhere in a corner,—but, besides the huge golden Thomas Cole in the shadowy hallway of the Tweedy house, there was a supposed Canaletto and a supposed Bronzino. I say "supposed," for no actual claims were made for them; and who, in those almost pre-expertizing and altogether pre-Berenson days, was really sure of the provenance of anyone's "old masters"? I mean, of course, in provincial collections, though these had all come from the Newport house of "Uncle Edmund" Tweedy, of whom Henry James wrote in *A Small Boy and Others*; and, for that matter, at Hampton Court in 1899 the pictures were still attributed virtually at random. One by an unknown Flemish painter had been labelled in the dim past a portrait of Raphael by himself and was still so labelled. But, authentic or not, the Tweedy pictures were as magical for me as one or two under the skylights of the town museum, the "Job Male Art Gallery" that never quite lost its terrors for me because of an early encounter with the donor in person. When I was three or four, Job Male had lived opposite my grandfather's house, behind a fence with pickets that bulged at the sides, and I somehow took it into my head that these bulges ought to be removed and crept across the street, with a hatchet, to remove them. How I found the hatchet I cannot guess, nor can I remember how I evaded my nurse's vigilant eye; but it comes back to me vividly enough that I chopped off two of the bulges before relentless fate caught up with me. The door suddenly opened and there on the threshold stood Job Male himself, like an angry God with eyes fixed on the sinner. I had been seized red-handed, for there was the hatchet, and I did not have a chance to tell a lie.

The "art gallery" in question was meagre enough, though ample as to numbers, academy pictures of the fourth rank, battle-scenes and what not, like the little girl in a field of black-eyed Susans. But there was one Italian picture, "Cleopatra and the Asp," that might have been the real thing, though of course it was not, for one never knew where, in those casual days, in any odd corner, one might happen upon something interesting and even quite good. One picture there, for instance, though certainly not a masterpiece, was unmistakably better than any of the others, a picture with a history too, as I discovered later, John Vanderlyn's "Marius Among the Ruins of Carthage." I do not know whether it was this or the other version,—in San Francisco,—that Napoleon medalled at the Salon in 1805, but, quite different from the other, it was almost as good, and Vanderlyn, while far from great, was an early American painter who knew his trade. How had it strayed there and whither did it vanish when all these pictures were later auctioned off, victims of a local birth of taste, regarding the gallery generally, that also carried the Vanderlyn away? It was the great *revolution* in taste that had scattered elsewhere,—everywhere,—the remnants of the "gentlemen's galleries" of fifty years before when the Lewis Raycies of whom Edith Wharton wrote in *False Dawn* came into their own with pictures that Ruskin approved of. But not even these were above suspicion in the most instructed quarters, in the households of the Perkinses and their grandmother Perkins at Newport, the widow of the old Boston critic and historian of art. "Bruen Villa," which I knew later when I was at Harvard with Max, was virtually a museum not only of paintings but of objets d'art of every sort that sometimes turned out to be genuine and sometimes not. Assembled in the easy-going days when Charles C. Perkins had lived in Florence,—where Max's father was born,—a friend of the Brownings and a member of W. W. Story's circle, many of these objects were challenged later, even the superb Michelangelo drawing, a sketch for the "Last Judgment," that hung in the Plainfield house.

Max Perkins himself had a marked talent for drawing. I have lately found sketches of his in my college notebooks, and I remember that he sometimes carried a sketch-book in his pocket and constantly drew figures and especially heads. They were sometimes heads of Napoleon or his favourite Shelley or his later idol Mark Twain, with a corncob pipe; and they were often heads of a pure Greek type quite like his own, for he was a beautiful boy, Praxitelean. Had this gift descended from his grandfather Perkins, who had studied painting with Ary Scheffer?—studying music in Germany as well, for he had been a composer too, and his whole life had been passed in an atmosphere of art. Charles C. Perkins had been for a while the conductor of the Handel and Haydn Society, and he had given to the city of Boston Crawford's statue of Beethoven, the first statue of any sort of artist that was erected in the country. It was one of this grandfather's uncles who had discovered William Rimmer, the interesting sculptor of the statue of Hamilton in Boston; and I had read his own *Tuscan Sculptors,* as I was to read in time the book on Ghiberti and his school that he wrote in French. When Max and I were in college, his grandmother gave us, to hang in our literary club, a number of letters from various old friends of theirs in Italy and Boston, among them Browning, Longfellow, Lowell and Motley; and at Newport, in her atmosphere of early Victorian elegance, she talked about her old Italian days. She suggested to me the pictures of Salvator Rosa, for she recalled banditti in wild passes of the mountains and travellers robbed on the road in the middle of the night, along with musical *soirées* in Rome in the days of Pio Nono, Walter Savage Landor and *The Marble Faun*. The names of "Harry" and "Willie" James recurred in Mrs. Perkins's talk, together with the family of Charles Eliot Norton,—immemorial Newport friends,—one of whose daughters I remember as present in the house.

As for the Perkins clan whom I knew so well at home, I think of them as a raft of Boston culture,—one of those rafts that were to be found in many another American town, serenely riding the wild waters of the world around them. Not that our world was very wild or that they were the only Bostonians,—there were many New Englanders, at least, among our friends; but they somehow threw into the boldest relief the New York character of our own life, which seemed to me so different from the character of New England. I never ceased to wonder at the strength of the local atmospheres, the flavours that persisted so pungently for two centuries or more and kept the old provinces and colonies so distinct; for although my own grandfathers had been Vermonters they had both been absorbed in New York and I always felt like a foreigner when I entered New England. As it happened, I was taken every summer for two or three months to Kennebunkport, or to Saunderstown, Quisset, Magnolia or Maplewood, New Hampshire, usually travelling on the Fall River boat that might have been crossing the ocean so alien to me was the world in which we arrived. Exciting enough was the shuffling sound of the porter's feet in the corridor on the heavy red carpet outside the stateroom door, the tinkle of the ice-water pitcher and the knock that followed, the clanking of the loose brass key in the stateroom lock. And to what new sights and sounds and scents one wakened in the morning in that world of clambakes and lobsters and salt-water taffy, of Salem Gibraltars and briny smells, whiffs of hemlock, spruce and fir and the odour of fresh pine as one opened the wardrobe doors. Then there were the Indians who camped near the summer hotels and sold sweet-grass baskets, arrows and birch-bark canoes, and the buckboard excursions to some spot in the woods where the ladies gathered autumn leaves and read nature books aloud, sitting on the rocks. And the harvest fêtes at the mountain resorts, the flag-draped arches and the coaching parades, the huge floats decked with goldenrod and asters! Far away seem those young girls swathed in flowers as the "spirit of autumn" and those evanescent structures of cheesecloth and bunting, emblems of a summer scene that vanished fifty years ago and survive now only in Howells's novels.

Even years later when, at forty-five, I was writing about New England, I felt as alien there as I had felt as a boy, as an English boy might feel on his first visit to Scotland, for the Yankee dialect was as palpable as the language of Burns. Especially in Maine I felt this in those dying seaports that never died, in the rough-shingled fish-houses on the dilapidated wharves,—which were always falling down but never fell,—where the old sea-captains, basking among the lobster-pots, seemed to have been fixed for all time in their stage of decay. They liked to sleep in hammocks, though their houses were full of good beds and their wives made every effort to keep them indoors; but, as soon as their wives were asleep, back they went to their hammocks again, for they lived, as one saw in their dwellings, in a dream of the sea. Like ships, these dwellings were covered with hatch-ways and companion-ways, ladders and piazzas that were built like bridges and decks, climbing as it were all over their fronts and sides, with captain's walks to survey the ocean and masts for the flags that waved from them,—every house, in fact, a Yankee vessel. All this, of course, delighted me, but it could scarcely have seemed more foreign; and, for the rest, I had been brought up on the usual pleasantries about New England that in those days filled the pages of the comic magazines. I had heard virtually at birth "Mr." Choate's toast to the Pilgrim mothers who endured all the troubles of the Pilgrim fathers and had had to put up with the Pilgrim fathers too, the climax of the New York jokes about baked beans and the "Boston look" and little boys with goggles and bulging foreheads. *My* only immediate scholarly forbear,—oddly enough, as it seemed to me, inasmuch as both my grandfathers had come from New England,—was my father's Irish grandsire, whose nose was always in a book, as an uncle who remembered him told me later. He had read not only Latin and Greek but Hebrew, by no means to his advantage as an importer of woollens; while "thoughtful" New England was generally regarded by the little world I knew as in some way cold and dry, pedantic and forbidding.

I only dwell upon this now because these distinctions of atmosphere seemed to count so much in the small world in question, in which at the same time "the West" was a kind of wild Siberia that swallowed up unsuccessful uncles and cousins. I somehow identified Boston with too many books, and my grandmother, who was well aware of the world but totally detached from scholarly circles, regarded my liking for these with a faint touch of scorn. She had a story about one of her brothers who had gone to a New England country college,—Dartmouth, I think,—and come back for his winter vacation with Gibbon's *Decline and Fall* for "light" reading, which was not the kind of lightness that our New Yorkers understood with what Howells called "the levity of their old Dutch blood." For while the English element in them generally predominated over any other infusion of whatever other strains, their racial intermixture,—as I was happy, later, to know,—was precisely that of the two greatest New York writers. Like Melville and Whitman, they were equally English and Dutch. Because of all the influences that played over my childhood, I felt that I was myself an ingrained New Yorker, and I had the sense of coming home when, writing my literary history later, I turned from New England to the world of Washington Irving. But when I think of New England now in relation to this other scene, I remember Fenimore Cooper's attitude towards it, for Cooper, although born in New Jersey, had spent his whole life in New York state and knew, none better, what he called "New York feelings." He scouted the "Blarney Rock of Plymouth" and said "Nothing Yankee agrees with me," while most of his New England characters were either mean, like Ithuel Bolt, or, like Remarkable Pettibone, figures of fun. But he was obliged to praise whole-heartedly the intelligence of the New England folk and recognize their "high and honourable distinctions." Could anyone have quarrelled with him for that?

Now the Perkinses were not only New Englanders, they were even doubly so, for they united the two great lines of Boston and New Haven,—Harvard and Yale,—the twin immemorial schools of the mind of New England. Max, descended on one side from the old East India magnates,—some of whom had been Loyalists in the Revolution in Boston,—was, on the other, through his grandfather Evarts, the Senator and Secretary of State, descended from John Davenport and Roger Sherman. I mention this merely because I have known few other Americans in whom so much history was palpably and visibly embodied, so that one saw it working in him, sometimes not too happily, for his mind was always in a state of civil war. And this was the old *English* civil war that he never quite fought through, the war between Roundhead and Cavalier one or the other side of which constantly came to the front at crises in his life. How often Max talked King Charles to me to make me talk Oliver Cromwell, beaming when I did so because I was putting into words what he,—or the other side of him,— really felt. One side was the romantic adventurous boy, indolent, graceful and frank, all gaiety, sweetness, good spirits and animal charm, drawn to the John Reeds of his time and the heroes of Richard Harding Davis, soldiers of fortune who lived a knight-errant's life. This was the Max who arrayed himself in splendour, whose appetite for pleasure was unending and keen, and who liked to remember that one of his forbears had ridden against Paul Revere and beaten him in a horse-race once in Boston. This side drew him to Scott Fitzgerald, while the other was the side that rose in rebellion in London when he met three young swells in Parliament Square. I remember his picture of them swaggering towards him, and I saw that his fantasy clothed them in the plumes and ruffles of King Charles's men while all his Cromwellian blood rose up against them. This other side of Max believed in living against the grain and doing the "hard way" whatever he had to do, and he might well have said what his grandfather Evarts really said, as Henry Adams reported in the *Education*. "I pride myself on my success in doing not the things I like to do but the things I do not like to do" was the motto of the old Roman statesman whom I saw sitting at the window once in his house on Second Avenue below Stuyvesant Square. For one day when I was in town with Max we visited this house, then lost in the slums, with the wide tessellated pavement in the entrance-hall, so large a house that when it was demolished two apartmenthouses, the "U.S. Senate" and the "Evarts," were built on the site. *This* Max was always scolding me for following the line of least resistance, setting out in cold blood to do what I wished and liked instead of what, so obviously, I *ought* to do. Here was the descendant of Jeremiah Evarts who had preached abolition even in the South and in consequence spent a year in a Georgia gaol, the foil of the child of the art-loving grandfather, along with the uncle who discovered Rimmer as Max himself discovered so many writers. One side appreciated the writers, the other side helped them, an ambivalence that explained why Max never became a writer himself and why he became the rock on which others leaned. He was himself a character in some of their stories; and sixty-eight books were dedicated to him.

When the novelist Galsworthy visited this country he told a common friend that Max was the most interesting American whom he had ever known, and not the least interesting thing about him was this perpetual war with himself that made him in the end a "prey to sadness." For it seemed to me that he fulfilled Kierkegaard's phrase for accidie, that malady of so many monks in the Middle Ages, the "despairing refusal to be oneself" which really means that a man "does not give the consent of his will to his own being." It struck me as symbolic that, in his office in the publishing house, two pictures always faced him on the wall behind the desk, a photograph of an old schoolmaster, an austere New Englander, and one of the Saint-Gaudens monument for Mrs. Henry Adams. For me the old Yankee head, which I too had known in life, evoked Dr.

Arnold of Rugby's well-known phrase, "the silent pleasure, so dear to every Englishman, of enduring, resisting, and struggling with something, and not giving way." Alien as the sentiment was to me, I always admired it in Englishmen, in the classic type of the civil servant working with selfless devotion, in jungles, in deserts,—wherever,—for the "natives" and the Empire. For Max the Empire was the publishing house and the natives were the authors, the authors who kept the Empire going and whom he served devotedly but also with respect and frequently affection. So he served Thomas Wolfe with and for whom he spent hundreds of hours labouring through jungle-like nights in the middle of summer. He even told Wolfe that he regretted not having kept a diary "about the work that both of us were doing . . . the triumphs and surrenders that went into the making of a book,"—as a nurse might keep a diary about the progress of a fever-patient or a consul in the tropics about some local insurrection. But heaven knows how many repressions this involved for the other Max, one, for instance, that recalled to me Dr. Johnson's saying, "Every man thinks meanly of himself for not having been a soldier." For I know there was an anxious time when Max would have been a soldier, and would have thought better of himself, *except* for the Empire.

It was this kind of resignation that produced the "sadness," the fatalistic sadness of the veiled figure designed for Henry Adams, the old friend of his grandfather's family in Washington whom Max's mother had known so well and who in a way had been part of his own life. So Saint-Gaudens had also been, across the Connecticut river from Windsor, where he made the bust of the Senator in his summer White House and where Max had met General Sherman and Benjamin Harrison when he was a boy and learned to take presidents and generals almost for granted. There, in old houses beside the lake, the clan gathered in the vacation months, the Thackerayan uncles and the aunts and older cousins who might all have stepped out of *Punch* in Du Maurier's time. Many weeks I spent there with Perkinses and Evartses and the stream of little girls in pigtails, faintly suggesting the *Peterkin Papers*, that flowed on, unchanging, from decade to decade. It seems to me that, even now, if I were to drive past, on the long road from Canada that runs through Vermont, I should still see them there, in white dimity and sashes, an endless succession of Alices in Wonderland, playing croquet on the lawn, all in the golden afternoon.

No one could have known Max who did not understand what Windsor, or Vermont in general, meant for him, the deep stake in the old rural America from which the foreground of his life was in many of its elements so far removed. One of his visions was to own and edit a country newspaper, such as Bowles's *Springfield Republican* once had been, and in Windsor he had been the boy who knew guns, hunting and fishing and the "wonderful river trips" that he remembered in a letter. All this drew him to *The Yearling* of Marjorie Rawlings, as to Hemingway, Thomas Wolfe and *Huckleberry Finn,* for which he shared the passion that, more than any other of a literary kind, bound the American novelists of the new time together. "The best part of a man is a boy," he wrote in a letter to one of his authors, some of whom were boys themselves and who found in him a father, just as he sometimes found in them a son. It is with "young authors . . . that our great hopes lie," he said, for old authors "never surprise" while "young ones *can,*" and he seemed to be naturally inclined away from the old and the traditional and towards the experimental, the native and the new. It was not surprising that he should have felt, as he wrote to Wolfe, "There could be nothing so important as a

book can be,"—what *might* have seemed remarkable was that
he should have recognized at sight such un-Thackerayan talents as Ring Lardner's, for instance. It was still more remarkable that he was the first to recognize them and that he led the
movement away from British standards in novel-writing in the
most conservative publishing house in New York. There for
years W. C. Brownell had vainly struggled with his own belief that America was merely a "literary dependency" of England, and Max's family atmosphere had perfectly borne out
Emerson's phrase that we had our "culture" from one continent and our "duties" from another. His eyes had scarcely
rested on anything more American than Arundel prints, Elze-
vir Ciceros and Horaces, Méryon etchings and seventeenth
century Italian bookcases and chests, brought back from the
city of Dante and Ghirlandajo, and his father had a way of astonishing the natives with remarks about art that left small
room for anything likely to appear on their own scene. One of
his father's dicta was that "bad art" was not "art" at all, and he
applied this to E. A. Abbey's Boston frescoes, the praises of
which at the time were in everyone's mouth. One might have
expected that Max's taste, when it developed, would be severe;
but who could have guessed it would be so direct, so uninflu-
enced by prejudice, so unclouded by secondary feelings, so immediate, so fresh? Had not Windsor and all it stood for done
this for him?

There were many of us later whose "culture" was originally
European and who found ourselves "turning homeward," as
Emerson put it, because of elements, deep in ourselves, that we
were unaware of but of which we became aware as time went
on. For the rest, Max's epistolary style was distinctly eighteenth
century, and so it remained, as one saw when his letters were
published,—the result of a taste I shared with him for the

world of Swift, Addison, Defoe and Pope that especially included the circle of Dr. Johnson. How well we seemed to know these men, as characters and writers, just as we knew the poets and critics of a later generation of whom Max's favourite was Shelley and De Quincey was mine. The legends of these English authors were all as vividly real to us as the lives of any of our friends. But it interested me, when his letters appeared, that what he remembered from the life of Swift was not the romance of Vanessa, which everyone talked of, but something a novelist would have observed, that Swift liked to sit in taverns on greens listening to the talk of teamsters and coachmen. Just so Stephen Crane had sat by the hour in Bowery saloons, fascinated by the rhythm and tempo of living speech, and this went far to explain to me Max's intuitive understanding of the writers of his own time in his own country. He knew, knowing the eighteenth century, that the most enlightened ages had been, as he said, the most free-spoken,—which opened him still further to the young mind of his time,—as he knew that good writers "always feel anxious" and "ought to have trouble," as he put it, "getting under way" with a fine book. No one was more aware that, with their "subconscious confidence," good writers have vastly less confidence in beginning a book than men who merely follow the trade of writing; and he always found it a good symptom when a true writer felt greatly discouraged and even, at moments, desperate in writing a book. He knew that books, like people, should be "sized up in their own terms" and in terms of the particular writer's capacities and interests, and he was always on the side of the author not only against the public but against the publisher as well. Less than a handful could understand the writer's point of view, he said, while "the true artist has always insisted upon making his book what he wanted it" and should never be censored by edi-

tors or any outsider. This understanding enabled him to out-
line whole novels more than once that subsequently his authors executed or to suggest that in writing their books they
should follow certain forms that proved to be entirely respon-
sible for their ultimate success. Meanwhile, he affirmed that
"the only important things" were "loyalty, fortitude and honour," and he felt that to be "born knowing this" meant going
at least a part of the way towards being "a great writer in
more than the technical sense."

What, after his death, came back to me as chiefly character-
izing Max was a certain unwavering nobility,—an elevation
that many who did not possess it revered in him,—with the
kind of "high gentlemanlike bearing" that Thackeray ascribed
to Pendennis, whom in various ways Max followed as a model.
This in turn recalls to me the influence, in our time and place,
that novels seemed to possess over manners and behaviour, especially Thackeray's, written "in the gentlemanly interest," although Dickens's characters were the best known of all. But
the names of the people of Dickens were commonly used as
epithets, Micawber, Pecksniff, Murdstone, Uriah Heep, and no
one thought of acting out these characters in real life, as they
acted out Thackeray characters and the women of Jane Austen.
The only exception that I remember was Sydney Carton in
A Tale of Two Cities, the young lawyer whose labours we had
in mind when, grinding for college examinations, we wrapped
wet towels around our heads at night. But at home I felt
sure that Colonel Newcome was always in General Sterling's
thoughts as he passed our house with stately tread, always appearing in mid-afternoon, bent slightly forward, with long
drooping moustaches and his pearl-grey gloves draped over his
walking-stick. He was on his way down-town for a chat with
the bookseller Mr. Estil, and it was on one of these afternoons

that, in the post-office, he observed Mrs. Perkins licking a postage stamp. Approaching her boldly, he exclaimed, "Mrs. Perkins, that is something I never expected to see a lady do in public." Had Thackeray ever aspired to that altitude of manners?

But our whole scene comes back to me as a pageant of Anglo-American fiction, beginning with the rector of Grace Church, benign, with his shovel hat, who was surely the walking image of the Vicar of Wakefield. We had not yet reached the time when the Vassar girls all went Botticelli, with Primavera draperies and languishing postures, still less the bar-fly days of nymphomaniacs and alcoholics that followed the publication of *The Sun Also Rises*. Nor were young boys given to emulating Huckleberry Finn as their great-grandfathers had emulated the heroes of Plutarch, though I knew more than one whose later life was crippled by the Little Lord Fauntleroy fever that possessed their mothers. They were kept, with hair in curls, in black velvet and lace until they were ripe for analysts and sometimes asylums. There were also not only Gibson girls but Trilbys and Isabel Archers, studied from Henry James's *Portrait of a Lady,* and dozens of Miss Poles and Miss Matildas, in grey or black mousseline-de-laine, who might have been characters in *Cranford*. They too had sometimes persuaded themselves that to be a "man" was virtually, by definition, to be "vulgar." But in general these characters owed nothing to a book. In America and England alike they had grown that way.

CHAPTER III

# AT THE SEMINARY

THERE WAS scarcely more than a touch of *Cranford* in the
nunlike circle of the Seminary, the big brown school for
girls with the cupola on top, and only when some widower,
who had perhaps a daughter there, laid siege to one of the
younger and prettier teachers. Standing in a grove of chestnut
trees, with winding walks and flowering shrubs, and with rustic arbours and a playhouse near the garden, this was Miss
Kenyon's peculiar domain where the abbess and her flock instructed three generations of the daughters of the town. There
lived, moreover, for a winter, a year, or even for two or three
years, while they were building new houses or abandoning old
ones, a handful of families who were more or less congenial
but who kept to themselves for the most part in their own sets
of rooms. Among these for a while were the Perkinses and my
own family, too, and Rockwell Kent with his architect father
and mother. There was an extension, with wings, at the rear,
and three large verandahs over which the wistaria vines climbed
up to the roof, and, within, two staircases curved upward from
the entrance hall, with Boydell prints lining the walls under
the high ceiling. At one side was the library of which the lady
from Pittsburgh said that "culture stuck out all over it"; and
there, on Saturday evenings in winter, one of the gentlemen
read aloud to a circle, grouped round the samovar, drinking

tea. For gentlemen were never referred to merely as men. I remember hearing, as I passed the door, phrases of Kipling and
Lafcadio Hearn, the favourite authors of the moment.

In summer, in the shade of the vines, on one of the verandahs, Miss Kenyon seemed always to be reading Browning or
*Faust*; for she not only personified culture, in the nineteenth
century sense of the term, but she was a missionary of culture
to the town as well. It was she who had founded the women's
club in the parlour of the Seminary,—"to pursue all the means
of culture within reach, whether by study or writing or listening to others"—in the days when lecturers began by saying "as
Emerson says" or "as Lowell says" and ended by discussing
Agassiz, botany and what not. This was in the strenuous earlier time when there was a Plato Society too, led by an Irishman from Trinity College in Dublin, an eccentric schoolmaster, an Episcopal clergyman,—Dr. Johnstone was his name,—
who had long since entered the fold of Tammany Hall. As I
heard of the Plato Society, its meetings always suggested to me
the austere Athenian raptures of a still earlier Concord and I
pictured them as taking place in the light of white lamps and
gas-jets that exploded, at the touch of a match, with a loud report. They expressed, meanwhile, states of mind, remote indeed from the Wall Street world, that now persisted only in
the Seminary, whither Miss Kenyon had brought back her
own recollections of Concord which she had visited in the seventies on more than one occasion. She had witnessed, at the
School of Philosophy, the assemblage of the sages, the venerable Alcott, Elizabeth Peabody and Emerson, in his slat-
bottomed chair, listening with pleased attention, though he
seldom spoke. Since then she had drawn to the Seminary, sometimes to address her girls, a number of writers and scholars who
were famous in those days and some of whom came for annual

visits and even stayed for a week or two because they enjoyed Miss Kenyon and felt at home there. Marion Crawford came, for one, and Julia Ward Howe, his aunt, who lectured,—with the daughter who lived in the town—on the art of conversation and on Dr. Howe's adventures in the Greek Revolution. (Arriving on the very day when Byron died at Missolonghi, he had become, as everyone was supposed to know, the surgeon-general of the navy of the rebellious Greeks.) Others who came were Mrs. Custer, the widow of the general, who talked about garrison life on the northern plains, and Thomas Nelson Page, who read *Marse Chan*. A constant visitor was John Fiske, who sometimes brought his music with him, for he liked to play in the evening and occasionally sang.

What did Miss Kenyon think herself about these unusual guests of hers, and what was her own life during all these years?—questions I never thought of asking and never would have asked if I had not come into possession of her journals and letters. I had later married her grand-niece who had lived as a child in the Seminary and who was permitted to come to the table with John Fiske, when she was four or five, on condition that she was to remain absolutely silent. For Fiske was by then grotesquely fat in a manner that excites a child, and the situation was not improved when the child in question whispered, "Would he mind if I said something *nice* about him?" Miss Kenyon herself was devoted to Fiske and the something large about all his views that was very reassuring after the pettiness of others, and she delighted in his series of lectures on American political ideas, for one, and his talk about Huxley, the generous, his friend in England. But she felt the lack of a certain something in Julia Ward Howe that would have made her a really great woman, something, as she said, that slips over the boundary of selfishness or prudence and creates the complete devotion which runs all risks. And why did she lament, in her poem "To the Brownings" their indifference to her poetry when she had done so much to interpret *them?*—which struck Miss Kenyon as rather weak, especially in one who had followed so well her own unique vocation, which was not the poet's.

Miss Kenyon could scarcely have expressed her feeling for the Brownings. She had shelves of early editions of both these poets, and she was given to reading them religiously with the "Browning Encyclopædia" sometimes at her elbow. One day, with a special friend, she spent an afternoon in honour of Mrs. Browning's birthday, setting out pictures of husband and wife on a table in her room, with their books and vases of violets placed among them. Then the two read together the Portuguese sonnets alternately, with passages from Mrs. Orr's biography of Browning. "O for Browning's courage!" she exclaimed in her journal at the end of a day when her life seemed to be a failure and she asked, "In which direction shall I look for the light?" Browning for her was "Shakespeare's equal in versatility," and she felt that, writing for an age to come, he could easily afford to be so little understood during his lifetime.

But Browning was only one ray of the great sun of culture that was represented for her, as for so many, by Goethe, one of whose apostles, another of her friends, was also a frequent visitor at the Seminary. This was Thomas Davidson, the peripatetic Scottish philosopher whom William James called "a knight-errant of the intellectual life," and who had established in London the "Fellowship of the New Life" of which the Fabian Society was presently an offshoot. The "most intensely alive man whom I had ever met," as Havelock Ellis was to call him a few years later, Davidson conducted schools of philosophy in the Adirondack mountains, at Farmington and at Saint

Cloud, near Orange, New Jersey. He lectured at the Seminary on the "four great religious poems," Job, the *Oresteia*, the *Divine Comedy* and *Faust*, while he talked, as he wrote, on the frieze of the Parthenon also. His great theme was the course of European thought,—"with regard to the highest things,"—together with the "heroes of spiritual thought" and the problems which the nineteenth century was leaving for the twentieth century to solve. He asked Miss Kenyon to accompany him, with a party of friends, on a walking tour through the Black Forest, through Switzerland and over the Alps.

As a local apostle of culture herself, Miss Kenyon read Dante with a class of her own, while she started another to awaken an interest in Homer, and one day two ladies waited on her to suggest a class for the study of *Faust*, the book to which all roads led in the world of culture. To herself she read Aristophanes, *Obermann*, the *Iliad*, Fanny Burney's journal, the life of Landor, while she conducted an inner life of which she recorded day by day the discouragements, the efforts, the resolutions. She dreamed that she was "smothered under the rubbish of circumstances" over which she seemed to have little control, feeling that there was a power within with which to free herself if only she could discover how to use it. She was oppressed with a sense of hurry,—"I think in a jerky fragmentary way. I move with nervous haste, head, feet and tongue"; and, endeavouring to correct this, she looked into William James again and copied out parts of his lecture on Habit. Then, consciously moving and speaking more slowly, she wrote with deliberate motions of the hand to overcome this "hurried and spasmodic action." Another problem was what to do with girls whose "want of delicacy" betrayed them into foolish escapades and whom she would gladly have given up if this had not been to confess that she lacked the wisdom and the strength to convince and conquer.

Among the many questions that Miss Kenyon asked herself was how to achieve real solitude for meditation,—and was she not making too great an effort to live up to an ideal when possibly the real that she had was better? She wondered what would have been the result if she had been encouraged to live a writer's life rather than a teacher's, and she wrote in praise of silence,—"Let me learn to voice only what I wish to continue resounding in the atmosphere." One whole rainy afternoon she spent walking on the southside verandah, thinking of Thoreau and listening to the rain, and, looking through the rain, she seemed to feel a soft veil fall suddenly over the hard practicality of life. She often had these moments of illumination. It was all she could do to control herself and continue a conversation when she looked at some dry oak-leaves, on another occasion, through an upper-storey window, against a background of pine; and she was carried away by the charm of the coming and going of vehicles, depositing the girls at the door, on a winter morning. How picturesque this bustle of omnibus, carriage, hack and sleigh amidst the whirling snow and biting wind. She responded to the first note of the woodthrush in spring as well as to the woodbine leaves, the white orchis and sumac that she brought home from walks in the woods in October. Sometimes William Hamilton Gibson came out for a Sunday at the Seminary, talking about fungi, spiders, flowers and birds, and then everything that had life crept or flew for her or expanded along the horizon of his conversation. An occasional moment seemed to her "wholly divine," when she stepped to the window, for instance, while her classes were changing, and looked at the phenomena of nature out of doors. The dry rustling of the brown leaves reminded her of her rela-

tion to it, or the silent slow falling flakes against the evergreen
hedge; and a golden branch, struck by the sun, opened the
portals of an unseen world for her as well as for Æneas. Then
the sudden clashing of the school-bell brought her mind flut-
tering down again to scratch among the gravel for grains to
nourish her brood.

Once, in her sitting-room, while she was reading Lowell
aloud, she felt a sudden thrill as if her "friend" were near, and
she was so affected that her face flushed and her attention
wandered from the reading. The thought flashed through her
that he might have left the body simply in order to share in her
pleasant employment, and she made no effort to repel the influence when her companion asked for the time,—it was five
minutes before ten o'clock in the evening. Was this the result
of their recent discussions of the Psychical Society, or her
reading of Balzac's *Ursula* or what not? Or was it one of
Wordsworth's "strange fits of passion I have known"? Minutes
became hours before she felt "wholly withdrawn from the influence." It happened that her circle had been for a while concerned with planchette, which sent messages from an unknown
cousin in Constantinople, while, saying that its own name was
"At No Man's Disposal," it talked about "Nefter, the place
where undeveloped souls go." The circle, however, did not
long encourage these peeps into the spirit world when Miss
Kenyon's niece from Radcliffe began to hear raps, and, meanwhile, her "friend" made bodily appearances every year,—he
was a regular visitor at the Seminary.

Who was this "Mr. B." to whom Miss Kenyon referred so
often? He was Harrison Gray Otis Blake, Thoreau's most intimate friend, perhaps, to whom at least he had written most
constantly and fully. The two had camped out on Monadnock
together, and Thoreau had used in *Walden* long passages from

his own letters to Mr. Blake, who had been appointed executor of his literary papers and had published a series of volumes selected from the journals. One of those Unitarian ministers who had withdrawn from the pulpit because the least weight of theology was too heavy for them, twice married and twice bereaved, he had retired with an income to a life of literary leisure in his birthplace, Worcester. There he discussed with a friend, on Sunday afternoons, the theory of evolution and metaphysics. He had been one of the seven members of the Harvard class at the Divinity School whom Emerson had addressed in 1838, shocking the old guard in that "refulgent summer," and he found, as he wrote to Miss Kenyon, that for him at sixty-five life had a profounder beauty than when he had been young. With all his fluctuating moods, he still agreed with Emerson that "the night was made for the day, not the day for the night," and, telling Miss Kenyon the story of his life, he asked for hers in turn,—what had been her history, what had been her experiences? "I felt hardly worthy," he then replied, "to be the correspondent of one who has struggled so nobly and conquered so bravely . . . somewhat as Thoreau may have felt after receiving a certain letter from Mrs. Emerson." He quoted Thoreau again as "expecting the visitor who never came," meaning that no one living could approach his ideal, but for seventeen years before he died he wrote to Miss Kenyon constantly and almost as constantly came to see her. It pleased him, as he drew near the town, to leave the train at some station near by and approach his friend on foot, walking into Plainfield.

When and where had they first met? At Concord in 1879, at the sessions of the School of Philosophy and the house of the Alcotts, where Louisa Alcott had remarked to them that men were "not practical" and that she was "not philosophical," neither were her sisters. At the school, Miss Kenyon wrote, "Mr. Blake's silence was the finest thing said," and they walked together to Thoreau's grave and rowed on Walden pond, which was desecrated already by human innovation. For there were boat-houses on the beach and boats full of noisy girls profaned the spot where Thoreau had once embarked. They picnicked on the river, botanizing, even discovering arrow-heads of white quartz, and, sitting on the bridge that arched the flood, Mr. Blake read aloud some of the letters that Emerson had written to him. They read *The Ring and the Book* together in a grove of hemlocks beside the stream, for Browning was his favourite poet as well as hers, and he was happy that there was "another so grand realm in which we may meet," as he presently wrote in one of his letters from Worcester. They looked forward to many such readings, talking freely as they read, prepared for disagreements on other matters, permitting the widest differences so that their intercourse might rest on a basis that could not readily be shaken. He gave her fragments of Thoreau's handwriting and first editions of all his books, and she suggested that he should make the pocket edition of "Thoreau's Thoughts" that was to find more readers than any of them.

Meanwhile, they discussed in their letters all manner of questions, hoping, as Mr. Blake wrote, that "we may seek in the right way and help each other by our experience and insight." He was devoted to Fénelon, who seemed to condemn him for being "too eager and anxious for celestial moods," defeating his own aim thereby, but, although he enjoyed the long walks that made one content with life and the world, he still believed in "the attitude of expectation." He had found in certain late experiences "hints of eternal life," as if "time and the world might be dropped without any real loss." She, on her side, compared Carlyle and Emerson. With what noise and how much smoke Carlyle drilled and blew up the rocks in his way while Emerson remained quietly and serenely the master, putting down into the crevices the delicate rootlets that silently grew so that the rocks were broken without noise or smoke. When the correspondents were unable to meet they wondered if this, in itself, might not in some way enhance their relation because it would increase the "other treasure"; and they reciprocally thought of themselves as prisms that "sift the sunbeams," unlike the sort of people who "intercept the light." Rejoicing in his "calm exalted nature," Miss Kenyon wrote poems "To H.G.O.B.," and once she blamed herself because he had not come. "Had I set myself to the music which he hears," she wrote in her journal, "he would have drawn near to listen; but I have deliberately filled my hours with the worldly activity and bustle which he abhors. How could he approach? He will scarcely come until I call him, strongly, irresistibly. Shall I? Can I? Let me not tempt an adverse destiny by anxiety or haste."

Elsewhere she spoke of Michelangelo and his relation to Vittoria Colonna as "more beautiful to me than ever"; and did she not perhaps feel that her relation to Mr. Blake had somewhat the same character as theirs? Michelangelo had been sixty-three and the austere Marchioness forty-six,—virtually their own ages,—when the relation began; but there came a moment in Miss Kenyon's case when she must have been aware that her own feeling was not entirely Platonic. One day she found on the table downstairs a letter from her friend which she slipped at once into her black silk bag, planning to read it when the tumult of the day was over,—conscious that his summer visit had not been what it should have been, she had urged him to repeat it in October. Then, at last opening the letter, what did she find?—that he had gone off to Mount

Mansfield and another lady had written to him, asking him to visit her in New Hampshire. This lady had sent him a mere postal card, yet he had spent a day with her, and she had joined him for another day's trip in the mountains. What two or three earnest letters of her own had asked for and not received, a simple postcard from another had gained,—his presence; and, well as Miss Kenyon knew that she herself lacked beauty and charm, she felt nevertheless stung to the core. Thoughts, many of them no doubt unjust, surged through her and kept her awake all night, and she rose thinking of what he had said, that every friendship ends in tragedy, to which she had replied that *theirs could not*. For, she had said, "We only wait for what is given, demanding nothing." And could she say this now?—could she think it any longer? "Here," she felt obliged to think, "here is the fitting and final end," for "I see I have expectations, demands even." Yet this was not the end, by any means. His visits increased, on the contrary,—his letters now came every week,—and she wrote, "We are both older and calmer every year," though she noted that his birthday, April 10th, was usually cold and snowy and the buds of the cherry tree seemed always late. On his return from the World's Fair in Chicago in 1893, they still read Browning together,—*The Ring and the Book*,—and on the verandah after dinner they talked about the "angel guest, seeking the angel in every human being." Even after his first stroke and against the judgment of his friends he insisted on coming to see her and stayed for a week. She met him in the city and took him back for a last good-bye, for they both knew they would never meet again.

Years before this, on a tour of Europe with George P. Bradford, the old Brook Farmer, Mr. Blake had gone out of his way to stop at Turin to meet Miss Kenyon's other great friend, to whom she had given him a letter, the "Martha Washington of Hungary," Louisa Ruttkay. "I know well what you say," he wrote, "that to meet a true and noble person is better than seeing Europe," and he was not disappointed, nor was Madame Ruttkay, who was living with her brother, the "Liberator," Louis Kossuth. In glowing terms she wrote to Miss Kenyon about him. At that time, in 1881, he had seen Miss Kenyon only once, although they had since exchanged photographs and letters, and he was bursting with curiosity,—"Tell me *all* about Miss Kenyon!" he had exclaimed at the outset of this meeting in Turin. "I will not repeat what I said," Madame Ruttkay then wrote. "You know so well what my heart, overflowing in love to you, can dictate. His face (that noble face!) was beaming with joy and he said, 'That is just how her letters have impressed me'. The clear ringing laugh which burst from his lips every time I touched upon your individuality sounded to me like the fresh irrepressible joy of one who had found a treasure for which he was searching a long time. How well I recognized the young soul in that eye arched by a time-bleached brow. Your tact will tell you what use to make of the description of the short but very pleasant call. Only do not let prejudices enter into your decision. Those are only fit food for the crowd, and its mediocrity, but not for your developed soul."

What were these prejudices that Madame Ruttkay had in mind as she fostered this little romance through the middle eighties? Mainly, of course, the question of age, for "it is hard to be ridiculed when time," as she wrote, "has bleached our hair." She knew this well herself, for she was as old as Mr. Blake, and "only when you have attained our age will you understand the trials of a pure aspiring soul imprisoned in a withered frame . . . Do not condemn him, my dearest." As a widow, she too had known all this, "in contact with a gifted person of unusual intellect, a kind heart and attractive manners and appearance." Was this conceivably Colonel T., her brother's younger comrade-in-arms who had lived with them so long in the country near Turin, in the villa with the terrace that faced the Alps? Mr. Blake's demeanour was contradictory, but her friend should not be surprised by that, for the more contradiction there was in it the more affection he had for her and the battle he was fighting against prejudice so much the harder. Let her friend be careful not to break over misunderstandings in letters, "for I should be very much mistaken if there is not *real* congeniality in your characters . . . He who through his soul to triumph over feverish excitements continues to love goes to the grave fresh and young, if he has lived a proper life. But because the majority of humanity does not live the proper life the world looks on love in advanced life with ridicule . . . You do not know how often I am looking at you, in the abundance of my love, praying for you and fearing for you that the battle will be hard because, according to the light, the shadows must fall!"

As the years continued and the battle went against them both,—for Mr. Blake was, as he said, an "undecided person,"— this question dropped out of a correspondence that was prolonged for twenty years, from 1875 to 1894. In that year Louis Kossuth died,—"my brother, protector and loving companion," as Madame Ruttkay wrote to her "darling friend," and she herself, at seventy-eight, returned to die in Budapest, from which she had been exiled for forty-five years. Her friendship with Miss Kenyon had begun just after the Civil War, in which two of her sons had fought, the boys she had brought to the United States who had joined the Northern army, one becoming a major, another a colonel. She had followed Kossuth

when he came over in 1851 and toured the country in triumph like another Lafayette, the "guest of the nation," the
romantic hero that Garibaldi also was and virtually as much in
England and France as well. His family had been banished
from Austria with him, and Madame Ruttkay had fled with
him to Turkey,—in 1849,—where he had been imprisoned for a
while. She had lived in Plainfield off and on, where one of her
sons continued to live,—although she was to survive all three
by many years,—and where she had found with Miss Kenyon
"a home in days when I needed it most," she wrote, "suffering
from loneliness, crying for companionship." For the last fifteen years of her brother's life she had lived with him in Italy,
returning for brief occasional visits to this country,—to "my
only friend," as she called Miss Kenyon, "to whom I can open
the recesses of my heart," for "you are to me *what none* of my
friends are." She visited the Concord School of Philosophy
with this "precious daughter of my love," sending her regards
later to Mr. Alcott, and she too read Browning aloud with
Miss Kenyon, delighting also in "Thoreau's Thoughts," which
she read fifteen minutes every day. On her bookcase in Turin
stood likenesses of Ruskin and Herbert Spencer, and she asked
Miss Kenyon for a photograph of John Fiske, together with
one of Emerson, to place beside them.

Her earlier letters had been written from the villa, with the
fish-pond and the terrace, which they had been obliged to
abandon, outside Turin, after Louis Kossuth had brought back
from his botanical excursions no less than four thousand Alpine
plants. Fourteen years older than herself, he was still able at
eighty-seven to walk, without stopping, more than three hours
a day, and every year he had gone for a while to one of the
Swiss valleys,—"full of the spirit of excursions,"—or perhaps
Lake Como. Once he had spent two months in Naples, visit-

ing his son, who was the director of all the railroads there, watching an eruption of Mount Vesuvius that interested him greatly, for he was deep in the study of natural science. But he preferred the mountains, loving those "high locations" that did not agree with Madame Ruttkay,—so that she preferred to stay at home,—always returning with fresh plants to replace some of the older ones that had been "contaminated by civilization." Madame Ruttkay loved what she described as "the charming little tribe of crocuses, primroses and lingering snowbelles" that tried to "lift their little heads above the snowy ice-cover" in March, "facing the chilling blasts of the wind." There stood the touching snowbelle, as she called it, with dark clouds overhead, while it gave gladness and joy to the human eye, bearing up against adversity with courage and submission. It was "easy enough for the rose to be bright and beautiful in the sun." But the snowbelle!—no other flower taught her so much as "this little pilgrim solitary." With all her disappointment and sorrow over the indifference and the death of her sons, with whom her relations had been clouded, she said, by distrust, she had to keep up her courage in the presence of her brother, for he was "easily influenced by sadness."

When the weather had forbidden her taking part in Louis Kossuth's long daily walks, she had walked herself in the greenhouse, with the flowers for companions, joining him when he returned in the study, for he went out in all kinds of weather, even when he was obliged to carry an umbrella. But his brain was busy with astronomy now, with cipher-filled papers spread out before him, and they scarcely exchanged a word before sitting down to dinner. Her brother had a favourite dog, an immense white Newfoundland, that had his own plate by the table and a portion of each dish,—be it the finest dessert, he must have his share,—and, not to be without dainties, as he did not eat pears or grapes, he had his portion of the cheese. Then Madame Ruttkay was obliged to peel chestnuts for him, after which the cat Minnie had to be fed, and all this took an hour before they went into the billiard-room, where her brother made the balls fly for an hour or so. At eight they took their seats at the whist table. Her brother was kind and affectionate,—even as she was writing he came into the room to show her some rosebuds plucked in January; but they had no neighbours there and, as Madame Ruttkay said, "Seclusion is uncongenial to me . . . I chafe under the separation from the great imperfect human family, and my soul cannot expand without human sympathy and contact." Her brother himself had been in frequent intercourse with Mazzini until his death in 1872, but he had become so accustomed to solitude that the effort of conventionalities had now become almost unbearable to him. Mr. Blake had also had this "obstinate love of seclusion" that so many superior men shared with him, and this was the only fault she had found in Thoreau, who was "one of Nature's high priests." How much deeper in the human heart he would have planted his beautiful thoughts if he had lived closer to humankind. Her brother also turned his back on sympathetic gestures that would have influenced humanity, as it seemed to her. But, lonely as she was, and remained in Turin, she had drawn lessons of endurance and calm from the view on their terrace of the range of snow-covered peaks. How the Alps proclaimed the power of God with their shining granite faces! The setting sun tinted them every minute with a different luminosity, from the soberest purple to the brightest yellow and red, raising and expanding her heart with that glorious sight.

But they had been driven into Turin by an untoward incident that made it impossible for them to continue in the village. They were Unitarians, and when their friend Colonel T.

died the villagers rose against their Protestantism. While the Vaudois minister was reading the burial service, they shouted insulting remarks into his ears, hooting and laughing at them all, in a demonstration managed by the priests, so that they almost expected to be assailed with stones. "My poor old brother said, 'Such an insult was never done to me in my life!' You may well imagine our indignation," Madame Ruttkay wrote; and Louis Kossuth and his sons decided that the coffin could not be left, exposed to some further outrage, in the village. So they at once arranged for a proper funeral in Turin, "with all the military pomp due to their old friend's station." The burial took place in the Protestant cemetery there, and then, for two weeks, for a change of scene, they had all gone to San Remo. But Louis Kossuth had been deeply moved, he had wept like a child at his friend's death, and the emotion had been prolonged, as Madame Ruttkay said, by the inhuman action of these soi-disant Christians. Inasmuch as, besides, they were remote from medical assistance, the sons were unwilling for them to remain in the village, so, selling the villa, they had settled in the city, laboriously moving her brother's collections and his library of more than three thousand books. The solitude of the winter would have been almost unbearable without the society of their dear old friend, and Turin had so many public gardens that one did not miss the country there as much as one might have missed it in other cities. They had taken an apartment with windows opening on one of these beautiful parks with flowers and a great fountain facing their parlour, "shooting high its lively drops that chase one another like so many flying diamonds," as Madame Ruttkay put it. "When I step on the balcony I feel I am in a garden. But I miss my beautiful Alps with their snowy caps and their shifting shadows and clouds gilded by the rays of the sinking sun."

There, as before, she had few social pleasures,—in any case, difficult for "one of my age and my past,"—partly because she hesitated to accept invitations when she was so seldom able to return them. Her brother never went anywhere and he was disturbed by the least social interruption, and she rarely went out in the evening because she did not "like to come home with the valet." She met a few French people of the Vaudois society, a few Italian countesses and the English in Turin,—she visited on Lake Como the wife of the English consul; but she had found society very limited in this town, where almost everything "overstepped the boundaries of womanhood." It was restricted to tea and whist, a little mediocre piano-playing and a few admiring remarks about pretty toilettes; while, as for her own toilette, she was not shabby, and that was really all one could say about it. However, if her family life had not been so frigid, it would all have been quite pleasant; but her brother had no time for demonstrations of affection. He was very good to her,—he had just left the breakfast-table provoked with himself because he had eaten a peach which he was afraid was the best in the dish,—but he was absorbed in his books and manuscripts, writing his memoirs, volume by volume, and working regularly nine or ten hours a day. This harrowed up the past for him, he came to his meals "with a flushed face as if he were in a fever," and "emotion," as Madame Ruttkay said, "is dangerous for aged people,"—she knew that her presence and care were essential for him. His only diversion was to go to his billiard-room with two Italians who came to play with him; but, approaching ninety, he was without any other relation to help in a foreign land in time of need. It was hard to be old, weak and alone in exile! To be sure, his son, Francis Kossuth, the statesman of later years, already famous in Italy, was there at times, but he was a busy civil engineer, director of the sulphur

mines and building steel bridges in Egypt over the Nile. Even
their good friend Dr. Basso had become unpunctual, fighting
with filial devotion against an infirmity that made him a "most
pitiable spectacle," Madame Ruttkay said. For he was infatu-
ated with a red-haired Irishwoman in Turin and in consequence he was as negligent as he was distracted. For the rest,
"By what trivial means are we often enslaved in our life!"
Madame Ruttkay exclaimed in her solitude, as she worked on
her memoirs. The servants,—two men, Italians both,—did not
understand the Hungarian ways to which her brother was so
partial, for, with all his wanderings through the world, he had
never changed his habits or his love for "our Hungarian mode
of cooking." Changes of diet were impossible at his time of
life, so she had to assist in the kitchen, which she found dis-
tasteful, "inseparable from bad odours and grease spots on my
dress." This kept her, besides, in a nervous condition that was
disadvantageous for all mental work.

In her secluded monotonous life, she therefore turned more
and more to the "darling friend" who, "though a daughter in
years, so thoroughly understood" her "thoughts and foibles,"
knowing that when the old lame postman brought her one of
Miss Kenyon's letters "many a wave" would be "lulled to rest
in my tired head." For "you are always the first," she wrote
"to whom I send my message of love . . . Your letters are the
water of life to me." She only regretted that prolonged separation, while it did not eradicate the love from one's heart,
took away some of the "eloquence" of letter-writing, and she
craved "the trifling details of daily life to chain our thoughts
together . . . You see how persons of Mr. Fiske's mind are attached to you. What attracts people to your house? The intellectual atmosphere which your individuality has diffused
there." Had she not known this herself? She had never since

found anyone with whom reading, for instance, was such a delight, and there was nothing in Turin to compare with her friend's society, "nothing above kindly everyday chattering." She mentioned a French weekly paper, *La Nature*, which her brother took, suggesting that if her friend subscribed to this review of the sciences it might further their interchange of thought. Then she continued with a word of counsel about managing the school and "your noble and religious work, the education of young children." It was true that in 1874 she had urged Miss Kenyon to give up the school because "systematic occupation fetters high natures,"—why not devote herself to literature?—and Madame Ruttkay had suggested that they might take a house together in which she could spend half the year. She would have to spend the other half with her brother in Europe, but they could support themselves by raising silkworms. Meanwhile, she discussed the authors she was reading, Amiel, who had just died in Geneva, Edgar Quinet's histories and Emerson, whom she enjoyed "beyond expression." How had her friend felt about Emerson's lectures? And was not the true greatness of Herbert Spencer that he put "sympathy" as the regenerating power foremost to lead humanity to final perfection? Miss Kenyon, in turn, sent Madame Ruttkay reports of the Dante lectures she had just heard in Concord, together with some of the American poets whom her friend was eager to know and especially John Fiske's philosophical writings. It was Louis Kossuth who had begged for the photograph of Fiske, for he had been delighted with *The Idea of God*, and he cherished other connections with Miss Kenyon's country. Madame Ruttkay had bought for him *Picturesque America*, which he enjoyed, as she said, "beyond my expectation," and his son Francis, who was pleased with the book, said he would make some oil paintings after a few of the charming woodcuts in it.

How many other questions rose in this lively correspondence, in the seventy-nine long letters of Madame Ruttkay that I was to find years later in a bundle in a trunk,—among them the question of the education of women beyond the role of being wives and mothers. Sad was their state in Europe, or in Italy at least. There were in Turin only three married ladies who did not have lovers,—so her Italian friends told her,—and, alas, for the unmarried. What was to be done for the elevation of women? Then there was Fénelon, Mr. Blake's favourite, whom she had read in the dark hours when her own sorrow had seemed too great to bear. His theme was self-crucifixion, but she herself could only believe in the kind that promoted self-respect. He saw human nature too much as depraved and debased, while she felt that instead of frightening people with overdrawn pictures of corruption and vice one should show the heights it can attain by self-discipline and love. She quoted against Fénelon other French writers who said that his pictures of depravity were unreal and false, existing only in the writer's mind and swallowed by the reader only because he was unwilling to confess that he had less experience of life. Then, regarding the love of God, which meant for her simply the love of virtue, she disagreed again with Fénelon, for, while he taught that to do God's will we must renounce ourselves, for her the divine will was in harmony with our own nature. Why, if we lived rightly, should there be any antagonism between our nature and God's will? Then Madame Ruttkay discussed Rousseau's *Confessions*. Miss Kenyon was reading this, and she was impatient for her friend's opinion, for so many turned away in horror from the book. "I could not find in it this abomination." At one time when she herself had thought of opening a school, a friend had warned her not to leave it on the table, not that she herself had read the book!—O no!— whereupon Madame Ruttkay had given her a lesson. She had felt obliged to say, "You know we can become virtuous only after knowing good *and* evil and *choosing* the good. Otherwise we can only be ignorant."

Madame Ruttkay went on to praise the thirst for knowledge that linked one with the teachers of humanity in a brotherly circle. How much more precious it was than worldly posses- sions! Then she exclaimed in 1889, "I am sure our spirits have met at the grave of Browning. A shining star has set in the intellectual world." Ten years before this she had opened her arms to Miss Kenyon's niece who, as a young art-student, spent a year with her. When this niece became my mother-in-law, I marvelled over the variety of games, each more ingenious than the last, that she knew how to play, games of solitaire that she had learned from Louis Kossuth, who had contrived them to while away the time in prison. Under surveillance in his cell, he had found a place behind the door where the guard could not observe him, and he felt he had saved his mind by inventing these games. My mother-in-law well re- membered the noble-looking old man, with the black velvet smoking cap and the white beard, in the library, with his herbarium, the bust of himself in military dress and two or three good pictures, among his books.

There came a time when Madame Ruttkay wrote to her friend in America, "You must fix me in your memory as hav- ing grown very old." She added that she took comfort in the promise, "According to your days will your strength be"; but she heard the warning, "The evening is at hand, fill your lamp." Those moments of enthusiasm that had once carried her soul above persecution, penury and sorrow appeared now only like so many falling stars, making the darkness more visible after they vanished. "My soul," she said, "is like a harp, the broken cords of which show what it was, not what it is." For a number of years her mind had been turning back to Hungary. To her great joy a Hungarian family had become neighbours in Turin,—the father had shared in the rising in 1848,—and she listened, bowed with emotion, when the daughter and the niece played Hungarian airs on the piano. In fact, she said, "I burst out crying." She noted the excitement over the discovery near Budapest of a great Roman amphitheatre, and, regretting that "our language is not spoken in any other country," she mentioned some of the new Hungarian writers. There was, for instance, a great new work, *The Tragedy of Man*, which her brother considered superior to *Faust* and which was less burdened with the metaphysics that had made Goethe's poem so difficult for her. Then, knowing how poor her country was, without any guide-book to speak of it, she compiled an article to draw the attention of travellers to it, as they were drawn to Italy, Switzerland and France. She meant to show the advantages and the practicability of a trip from Vienna,—so much frequented,—through Budapest to Constantinople; and, touched by the attention and the praises of "our people . . . showered on me by their letters and papers," she longed to go back to her own country.

Perhaps, Madame Ruttkay said, where there was so much to be done,—in Hungary, especially for women,—she might "drop the seed of future harvests." Touching were the manifestations of love and admiration that came to her brother on his birthdays, sheaves of telegrams, hundreds of banquets held at home and albums signed by more than thirty thousand people. In 1889 a delegation of eight hundred and fifty Hungarians came to Turin to protest their loyalty to Kossuth, sending a deposit to the bank of forty thousand lire in order to guarantee their expenses. They were all of the educated class, judges of the supreme court, deputies, professors, lawyers, journalists and artists, and, together with a poet who read an ode, they had brought with them a large iron caisson filled with Hungarian soil. On her brother's ninetieth birthday another delegation wished to come, but a public dispute had arisen about the date. Was it September 19th or was it April 19th? Alas, they could not remember themselves precisely, and the Bible in which their parents had written down their birthdays had been lost when misfortune had scattered them all. Had the Austrians thrown this away, or had it been sold along with her brother's furniture at the public auction? They had been able to remember only the year; and, strange to say, the parish church in which her brother was baptised had been burned with all its records.

Already, when her brother was away at Lake Como, "to still the craving of my heart to live in my native land" she had gone back for a visit, receiving "ovations of an astonishing grandeur," beginning at their father's grave where she found hundreds of people waiting for her. Crowds met the train at every town, with veterans of 1848, deputations, choruses, banquets, torchlight processions, and she was escorted everywhere with banners and throngs of peasants in their native costume. Whole villages had turned out to meet her, and from dawn to dusk she had had to wear her best dress!—and her friend knew that her wardrobe was very slender. But how ironical her life seemed, "a farce of the first order," after those "months of ovation befitting only the most illustrious people," when she returned to Turin. She found her poor brother, at eighty-eight, bent, as usual, over his desk, toiling from seven to eight hours a day to earn his daily bread, finishing the fourth vol-

ume of his memoirs. For he had refused pensions from Victor
Emmanuel and Napoleon III and would not accept alms from
anyone. Besides, she had found the visit very disappointing.
The people seemed to have lost all their principles and courage, and her old friends disgusted her by their hyper-loyalty
to the present regime to which, in order to hold office, one had
to belong. "I saw their eyes looking round to ascertain if there
was anyone near to see their hearty welcome to a sister of
Kossuth . . . I am willing now to stay and die away."

Nevertheless, when her brother died in 1894, Madame
Ruttkay returned to Budapest, and there she remained to the
end with her nephew Francis, who devoted the rest of his life
to the welfare of their country. Great was the excitement when
a crowd of a hundred thousand people met them at the station
for the funeral procession, with a specially constructed hearse
and six black horses and with nineteen funeral cars and two
thousand wreaths. There were black flags and drapery everywhere, for the whole population was in mourning, and Maurus
Jókai delivered the funeral oration. But what did this mean
for the future of Kossuth's son Francis? Honoured and happy
in Italy, he had left that life behind in order to maintain the
principles of his father at home, and, as leader of the party of
independence, he found himself thwarted at every turn, for
the ministers were all sycophants and toadies of the imperial
regime. For the happiness of their people how little her dear
nephew could do! To the last Louisa Ruttkay was constant to
the spirit of 1848,—she remained a child of the year of Revolu-
tions,—faithful as well to her friend in America, that "accom-
plice of Prometheus," as she called Miss Kenyon, "in stealing
the heavenly spark."

## CHAPTER IV

# MY FORBEARS

IT WAS in the nature of our suburban world that everybody had come from somewhere else, from Philadelphia, New York or Boston or the pre-urban countryside that for me meant Lake Champlain and the valley of the Hudson. At that time attics were domestic museums that evoked a family's past, with spinning-wheels and broken old portraits in corners, and one I knew contained an ark that was packed from the bottom and overflowed with straw-coloured paper money of the continental congress. In ours there were piles of Plutarch's lives, Burns and *Godey's Lady's Book,* Griswold's *Female Poets,* the *Sparrowgrass Papers* and a red morocco music-album including the "Battle of Prague" that my great-grandmother had used at Emma Willard's school. I looked with horror on these mouldy old books, among them the *Travels of Mungo Park,* in "Harper's Family Library," stacked near by, published in the days of Andrew Jackson for whose prodigious hirsute head on certain old stamps we plundered trunks of letters. There was a portable writing-case containing grisly souvenirs, the locks and curls of ancestral hair that literary circles a century ago passed from hand to hand and memorialized in poems, among them curls of the same great-grandmother who had died when she was very young, a friend of the "poetesses of Plattsburg," the Davidson sisters. Her papier-mâché sewing-table, inlaid with mother-of-pearl and lined with old-rose satin, stood there too, suggesting scenes as remote from our Wall Street suburb as any scene, still American, could well be.

Outside there were pink and white peonies brought down from Plattsburg. There they had grown for generations in the legendary garden, the paradisaical garden of which I gathered as a child that people had driven from Albany in flocks to see it. There my great-grandfather had raised figs by some miraculous method of his own, outwitting Nature ten miles from the Canadian border, inventing the apples and the grapes that sometimes bore his name and for which he received the medals that are still in my possession. His grandfather Platt and his three great-uncles had founded the town in 1784, and it was generally assumed by us that the fruit-clusters in the trees there were more splendidly ripe than the fruit in other gardens. Along with my mother's Eastlake furniture and the relics of the blue china craze that had raged at the time of her marriage and were scattered through the house, we were surrounded with Plattsburg spoils, old Canton china, Duncan Phyfe chairs and engravings of Trumbull and West in walnut frames. These scenes from history recalled the part the engravers played in naturalizing an American mind that had broken away from England.

Plattsburg was always to remain for me an emblem of the old agrarian world that seemed more normal for Americans than the world of trade, a European interest, comparatively speaking, when ours was a nation of farmers almost to a man. Had we not lost much in serenity and depth when "business" triumphed over agriculture? I wondered if this older life would not have suited my family better than the life which they had known for two generations since my two grandfathers, "Green Mountain Boys" both, had come to try their fortunes in the

city. They had arrived at about the same time as Horace
Greeley, who had also come down from Vermont, for the
Yankees of this inland state drifted as naturally to New York
as the Yankees of the eastern seaboard drifted to Boston. Both
had prospered in business there and both had married New
York wives,—my Plattsburg grandmother was one of these,—
and they had in time become so absorbed in the metropolitan
atmosphere that they had lost most of the traces of their original New England. As a child, at least, I heard little of this,
while I heard much of "old New York," for even my Plattsburg grandmother had gone to school there, at "the late
celebrated Madame Chagaray's," as Henry James called it in
one of his stories, where she had acquired her wondrous
"Chagaray French." This was a joke with all of us, for my
father, who had spent five years in France, had learned *not* to
speak the French of Stratford-atte-Bowe, in which, as I later
read in a novel of Constance Fenimore Woolson, the girls were
taught to "grimace" at my grandmother's school. Miss Woolson, who was also a pupil there,—Fenimore Cooper's grand-
niece,—described the school in *Anne* as Madame Moreau's,
where "the extreme of everything called accomplishment" was
taught, with a "vast deal of nonsense in the latest style." With
grimacing in French this included "squalling" in Italian,—as
an ill-natured parent said in the novel,—actually taught by
Lorenzo da Ponte, who had written the libretto of *Don Gio-
vanni* and of Mozart's *Figaro* and *Così fan tutte* as well. Julia
Ward Howe had been his pupil at Madame Chagaray's, that
good-hearted little old Frenchwoman whom everyone called
Tante, with a plain black satin dress and a shrewd face. A
special friend of my grandmother there had been one of the
granddaughters of Fenimore Cooper, whom she visited at
Cooperstown in Otsego Hall.

During these years, off and on, my grandmother had lived with her "Uncle Nat," the universal family benefactor, whose villa at Fordham was to house in time the priests of the Catholic Orphan Asylum that stood in his old grounds overlooking the Harlem valley. His venerable relict Aunt Eliza was one to whom my brother and I were obliged to pay an annual visit of obeisance in the upstairs cabinet in which she sat, in lavender satin and lace, looking out at the Stanford White tower of Madison Square Garden. I recall this daughter of Jacob Lorillard as like some ancient bonze, enthroned, presumably forever, in a Buddhist shrine, one to whom only words of ceremony were ever addressed by anyone, to thank her, in our case, for the goldpieces that she sent us at Christmas. Then there was Cousin Walter Jones upon whom we had to call because he also gave us goldpieces at Christmas and whose middle initials, "R.T.," signified "Returned Twice," whereby hung a tale that had once been told me. But how many dim cavernous New York abodes, crammed with bric-a-brac, draped with plush, with tasselled sofas and whatnots, knickknacks and easels, filled with vague awe my suburban eyes, accustomed to the bright openness and the unencumbered windows of our semi-rural dwellings. These dusky domestic interiors put me in mind of Egyptian tombs, each more Cimmerian than any of the others, dark indeed yet not too dark to be filled for a child with colossal shadows that sometimes materialized as the widows of old-fashioned merchants. Nebulous pier-glasses mounted upward until they were lost in cloudy ceilings, and there were massive doors that were never opened or that, being open, were never shut. There were pictures, spoils of the old world and redolent of grand tours that had culminated in Rome and Raphael, or sometimes native products of old New York, relieved by portraits of gazelle-eyed young women with naked drooping shoulders and with lyrebirds or parrots perched on their uplifted hands. How often in later years I wonderingly passed those brownstone fronts now plastered with the gilded letters of retail trade. I scarcely knew how I was related to the multitude of cousins with whom my parents cherished their connection, even as I gathered, to the third and the fourth generation, and with whom they talked about Dr. Dix or Mr. Dodsworth, the dancing-master, or the organist of Grace Church, Mr. Helfenstein. Or about Miss Comstock's school where my mother had gone in West Fortieth Street and where, as one of her old beaux told me when he and she were both eighty-six, she had let down little notes on a string from her window.

Of my Brooks grandparents I knew little, for both had vanished before I was born, but they too savoured in their fashion of old New York, where my grandfather had been a cotton-broker, buying his cotton in the South, storing it in his warehouse and shipping it to England. An old law-clerk of one of my uncles told me that his first house had stood on Broadway near the corner of Rector Street, where his family had lived on the lower floors while the third floor was the loft where the cotton was kept till the ships were ready to receive it. Sometime in the eighteen-forties he had moved to "modest" Macdougal Street,—as an old New York story-teller called it,—where my father was born, rising as his fortunes rose to the house that he built on Lexington Avenue, 279, just above 36th Street. But his fortunes fell when the Civil War destroyed the Cotton Kingdom and ended his own connection, as a merchant, with England, so that he was obliged to declare himself a bankrupt, though he subsequently repaid his creditors dollar for dollar when he had become the manager of a department-store. I assume from this that he was not only what Ruskin called his father, an "entirely honest merchant," but able as well, though beyond this I know little about him except what I find in the portrait of him that Charles Loring Elliott painted in the eighteen-fifties. In its Washington Irving pose this typifies the moment.

As for my grandmother Brooks, she was half of Dutch descent, while her father was the Irishman of whom I delighted in hearing as a child because, as I was told, he had come over in a barrel. Had he *lived* in the barrel for weeks and weeks, and, in that case, how had he been fed? Or had he been merely *rolled* on to the ship in a barrel, after which he had emerged on deck like a robin from its shell? No one could answer these questions that simmered in my mind. My great-grandfather was one of those rebels who had fled from Ireland with a price on their heads,—in Emmet's rebellion, I think, though of this I am not sure,—escaping as Hugo Grotius had escaped from prison in a chest that was carried out supposedly filled with soiled linen for the laundry. During his last illness, my father told me, the doctor had purloined his books, two or three of these each time he came,—the more valuable Greek and Latin books,—depositing them in the library of the New York Historical Society, which was then down-town. I tried to find them there years later, but could not trace them in the multitude of books,—I might have been looking for minnows in the open ocean. On her other side, my grandmother was a great-granddaughter of Henry Wisner, the well-known powder-maker of the Revolution who brought the great chain down from Poughkeepsie with his friend Gilbert Livingston and stretched it across the Hudson to stop the British ships. Greatly affected, as he wrote, by Thomas Paine's *Common Sense* and possessing a "strong predilection for republican institutions," he was the only New York member of the first Continental

Congress who voted,—against instructions,—for independence.

Not only had my father's father and mother died some years before I was born but my father was a semi-invalid in the years when I knew him, so that his youth and his family connection were more or less veiled for me and came to me rather like scenes from some old novel. I remember the office in Nassau Street in which he carried on a business that every day grew more fictitious as the "National Nickel Company," whose name was blazoned on the door, along with my father's name, faded out. With the big seal and the letter-press, a hogshead of ore stood near the desk to show the quality of the nickel that existed in the mine, but I was told that the nickel was too far down to be readily worked and the mine itself was too far from the Nevada railroad. How to finance it all, how to get down far enough and how then to transport the precious metal, this was the problem that wore my father to the shadow he became, he who had once been so gay and who remained so witty. The mine was like Colonel Sellers's Tennessee land or Colonel Carter of Cartersville's visionary railroad, and almost every family we knew followed some such mirage in the West, oil in the Indian Territory, copper in Montana. For years my father had lived like Tantalus plunged in water up to the chin with unreachable fruit-laden branches over his head, and the worst of the irony of it was that he had once owned a world-famous mine and traded it for this chimera in the Nevada mountains. I still have an indenture showing that he had bought in San Francisco, for fifteen thousand dollars, in 1880, the Arizona copper-mine from which a Boston company later drew sixty-eight millions supplying the United States mint.

Had my father been miscast in life? Had he chosen the wrong role to play or had he been assigned this role by "Mr.

Leighton," the partner, seventeen years older than himself, who had snatched him at the college gate and thrust him, like the devil himself, into the Wall Street inferno? For so I read the story, filled as my own fancy was with scenes from four-teenth-century Italian painters. It was Mr. Leighton who, tak-ing my father as a junior partner in his early twenties, had sent him to Europe for ten years to represent the firm, but, sure as I felt that my father should never have been a business man, I was melodramatic, no doubt, in my view of the case. I feared and hated business and saw it as the Moloch that devoured whatever was best in the American mind,—which prepared me to become a socialist a few years later,—but in all probability Mr. Leighton was in no special way to blame and really got less out of life even than my father. For, caring much for money, he lost his great place on Long Island, where he had had a stud of racing-horses, and, condemned to living obscurely uptown, he could not pay the German "boy" who continued, without wages, to care devotedly for him. I remember the old man,—Stutz beside him,—in his small office near Printing-house Square, with the glittering eye of a Quintin Matsys miser, hovering over the ticker-tape as if at any moment some number might mean millions again for him.

But, thinking of my father's youth, I can imagine that he felt like Mark Twain's young man in *The Gilded Age* for whom there was nothing but success in all his wide horizon and to whom the paths to fortune seemed innumerable and open. It had never appeared so easy to "go into something," Mark Twain said, as it seemed on Broadway then on a spring morning when one was walking cityward past the long line of "palace shops," listening to the hum and roar of the multi-tudinous traffic. It was Philip Sterling who felt this way as he too thought of the mine in the West that ultimately made him a "person of consideration," in those days when the newspapers were full of mining news, the jargon of mining-camps and mining-stock quotations. What glamour Bret Harte's stories and Mark Twain's books threw over the mines in that epoch of great mining fortunes and the romance of the West, the glamour that haloed the paintings of Albert Bierstadt and Thomas Moran that were everywhere to be seen in public buildings. In the intervals of his life abroad, my father had known all of this when he too had gone to San Francisco, crossing Arizona in a Deadwood coach, surrounded, as I pictured the scene, with howling Apaches. I saw him later in Bret Harte's tales as one of the young men who appeared from New York representing "Eastern capitalists" investigating mines; and after his death I always carried the lucky silver dollar that he had picked up in San Francisco. It was a Mexican dollar with the Emperor Maximilian's head that had jingled in his pocket for thirty years and that I lost ten years later, after it had travelled over half the world, on the day when I arrived in the city where my father had found it. Wherever I went, in whatever I read, I seemed to find my father then, in Menlo Park, in far Wyoming, where one of his friends was a ranchman, in the Garden of the Gods in Colorado. Especially I thought of him in the dead mining towns with chimney-stacks standing forlorn amid broken walls and with furnaces built by New York companies to smelt ore that was never found and that lay now half buried in sand and sagebrush. One saw coyotes wandering through streets, once lined with churches and saloons, where lizards basked now on heaps of wreckage, ruins so time-worn, silent and grey that they might have been as old as the ruins of which Volney had written a century before.

My father had never gone West again after those first exciting years when he had already faced the other way, when "going to Paris," as people said, was almost the only alternative to going into an office or a store. How lucky my father must have felt that he was going to Paris, where he lived in the rue Gluck behind the opera-house, when he was not in London, or in Brussels, or The Hague, cities in which he also spent five years. I felt as if I had lived myself, in some previous incarnation, in all these enchanting places I heard so much of, places that in a sense I saw in the souvenirs of all of them that filled, with the Plattsburg relics, every corner of the house. There hung the big painting by Van Heemskerck van Beest that my father had bought in Amsterdam, where the artist, so amusingly named, had actually lived,—indeed, there were two of them, father and son, whose pictures were in the museum there, as a Dutch professor told me many years later. Wonderful to me, this name,—too good, or too Dutch, to be true,—endowing with humour and mystery alike the sea-scape in which I saw a survival, a last weak remnant, of the great Dutch school. This was the artist whom Thoreau encountered, strange to relate, at Fairhaven, near the Yankee port of New Bedford, as he wrote in his journal—"the well-known Dutch painter of marine pieces" by name "Van Beest," who "talked and looked particularly Dutchman like." The entry in Thoreau's journal was dated 1855; but was it the father or the son with whom Thoreau had fallen in and whom my father encountered twenty years later?

With how many other mementos of my father's life in Europe my infant eyes were familiar,—the red sandstone column, a copy of Hadrian's column, brought from Rome, the prancing Richard Cœur de Lion, the dancing figures, also in bronze, that turned into candlesticks when one removed their hats. There were albums of lithographic "views" of Paris and

Touraine, the châteaux of Seine et Oise in soft light colours, carved Swiss figures redolent for me of edelweiss and alpenstocks, bottle-stoppers also carved grotesquely. There were rows of French yellowback novels and a painting of Chillon, where the so much poetized prisoner languished in the dark, another of the falls of Schaffhausen and a chest brimming over with European scenes that one scarcely had to open one's eyes to see. There was the fountain at Brussels, so dear to Americans, the Mannikin, and pictures from the Musée Wiertz, the mad rich Belgian painter whose vision was a singular mixture of Rubens and Poe. How well I knew that chamber of horrors with the headless corpse on the guillotine, the suicide, the man buried alive, Napoleon in hell and the lunatic mother in the act of dismembering her child, which I was not forbidden to see as I was forbidden to read,—precisely because of its horrors,—the novel *Quo Vadis?* Then there were double photographs that one slipped into the stereoscope, still more thrilling so miraculously round were the objects and people one saw in this, so that one seemed to be *in* the panorama.

I never even began to guess how my father had spent these years abroad from which he had brought back certain ceremonious ways, removing his hat, for instance, not only when funeral processions passed but when he encountered men as well as women. Once he had had occasion to take his hat off to Napoleon III when he was crossing the park at Chislehurst in England and the exiled emperor, walking alone, approached on a diagonal path and gravely took off his hat and bowed to him. My father had bought at the Tuileries, at the auction of 1873, a set of Napoleon dinner-plates which we had in the house, together with a sable cloak that the Empress Eugénie had supposedly worn and that was kept in a box in a closet upstairs. What a part this imperial pair played in the American imagination, still played, indeed, when I was growing up and when we had neighbours who were second cousins of the Empress Eugénie, after whom my mother as a girl had named her doll. These neighbours were also grandchildren of the empress's American grandfather, the old consul at Malaga in Spain, and I remember hearing that the empress, who never wore anything twice, sent boxes of finery to these cousins in far-off New Jersey.

Nothing could have been more romantic than European royalty in American eyes,—the Bonnie Prince Charlie, for instance, after whom my father had been named Charles Edward, as others bore the ducal names of Clarence and Percy. But my father's old life was a mystery to me, his life at the Langham, for instance, in London, the vast hotel in Portland Place that stood through the second world war, bombed and gutted. There, where he had lived so long, where he took my mother on their honeymoon later, had he not often seen Mark Twain, who was living there at the same time, and Ouida, who had her salon in the same hotel? Its one discomfort, my grandmother wrote, when she had stayed at the Langham, was that she had only sperm candles in her bedroom, though she added, "I am told that the English like the gloom." My father had been quite accustomed to living without gas-jets. For the rest, to rebuke my lack of interest in something,—I do not remember what,—he told me of an incurious man he had met in London whom he had asked in the city one day, as he was passing the Monument, what this flame-topped tower represented. "Young man," the Englishman replied, "I have passed that tower every day for twenty-eight years and never thought to ask." One moment of my father's life deeply impressed me. He had arranged to sail home on the "Ville de Paris" in 1874, and he was on his way to the train that would have taken him to Le Havre when something in him warned him not to sail. This premonition was so strong that he went at once to the steamship office, cancelled his passage and cabled to his mother in New York that he was coming home on the following steamer. That was the voyage on which the "Ville de Paris" vanished. No trace was ever found of it again.

Earlier still, my father had belonged to one of the volunteer fire companies that raced to fires with gorgeous fire-engines, almost as gay as Sicilian carts, with scarlet ladders and vignettes that were painted by John Quidor and other good artists. He had witnessed the burning of Barnum's Museum,—he had a picture of the scene, the ruined building covered with icicles and snow,—in the days when he had learned by heart, as I supposed in my childhood, all the operas of all the Italian composers. For which opera did he *not* know by Verdi, Donizetti, Bellini, Rossini,—whom his mother described in her diary as "our favourite composer,"—from *Lucia* to *La Sonnambula* and *The Daughter of the Regiment*, from *Norma*, *Traviata* and *Aïda* to *The Barber of Seville*. They were the operas whose arias and recitatives had passed into the rhythms of Whitman's *Leaves of Grass*,—for Whitman wrote some of his poems while listening to them,—and for me this taste was always a part of old New York, where Lorenzo da Ponte had first introduced it.

Many a time my other grandmother had seen this old man at Madame Chagaray's,—the grandmother who brought me up or to whom I felt closer than I felt to my mother, for I was bound to her with special ties. She had married a son of Fisher Ames, the namesake of his kinsman, the Boston orator of the post-Revolutionary epoch. But, fond as I was of my grandfather, it was her forbears who interested me, for they seemed so vital and so picturesque, the admiral-uncle who had captured New Orleans as Farragut's second-in-command and others whose portraits hung on the dining-room walls. Near by hung a painting of my grandmother's great-grandfather "raising the first liberty-pole in the Revolution," the farmer-colonel who had lived in Poughkeepsie where the Baileys and Platts intermingled and whence they spread to Plattsburg and New York. My grandmother's great-uncle Chancellor Kent had been living when she was a child in New York, where another great-uncle was postmaster for twenty-six years and where her brother, the lieutenant in the navy who died in Charleston harbour, was a young lawyer before the Civil War. There lived that other uncle, too, whose drawing-room Robert Weir pictured in the semblance of Scott's house at Abbotsford, with the family and their dogs gathered round the fire, a picture that worked, with others I saw, on a child's imagination like certain stories I heard of long-dead cousins. To one of these a "British officer," uncommemorated otherwise, had presented the "British Poets" in their greenish box, the fifty small volumes over which I used to pore,—"one of the greatest belles of the last generation," as Philip Hone wrote in his diary in 1839. This was the year in which she died, "a girl of seventy-nine years . . . lightsome and gay," as Philip Hone put it, whose Wall Street house had been the "resort of all the fashionable gallants of the day" and remained, he said, "the standard of elegance and taste." In her last illness she re-fused to receive any visitors, leaving orders that no one was to see her after death, unwilling as she was that those who had known her when she was beautiful and young should witness the progress of decay.

Although the links were growing thin that bound her to the Plattsburg past, my grandmother kept up her connection with it, and I dimly remember my great-grandfather, that Luther

Burbank of the north, with a Paisley shawl wrapped round him, sitting by the fire. In his youth he had been for a while a planter near New Orleans,—where my grandmother had been to a school that still exists,—at a time when so many men from New York and New England were settling in Louisiana and Mississippi. But, unable to endure the climate there, he had returned to spend his life in the old Plattsburg house with the long driveway that was lined with locust trees and a buckthorn hedge, the house that my grandmother sold after his death, destroying the barrels of papers that she found in the attic. She had these brought down and dumped in the garden, where they were burned like leaves, though a few of the papers blew off in the wind, and someone noticed that one of these was a letter that George Washington had written to my grandmother's great-grandfather in Poughkeepsie. When I saw this later in an uncle's house, I wondered what else had rekindled the flames of this all too final holocaust in the ancestral garden.

As for my own great-grandfather, I was five when I saw him, as he had been seven when the Battle of Plattsburg occurred, and I recently discovered an old interview with him in which he related his memories of it. He had picked up on the family grounds, after the battle, the cannon-balls that were piled in a pyramid in the circle of the driveway, although he must have had some help, for there were more than fifty of these and a few of them were 32-pounders. They were missiles of the American troops who had bombarded the old stone house because they knew the British had commandeered it. That was in 1814 when his father had taken the family away, seven or eight miles, to a neighbouring farm, for safety, while his grandfather, Captain Nathaniel Platt, refused to leave the place and stayed there with the British general and his staff.

During the Revolution, before he had gone to Poughkeepsie, he had raised the first company of soldiers on Long Island, and he said he had never turned his back on a redcoat yet and did not propose to do it then. When one of the younger officers insolently asked him who he was, he replied, "Captain Platt of the Revolution, and be damned to you, young man," and, when the Yankee ships won the fight, he said to the officers, "Wait till tomorrow and you will be 'Burgoyned,' every soul of you." They broke camp and left that night, burning the fences behind them. Yet after the war the British general sent the old man a dinner-service of which two plates remained when I was a boy. How little attention historians have paid to the indignation of the country squires as one of the main causes of the wars with England, the local notabilities who had ceased to feel they were subjects of the king and regarded the British simply as impudent invaders. Like all dependent people who have reached a certain stage of growth, they resented their own position as colonials or "natives," though sometimes, far from democratic, they thought of themselves as predestined to rule, while expecting other folk to vote as they were told. What led the Ogdens of Ogdensburg, the Gansevoorts of Gansevoort, the Coopers of Cooperstown and the Platts of Plattsburg to settle in these northern wildernesses? Partly the hope of perpetuating the landed aristocracy that was already dying even in New York state. The magniloquence of the inscriptions on some of their tombs matched the proud faces that one saw in the portraits of Trumbull and S. F. B. Morse, Sharples and William Dunlap who came up to paint them.

One could easily trace in the records of any of these families the inner struggle that marked the Revolutionary time, or the years after the Revolution when the old English element was at war with the American element of the new-born nation. How the new native point of view was evolving from the British I saw, for instance, in the record of the Baileys and the Platts before they went north as pioneers and when Poughkeepsie, where they lived, was for a while the capital of the republic of New York. There Governor Clinton also lived and Washington, Hamilton, Burr and Jay were present at the Poughkeepsie convention of 1788 that ratified, for New York, the Constitution; and the struggle between the old and the new divided the household of the farmer-colonel who had raised the liberty-pole in the Revolution. One of his sons was Theodorus Bailey, the United States senator who had joined Jefferson's party with the Livingstons and Clinton, while James Kent, later the Chancellor, who had married his sister Elizabeth, was his defeated rival in the same election. Kent, living in the Bailey house, had studied law in the library of this Jeffersonian rival, the brother of his wife, whose views he hated, calling them the "vulgar sophistries of the Revolution," for he was a passionate adherent of Hamilton himself. He had welcomed with rapture as they appeared the *Federalist* papers that upheld the "English party's" philosophy of property-rights against the "French party" of Jefferson that signified for him bad manners, low morals and rude dress. Riding circuits in Western New York, on horseback, following dim forest trails, he was disgusted with the backwoods democrats and with the liberty-poles they raised, no longer in protest against the king but against the taxation of the Federalists who were in power at the moment. Meanwhile, his closest friend was William Bailey, the brother-in-law who shared the views that formed the basis later of Chancellor Kent's *Commentaries on American Law*, views that owed little to the rebel "Enlightenment" from which was to descend in time the most distinctive and interesting thought of the country. It was with William Bailey that he went to Montreal, on a pleasure jaunt, in 1795, travelling from Plattsburg where the Platts, the Baileys and the Kents had bought four thousand acres, and more, of land. By the intermarriage of brothers and sisters these families formed a numerous clan, and, like Fenimore Cooper the novelist's father, their friend in the west of the state, they had thrown themselves into the land-speculation of the time.

To me as a child how picturesque was the tale of the founding of Plattsburg, when these forbears sailed up the Hudson and the waterways northward, ascending Lake Champlain in what they called their batteaux, the low flat boats that contained their possessions and their slaves. They manumitted these in time,—the last slave "Pete" in 1808,—while they brought seasoned Poughkeepsie timber to use, with the stone, in their dwellings and seeds of the Poughkeepsie poplars to plant by the lake. From these were to spring all the poplars of Plattsburg, Port Jackson and Cumberland Head. Only an occasional clearing broke the deer-haunted forests of upper New York where they built their blockhouses to protect them from Indian raids, with a forge, an ashery, a paper-mill, a grist-mill, a market-house and the first academy between Troy and Montreal. Nathaniel Platt was commissioner of roads and Charles Platt acted as a doctor whose fee for bleeding an Indian was a beaver-skin, for there were Iroquois all about, as numerous as the catamounts and sometimes no less fearsome to the lonely settler. To me the story suggested the legends that recounted the founding of cities in earliest England, in Greece, from the beginning of time when pioneers trekked up waterways, felled the timber and built their forts to secure them against hostile tribes or aboriginal marauders. As regularly as birds build their nests men had followed this pattern for thousands of years, the farmers succeeding the hunters in the waterside village.

Later it struck me that Fenimore Cooper had pictured the founding of Plattsburg in his tale of the founding of Cooperstown at just the same moment when his own father, the judge, had arrived in 1785 with the daughter who had had "advantages offered only by the city." His Templeton might have been Plattsburg in all respects, it seemed to me, from the dark forest of mighty pines to the French traders and Indian John, the emigrés, the sugar-maple boilers and the potashmakers. Among the Plattsburg settlers were the Saillys and the Fouquets, fellow countrymen of Cooper's Monsieur Le Quoi, and there the supposed "Dauphin," Eleazer Williams, published in 1813 his spelling-book in the language of the Iroquois nations. I seemed to see in Plattsburg another Leather-Stocking's hut and a tavern like the "Bold Dragoon" of *The Pioneers*, as I saw the same pedlar there with jack-knives and jew's-harps, calicos, tobacco, mirrors and potash-kettles. There were the sleighs and the skaters too, with the cutter on the ice that Currier and Ives were to picture in so many of their prints of similar bustling settlements in the northern forest; and I saw in the furniture of the Cooper "mansion" the clumsy mahogany tables and beds that I had known so well from the house at Plattsburg. Even in their politics Cooper's judge and my great-grandfather's father,—who was a judge as well, like Chancellor Kent,—would have agreed as heartily as I would have disagreed with both, sharing myself the views of the Jeffersonian brother. It was this judge with the opinionated choleric face whose bewigged portrait looked down upon me as a child and who, on a panel on his tomb,—in the name of the Maccabees,—asked us all to grant him "great honour and everlasting fame." I could see, more-

over, in the Plattsburg decanters the brandy, rum and gin
that were served, in *The Pioneers,* with the cider and flip at
those rustic feasts,—ending in custards and sweetmeats and
four kinds of pie,—of bear's meat and venison, turkeys and
fricasseed squirrels.

What a pity, it seemed to me, that we had no old novelists
to evoke this patriarchal life of the pre-urban past, no one
better than John W. De Forest in *The Wetherel Affair,* so
feeble beside Aksakov's *A Russian Childhood.* Fenimore Cooper
alone had recalled it faintly, and he had done little to body
forth a chronicler's remark about Plattsburg that it had "all
the luxuries of a seaport" in 1792. At that time, and later,
what might have been the "tune on the harpsichord," and what
the "philosophical conversation" that travellers were said to
have found there in "polite circles"?—circles that, to my fancy,
consisted of young ladies dying of consumption, with ringlets
that shone "black as the raven's wing." They were all symbolized for me by the flower-paintings and the music-books and
the youthful "female" poems of Emily Thurber, my grandmother's mother who had died so young, like the Davidson
sisters whom she knew and whose poems were extolled by Poe
and by Washington Irving. Had not the painter-inventor
Morse edited the poems of one of these, as Robert Southey
had written a memoir of her, comparing her to Chatterton,
while Mrs. Southey, the poet's wife, had composed a sonnet
addressed to their Plattsburg mother? The historian Prescott
had called Lucretia a "little flower of paradise" that had lived,
like Malherbe's rose, "for the space of a morning," this damsel
whose "bursts of poetic fire," in the manner of Ossian and
Thomas Moore, Poe had described as "wonderful" and
"thrilling."

Nor were these the only Plattsburg poets, or poets connected with the town in death; for what should I have discovered later, among the family gravestones there, but the name of the once famous and precocious John Blair Linn? This brother-in-law of Charles Brockden Brown, who wrote a memoir of him, had known that he too was "doomed to an early grave," and in fact he had died in 1804 after marrying another of the sprightly daughters of the old farmer-colonel of Poughkeepsie. A Philadelphian, like Brown, who had gone to New York with a passion for the stage and had had a success with a play when he was eighteen, he had become a minister who challenged Dr. Priestley for his Socinian attacks on the divinity of Christ. He had published several books of poems, the last of them *Valerian,* hoping "to promote the literature of his country," the pious wish of so many writers who flourished in the decades when the literature of their country was about to begin.

But how many names, with his, survive in letters that I have discovered in which oxen and apples and cattle-fairs are mingled with comments on "Pioneer Balls" at which other forgotten kinsfolk were evidently present. As my great-grandfather wrote of one, there were also "2500 others who are not particularly related to us," though I was to encounter descendants of many who were more or less related wherever, in years to come, I went in the world. For my grandmother's cousins, so called,—among them step-cousins and cousins-in-law,—were as numberless as the sands, it seemed to me, and I was to find them not only in New York but in London and in Dresden, in Washington, in Charleston and in San Francisco. Even at sixty-five, in Paris, I was to meet a family of them who had so far drifted away from their Anglo-Saxon base that they were half Dutch and half French. I had grown up knowing all their names, knowing that I was to visit them and always finding that they expected me, and they always seemed to me real cousins because my grandmother had brought them so vividly together. But, as I grew older, they grew more and more remote, until, for the most part, these shadowy connections were lost to me like phantoms that melt in the air.

## CHAPTER V

## "EUROPE"

IT was understood in the world I knew that a voyage to Europe was the panacea for every known illness and discontent, and I supposed that my father, who had crossed the ocean so many times, was versed in all the laws that governed travel. While, at a pinch, in foreign lands, one might go third-class on trains, only first class was thinkable on any kind of ship; and it usually took a day or two for one to get one's sea-legs and feel at home with the captain and the passenger-list. The French boats had the best cuisine, the White Star boats were excellent and made good time,—for men a desideratum, —the Cunarders especially were safe but not so attentive to the sick, and the North German Lloyd had its particular virtue. My father had a special cap for use at sea alone, with a little book in which he recorded the names of the ships on which he sailed and kept the log on all his ocean voyages. The "Bourgoyne" and the "Bretagne" were legendary names for me, with the name of the old and the new "Britannic" on which my parents had gone abroad on their honeymoon in 1882. If the most frequent illness we knew was the European fever, the Baedekers, more than thirty of them, that filled shelves with old Tauchnitz books, suggested an unfailing cure for this.

Was it merely a child's idea or did not Americans in general

feel that Europe was a realm of magic, permanently fixed, secure and solid as the Alps, regrettable in some ways perhaps,
but inviolate and sempiternal as a scene or a playground? It
was questionable morally and still more so politically from the
point of view of republicans who were children of the Pil-
grims, but it was incontestably a paradise of culture that had
scarcely known a beginning and would never know an end.
Did it occur to our elders, or would it have occurred to us if
we had been in their shoes, in their generation, that even
cathedrals might crumble away or that history, for them and
the world they knew, was not, in Toynbee's phrase, "com-
fortably over"? Whatever their circumstances were, or their
own personal ups and downs, for them the social order was
immovably safe and all the important wars had been fought
and finished long ago, for mankind had passed beyond the
cut-throat stage. How few realized that the underprivileged
who outnumbered them by a thousand to one were bent on
continuing history to their own advantage, for what reason had
they to be satisfied with it, or the subject peoples of Africa and
Asia who were no longer willing to be humble dependents?
This was the time when H. G. Wells, as I later discovered,
already felt that he was the one-eyed man in the country of
the blind, filled with a sense of the helplessness of flabby muscles and soft brains in the face of the general catastrophe that
he saw as impending. But no such feeling disturbed for Americans the iridescent fabric that was interchangeably thought of
as "culture" and "Europe," the continent every corner of which
stirred in their breasts an emotion evoked by some novelist or
artist, some composer or poet. The misery they saw on every
side, the cancerous mothers exposing their breasts in the
porches of churches in Italy, the cripples and the beggars were
preordained elements of the picturesqueness the painters had

memorialized. They were *tableaux vivants* that paralleled the pictures in museums.

To the child that I was myself when, at twelve, I was taken abroad for a year's frisk in these celestial pastures, there was no such thing as the cant of culture of which one later heard so much or what others called "unreal appreciation." It was all a bedazzlement, magical, simply, from the first rapture of approach, with the long black point of the Lizard running toward the ship, and, a day later, the ascent of the Scheldt, the red-tiled roofs of Flushing and at last the verdurous court-yard of the Antwerp hotel. My father, who had come over with us, knew Brussels, as he knew Antwerp, well, and, know-ing what pleased his imagination, whether it was good or bad, he took my brother and myself to the Musée Wiertz. He was a little amused, for the rest, by the fervour I displayed at my first encounter with "old masters," assembled in numbers, a fervour that mounted week by week and reached full flood in Dresden long after my father had left us to travel without him. For it was in Dresden that my mind first came to life, at the Zwinger, moreover, in the gallery that I learned by heart, so that for years I could close my eyes and see all the pictures on half the walls, or all except the cabinets of the little Dutch masters. From that day forward through the rest of the year, when I was approaching fourteen, wherever I happened to be, for a week or a month, in Vienna, Rome, Florence, Naples, Paris or London, I spent every morning in a picture gallery, roaming about from room to room, with a neophyte's zeal for the religion of the history of art.

Reading again, not long ago, the *Præterita* of Ruskin, I dis-covered that this idol of my childhood had been also thirteen when he was awakened mentally, as I was, by a book,—in his case, by Samuel Rogers's *Italy*, with vignettes by Turner, in my

case by Mrs. Jameson's *Italian Painters*. For this book confirmed the feeling that I had derived from the pictures themselves, starting me on a course of reading that,—to quote Ruskin's phrase,—"determined the main tenor of my life." It was
one of those popular handbooks, so characteristic of the nineteenth century when tens of thousands of people in the Eng-
lish-speaking countries were interesting themselves in a measure in affairs of the mind, another of which,—Mrs. Radcliffe's,
—ended with a descriptive list of the "twelve great master-
pieces of painting." Why twelve, and why just these,—among
them Paul Potter's "Bull"? Even a child could see the absurdity of it, as one could see the absurdity of all the flat assertions
in which the guide-books revelled in those days. One was expected to believe that a certain statue in the Lateran museum
was "the finest statue in the world," as one picture was "the
second finest altar-piece"; yet the list of the "twelve master-
pieces" was, in fact, no more absurd than Somerset Maugham's
enumeration of the "ten greatest novels." The mere specificity
of it focussed the mind on this object or that, like the stars
and double stars of the Baedeker guides. But Mrs. Jameson's
book, no other, was my open-sesame, and I might not have
read Berenson if I had not read this. I might not even have
discovered Ruskin, the favourite author of my whole adolescence, who illumined economics as well as art for me; for
*Munera Pulveris* and *Unto This Last* were to affect me later
as much as the Italian studies affected me at first. To what
fortuitous or trivial events, as they may seem, when one looks
back, one owes perhaps this first awakening, a view, a book,
a face in the street that strikes a prepared sensibility with the
force of a mystical message kindling the mind. It may be a
square of yellow light, on a dusty floor, on a morning in spring,
seen for the first time in the year, exciting the eye, that sud-

denly turns a boy into a landscape-painter, opening a new
world of desire for him. Up to that time, for my part, I had
collected birds' nests merely, pestering the birds themselves by
stealing their eggs, and I scarcely remember reading anything
but *Uncle Remus* and *Cudjo's Cave,* Frank R. Stockton and
Edward Lear's *Book of Nonsense.* It was my brother who had
been the reader and who had been found at three or four
reading Macaulay's history upside down.

As for Ruskin, I even unknowingly followed him in attempting to make pencil drawings of pictures in museums. One of
these was Fra Angelico's "Crucifixion" in the Louvre, where
Ruskin, on his first visit to the continent, had made his first
sketch. He had drawn Rembrandt's "Supper at Emmaus," ob-
taining a permit so to do, while I was stopped by one of the
guards and told that the lowest age-limit for this, whatever
the case may have been, was now fifteen. Ruskin had become
an admirable artist, as one saw in the drawings he made for
his books, while I had no luck at all with my few efforts,
sketching Roman ruins, street-scenes and what not; and moreover I outgrew the wish to write the art-criticism that I loved
and turned to another branch of this kind of writing. Not only
was I never an art-critic but I had an almost morbid dread of
so much as attempting to write about painting and painters,
although I have known more painters even than writers, and
although from the first I was convinced that criticism in some
form was the most delightful activity one could dream of in
this world. I even felt that everything might be expressed in
criticism, as others have felt about music or fiction or sculpture,
—in the last case, Michelangelo, as everyone knows; and certainly Ruskin, for one at least, expressed in criticism a good
half dozen sides of life. Years were to pass before I knew how
many Americans of my time shared, mostly on the economic

side, my feeling for this writer, for I never heard of the Ruskin clubs that flourished in the West and included among their members Jack London and Carl Sandburg. Nor could I have known that Charles A. Beard was founding Ruskin College at Oxford almost at the moment when I was discovering him in Dresden. Ruskin stood for the Utopian impulse that was deeply planted in the American mind and that awoke in me also in time; and it was this common impulse, fostered by Ruskin in both of us, that was to lead me to Lewis Mumford.

Meanwhile, Ruskin drew me to shelves of art-historians, who drew me into the study of history as well, and presently theology, from the Flanders of Thomas à Kempis to Cardinal Newman and even Jonathan Edwards. For years, when I was at home again, two engravings of Newman hung on my walls, and I even translated passages of Newman into Latin, while I also erected an altar in my room with a seventeenth-century Italian crucifix above it. Under the influence, in part, of a high-church clergyman whom I served for two or three years as an altar-boy, I vaguely intended myself to enter the Church, and I lived in a dream of the Middle Ages and of Italy and Catholicism, which somehow seemed to me one and the same. I shared the reveries of Marius the Epicurean when, as Walter Pater said, he "played at priests," playing "in many another day-dream" also, "replacing the outer world of other people by an inward world as he himself cared to have it." During those years, in New York or wherever, I haunted this Catholic church or that in order to recover the feeling of Italy again in the colour of the embroidered copes and stoles, the odour of the incense and all the intoxicating overtones of the liturgical words. I even carried in my pocket boxes of wax-matches because of their incense-like perfume when I blew them out, and I noted the feast-days of saints and involved myself in my

pre-college years in long theological discussions with two or
three friends. For the rest, I was engulfed in that "old world"
feeling which so many Americans used to share, a feeling that
was induced by their new-world living and that invested the
commonest objects, every fan-light or door, abroad, with its
own special exotic mystery and charm. How many books I
read as a boy, from *Romola* to *The Marble Faun*, from Byron's
*Childe Harold* to *Mornings in Florence*, bring back that feeling now at the turn of a page, as they bring back a time when,
in Leo Stein's phrase, I was "only concerned to know and not
to understand." I felt that nothing was expected of me which
I could not carry out some day and life seemed to consist of
moments that were never to end.

But, returning to Dresden, one moment there might well
have broken the spell for me, suggesting a twentieth century
that none of us dreamed of, when my brother and I were
stoned in the street by a gang of little German boys who, with
this angry gesture, signalized our country. We did not know
what was in their minds until Frau Schörke, who was teaching us German, explained that many of the Germans were in
sympathy with Spain and resented our victory, that year, in
the Spanish-American war, over one of the European countries. Centuries had passed since any outsiders had challenged
the power or the cultural supremacy of Europe, and these
Germans expressed what countless Europeans were feeling. I
might, but did not, realize then that Fra Angelico, whom I so
loved, had not uttered the last word on life or art and that the
comity of nations was not yet achieved, though I made in
Dresden one small discovery that everyone made in that generation, expressing it in the phrase, How small the world is.
For one day Colonel Ricardo, a British officer, and his wife
arrived at our Schnorr-Strasse pension with a Mr. Herdman, all

fresh from India and, like others in half the towns of Europe, seeking the kind of "economy" that we sought ourselves. Was it not on the very first day that Mr. Herdman, observing me, on my way out to the Zwinger, as I recall it, asking me to post a letter for him, held it up before my eyes so that I could not avoid reading the address? And what did I see there but "Sion Mills, County Tyrone," words evoking the Emerald Isle that I had written a score of times, assisting my nurse Rosie who was writing to her mother. And who was Rosie? Rosie Morris, whom Mr. Herdman had "always" known,—the Morrises had been "our tenants for generations"! There was Rosie, even then, holding the fort for us at home, while her name rang in the German air at this encounter of East and West, this meeting of India and America in far-away Dresden.

What ineffaceable other impressions Dresden was to leave in me before we turned southward in the spring to Vienna and to Venice, beginning with Christmas, more glamorous than ever in this land of lebkuchen and marzipan, of gingerbread mannikins, music and Hänsel and Gretel. All the old Northern mythology seemed to come to life then in the winter afternoons that darkened early, filling the glittering streets with mysteries and shadows, while the great flares illumined the snow that covered the booths of the Yahrmarkt with all their enchanting wares brought in from the country. What miles there were of pitchers and cups, wood-carvings, trinkets and porcelain pipes, grotesqueries of every sort, with peasant designs, delightfully irregular, often crude, poetic to the unaccustomed eye and savouring of Grimm's fairy-tales and Heine. There was the old king of Saxony, too, whom one saw sometimes in Prager-Strasse and always at high mass in the Dom on Sundays and who looked like Santa Claus himself with his long white whiskers and the air of grandfatherly benevolence

that radiated from him. I could not have realized how fortunate I was to have seen the Zwinger, the Schloss, the Dom and
the lovely Brühl Terrace before they were demolished; and
how often at the opera, to which I was taken three or four
times every week, I heard Frau Malten, still singing, the
original Brunhilde. Scheidemantel, too, in full voice also in
1898, was one of the old group of Wagner's singers. Among
the operas that I heard, thirty or forty of these at least, there
must have been a dozen that have long since ceased to be
performed.

I can scarcely think of Italy now, or of my first visit there,
without at the same time thinking of Arthur Ryder, later the
great Sanskritist of whom I recently read in Life as the teacher
of the atomic scientist Oppenheimer. He was at that time a
student at Leipsig whom we encountered in Venice, where he
too happened to be staying at Danieli's, then at Bologna, then
in Florence and finally in Rome, after meetings in railway car-
riages and the same hotels. Before we parted I looked upon
him as a youthful uncle or older brother, so much of my own
time I had spent with him, at Fiesole, in the Boboli gardens, at
San Miniato in Florence, at the Palazzo Vecchio and Santa
Croce. Together we saw Michelangelo's house and presently
in Rome we walked together, visiting the Mammertine prison
and the Palatine hill,—on a rainy morning in this case of
which he later wrote as "one of my best memories of Rome."
We drove together on the Appian Way and together we
sketched in the Forum, where I used the sketch-book my
mother had given me in Florence; and he afterwards referred
in a letter to "those days in Rome" as "good beyond anything
I ever experienced before." He recalls to me now the young
Americans in the early novels of Howells and James,—writer-
friends who for years were thought of together,—those culti-

vated young New England men who roamed through Italy
taking notes, discussing Lombardic architecture and Tuscan
sculpture. Ryder was certainly one of those types that still exist
in life, no doubt, but have vanished from the *dramatis per-
sonae* of the American novel. My mother attracted him greatly,
"more," he wrote later, "than I could tell her," adding in his
letter that he did not "distinguish her very clearly from the
other madonnas." He must have had in mind certain late madonnas who were decidedly mischievous and distinctly pretty,
for so she was, I think, at the time when he knew her. When
later he wrote this to me I was reading the journals of Gamaliel
Bradford, who had made me the executor of his literary papers,
and I discovered there that Bradford had pictured my mother
in the heroine of one of his unpublished novels. Fifty-three
years after he had first known her in the Adirondacks he still
remembered her frocks and their pinkness and blueness.

Just as in that Italian spring, wherever I went in later years,
I was always rediscovering Arthur Ryder, first at Harvard,
where he was teaching when I was a freshman there, and later
in California when he was at Berkeley. While one caught in
his Sanskrit translations the savour of femininity, he had come
to live the life of a guru or a sage, the gaunt lonely scholar's
life, wholly devoted to things of the mind, with its monkish
altitudos and renunciations. I saw in him a late survivor of
the New England Renaissance and the old Concord Oriental-
ism, a solitary like Thoreau and equally full of disdainful
pride, contemptuous of the machinery of scholarship and academic living. As in the case of so many ascetics, his perpetual
self-discipline had blunted his human sensibilities: he had
largely lost the capacity to sympathize with others and he had
small respect for his fellow professors. He described the head
of the history department, an Oxford historian, and his un-

derlings as "a sham giant surrounded by real pygmies," the
height of an academic wit that is touched with malice; and,
following the wisdom of the East, he thought Western philosophy "frivolous" because of its unconcern with the problem of
salvation. Ten years might go by before one knocked on the
door of his room,—a plain room like a Hindu hermit's cell,—
and the same voice answered from the same desk-chair in
which, when one opened the door, one saw him still sitting,
twisting the very same forelock. Meanwhile, indifferent to
renown, he carried on his real life-work, as one of those creative scholars, lost in this country, who might have been famous
in the England of Edward FitzGerald, for he was an artist as
a translator who, as it were, soliloquized through the medium
of the Indian poets and the Indian wits. All his translations
were flavoured with his own original personality,—*The Little
Clay Cart* and the *Shakuntala,* so often performed, in Ryder's
versions, at Harvard, in Berkeley, in New York, and the
Bhavagad-Gita, the Panchatantra and the versions in "Every-
man's Library" that introduced thousands of readers to these
writings of the East. I wondered in the nineteen-twenties why
they did not share the vogue which the Chinese and Japanese
poets had at that time, when Lin Yutang became almost as
popular as Mencken, dispensing the "cynically contented"
worldly wisdom of the earth-bound realistic Chinese mind.
But this, with its note of the art of living, was closer to an
American mind that had drifted far from Concord and the
Transcendental and that was Epicurean and also humanistic.
Confucius was congenial alike to Jefferson and Mencken.

Arthur Ryder remained for me a type of the Indian scholar-
sage, a sort of American version of the Oriental wise man; and
there were other characters of whom, as a child, I had glimpses
in Europe less fleeting than everyone's glimpses of the pag-

eantry of kings. As for this, at any hour, in Berlin, Vienna, Rome, a hush would fall over the street as the Kaiser flashed by, or perhaps the mustachioed King Humbert, with mounted guardsmen; and in this way I saw Queen Victoria twice, half covered with her parasol, on afternoons in spring on the Riviera. But were not Larkin G. Mead, the American sculptor in Florence, and the Greek widow of the old critic W. J. Stillman as remote from the twentieth century scene as the Widow of Windsor who had given her name to the epoch in which these two ancients had appeared and flourished? Both were connected with cousins at home in whose house I had often seen the Pre-Raphaelite paintings of one and the sculpture of the other,—a relief of their uncle William Dean Howells by his brother-in-law who was also their uncle, the last survivor of the circle of W. W. Story. This Roderick Hudson of an earlier time,—Larkin G. Mead of Vermont,—who had settled in Italy in 1862, had astonished the natives in Brattleboro with a colossal figure in snow that Lowell memorialized in his essay *A Good Word for Winter*. Since then he had sculptured the Lincoln monument for Springfield, Illinois, the original of which was still in his studio in Florence, where the old man, whose work seemed already archaic, was still the professor of sculpture in the Florentine academy in which Michelangelo had taught. Well I remember Larkin Mead, with his skull-cap and long white beard, surrounded by the Renaissance paintings that filled his house,—at least in appearance not unlike George Frederick Watts, whom I was to see in his studio on a certain afternoon. There, in London, I was taken to meet the astonishing Marie Spartali, who was only in her sixties then but whom I saw later, at eighty, erect and still young, with a red rose in her hair. It was easy enough to understand how Swinburne, seeing her in her youth, advancing across the lawn on a summer afternoon, could only murmur feebly, "She is so beautiful that I want to sit down and cry." She had outlived by decades the romantic Stillman who had founded the first American art-journal, *The Crayon*, though this perfect type of Pre-Raphaelite beauty who had posed for Rossetti's "Dante's Dream" still painted the pictures that could scarcely be distinguished from the master's.

Meanwhile, to return to Arthur Ryder, it was in Italy that I fell in with another sort of mentor,—six years later,—who scorned for quite different reasons the machinery of life. I was in college by that time and returned with my father and mother for a beatific summer by the Bay of Naples, a visit of which my impressions are now so entangled with those of the first that I am scarcely able to distinguish between them. My father was taken seriously ill, as it happened, in Sorrento, so that he and my mother were virtually prisoners there, and, roaming along the coast alone, I encountered at Capri an Englishman, a professional tutor in Italy who was taking a vacation. He was attached to a family, famous in Naples, who lived in a town called Penne in the Abruzzi, a mountainous wilderness, I gathered from him, horrid in the ancient Roman sense, a kind of Siberia to the Neapolitan eye. I pictured it as like Recanati, the dreary birthplace of Leopardi that evoked all those eloquent longings to escape to Rome, and G. E. Marshall had come to Capri, eschewing impedimenta, although not in Arthur Ryder's way. Nor did he share the guru-like scruples of Ryder regarding the acceptance of money for the teaching of wisdom, for he was an Epicurean merely with a "constitutional disinclination to work between meals," as I remember he put it. He wished only to be assured of enough to eat, an easy-chair, a bed, a fire in cold weather and a handful of books, and all his possessions were in one valise that he

opened whenever we stopped for a night, removing his white
linen trousers with his socks and his shirts. For I travelled
about with him to Ischia and a number of towns on the islands or in the neighbourhood of Naples. Whatever he had
worn he set soaking in a wash-bowl, hanging it out of the
window to dry in the night, so that, sans any underclothes,
garters, belt or necktie, he was always not only unencumbered
but impeccably fresh. For me the simplicity of it was a phil-
osophic lesson. He wore nothing else but a striped blue blazer
and a straw hat with the arms of Caius College, Cambridge,
embroidered on the hat-band. This emblem being a cardinal's
hat, various villagers with whom we fell in supposed that he
was some sort of ecclesiastic. They stooped and kissed the hem
of Marshall's sleeve.

He was, in fact, a Catholic, albeit an easy-going one who
used the Index, he said, as a guide to good reading and who
spoke of the priest at Penne, his friend, as the spiritual father
of the whole town and the natural father of at least half of
it. The prince and the princess there were by no means on
good terms because of their goings-on with servants and the
young men of Penne, and the princess, recently returning
from Rome, had found that her lover had been spending his
time in bed with an itinerant prima donna. Nor was their
heir to be outdone, Marshall's sixteen-year-old charge, who was
to be a titular archbishop when he came of age, as I understood
that one son was in every generation, or ever since the family
had produced a pope. But for a few weeks every spring they
all mended their ways to prepare for the annual visit of their
great Roman cousins, who had preserved, in appearance at
least, the austerity, the stately style, and even the puritan
morals of their antique forbears. Great was the awe they inspired in the C.'s, as Marshall represented them, minding their

P's and Q's, scrubbing up their manners, rehearsing their general behaviour like refractory children before the impending visit of some Aunt Henrietta. Had I not seen them, or supposed I had,—the Neapolitan upper crust,—in the dining-room at Sorrento where I was left alone when my parents were upstairs at the hour of dinner and when the great hall was full of guests the like of whom I had never met and who seemed to be a family party on some gala occasion? Who were all these little bejewelled men and these swarthy ladies in evening dress who were playing verbal tennis between the tables and who, to my crude adolescent American eye, suggested a lively chaos of bedizened monkeys? I presently discovered that half the *marcheses* and *principessas*, the great world of Naples, in short, spent every August,—and spends it still, perhaps,—in this Sorrentine hotel, the world of which, through Marshall, I had had a glimpse behind the scenes and in which I saw a species of *commedia dell' arte*. How easily one fancied these nimble shapes in masks and wigs and plum-coloured coats, or as figures in Guardi's paintings or the operas of Mozart or Casanova's eighteenth-century setting.

For I was at an age when one looks for types, for living illustrations of the books that one has read and the paintings one sees, finding them too easily, as I found in Marshall a Yellow Book type, a sort of Max Beerbohm character, which of course he was not. But why did he impress me? Because, in my second Harvard year, he confirmed my distaste for "efficiency" and the "strenuous life," for many of the ideas and ways that prevailed at home, living himself on nothing a year, and wholly "inefficient," yet making at the same time so much of life. He was a many-sided man, delightful on all sides. For several years we wrote to each other, while he drifted from Capri to Devonshire, to Algiers, the Canaries, Teneriffe, Rome and where not, to me recalling always my summer on the bay that supposedly inspired the wish to see it and perish. With him, at Dombré's Grand Hotel Piccola Sentinella,—of which who could ever forget the reverberant name?—I saw the sun rise over Casamicciola and the hollow of the town like an upturned seashell emptying on the beach. Behind rose the rambling mountain of Epomeo, surveying the ruins left by the recent earthquake; and I remember the grapevines of Ischia heaped one upon another with bulging clusters of fruit over-hanging the road. From every hillside along the coast ancient columns and mosaic floors protruded like so many plums from a ragged fruitcake, whether at Cumae or Baia or Posilipo, over the vine-clad stands of the lemonade-vendors with dilapidated wicker chairs assembled before them. How still were the hot afternoons, broken by the humming of insects alone and the quick darting of lizards on the white-washed walls, hung with purple morning-glories, over which the oleanders spread their spear-like leaves and bright pink flowers. Among the great oaks and the olive-trees in the cloisters of old monas-teries tattered frescoes clung to the broken walls and massive doors led into courts where the Middle Ages had not awakened to the nineteenth century or even to the sixteenth.

After that summer for several years I was obsessed with Italy, where I had filled my diary with Ruskinian pages about ambones and mediæval pulpits covered with mosaics and where, near Amalfi, I had read Rossetti all day long, looking out at the Isles of the Sirens. But I felt the oppression of so much that was beautiful and that overwhelmed one's own power to respond, and I could understand why artists, from motives of self-preservation, reacted towards the bitter and the squalid. I felt the danger of what Melville described as "falling into Plato's honey head" and, as he added, sweetly perishing there.

## CHAPTER VI

# HARVARD: 1904–1907

WHAT DREW me to Harvard, a stranger in a strange land
with which I had few associations? I went to Harvard
just as students in the twelfth century went to Paris because,
for me also, Abélard was there; for I knew I was a writer born,
—I seemed always to have known this,—and I supposed that
Harvard was the college for writers. It was intensely literary,
as it had been for three hundred years,—it was even more literary in my time than ever,—attracting many like John A. Lomax,
whose work was ignored by the Texas professors and who
came to study ballads with the far-famed Kittredge. While I
did not know what I wanted to write, I knew that write I must
and even the kind of writing that I was fit for; and for my
purpose Harvard was the greenest of pastures.

On the evening of my first day I was taken to a punch at
Holworthy Hall where a tumbler of unwatered whiskey was
placed in my hand, and, hearing the cry "Bottoms up!" I
poured it down my throat, swooning as I did so on the floor.
I was conducted homeward by a sophomore who later became
a famous Unitarian divine. On my second evening, at another
punch in the sanctum of the *Harvard Monthly,* I met the
poet John Hall Wheelock and various other literary men with
whom I soon found my natural level. But my loyal friend Max
Perkins, who had arrived the year before and wished to give

me a chance to know the "right" people, arranged to have me join at lunch the boys from the famous New England school where he had been himself for two or three years. What misery was that for me, tongue-tied and thin-skinned, not knowing how to escape from this purgatory, while the young barbarians at play threw crusts at one another and sometimes threw butter on the ceiling. Nor was I very much happier when I found myself launched into a "final" club where I was surrounded by oarsmen and football players. I was the "mollycoddle" among the "red-bloods,"—Theodore Roosevelt's words, much quoted at the time,—but, floating in a dream that was sometimes a nightmare, I learned at last where I belonged and what to frequent and avoid in the way of circles. I was glad, from that time on, to be an outsider everywhere except in the world that by nature I was *inside* of; and I always liked Ruskin's phrase for writers, that they should be "fit for the best society" and, being fit, should then "keep out of it." I agree that to be fit for it is not the easiest thing in the world, but to keep out of it was natural and simple for me.

The circle in which I felt at home gathered at the Stylus Club, the straw-yellow wooden house, 41 Winthrop Street, where I spent my last year in college living with Max. Downstairs, late in the afternoon, our literary friends met for tea, produced by Mrs. Amy, the Australian housekeeper who was used to boys and brought in piles of crumpets and other goodies. The walls were lined with the framed autograph letters that Max's grandmother had given us, while in my room upstairs hung my death-masks of Pascal, Canova, Thackeray and one or two others. There hung also the old engraving of John Quincy Adams, always my favourite president, that had come from Plattsburg. For a time, at least, Max and I rose every morning at six o'clock to read aloud together some book or other,—Herbert Spencer's *First Principles,* for one, though why just this I cannot say, unless it was for masochistic reasons. For Max was by no means a lover of early rising, and he had written for the *Advocate* an essay "On Getting Up in the Morning" that humorously expressed his detestation of it. But the Cromwell in him was uppermost then, and, sometimes wearing a Norfolk jacket, like Professor William James, he usually dressed severely in black and grey. He had given up gay neckties and corduroy waistcoats, and, while planning a novel, I think, like Pendennis, about his "griefs, passions and follies,"—another "Leaves from the Life-Book of Walter Lorraine,"—he had reformed like Pendennis when he had spent all his money. He saw little of his old Fencing Club friends, while he was kind in a hundred ways to various other students who offended his taste, teaching at the Social Union, where I also had a class, and going in for the study of economics. This was partly, it seemed to me, because he did *not* like to know about railway rates and fire-insurance statistics. One of our friends wrote to me, "If Max wants heavy thought without water or ice in the glass, why not mathematics?"—and again, "Tell Max to glance lightly over the faces of the star students in philosophy courses and ask himself if they are a race of thinkers." But vain were all such ironies and admonitions. Max slept in a tiny attic, with a table and a cot, that needed only a candle stuck in a bottle to reproduce the first act of *A Gentleman of France,* for at that time he idolized the "real soldiers of fortune" of Richard Harding Davis like the old Confederate officer General MacIver. Max too would have liked to fight under eighteen flags, living betweenwhiles in some casual room in a hotel with a trunk, a blanket and a sword for all his possessions. But he was indignant when anyone remarked that he also had a sense of the picturesque.

Meanwhile,—to continue for a moment with Max before I go back to the Stylus Club,—we spent dozens of evenings together roaming over Boston, dining perhaps at Marliave's or at one of a score of old-fashioned hotels of a kind that was rapidly vanishing in volatile New York. They were sometimes disreputable in a more or less amusing way like the burlesque theatres that flourished near Scollay Square or like the "Bell in Hand" where the sawdust that lay on the floor might have been there since the days of Samuel Adams. Having long since become a drinking-place for workingmen, the "Bell in Hand" enforced, to keep students away, the Massachusetts law against drinking for minors, and Max and I circumvented this by wearing large blond false moustaches. The barman could not challenge these without the risk of retaliation in the possible form of a suit for personal assault. We went to the Italian puppet-theatre where, night after night, for weeks on end, one could watch the *Gerusalemme Liberata* and listen for another thirty evenings to the *Orlando Furioso*. But I at least was not interested then in the old Boston culture that was to stir my mind in later years. Nor did I know that modern architecture had, in a sense, begun with Richardson in Boston,—the creator of Sever Hall, where I passed so many hours,—and with Louis Sullivan, the Boston boy who had settled in Chicago and developed the ideas of the old Boston sculptor Greenough. For the rest, for breakfast Max and I often went to the "Holly Tree," the coffee-house that so many of the celebrities frequented, among them "Copey" who uttered there an oft-repeated epigram comparing, in the matter of their freshness, poems and eggs. There too one saw Pierre La Rose, Santayana's friend who was also our general friend in the circle of the Stylus, although he was older than the rest of us and had once been an instructor,—he was a decorator now and a designer of

books. He was redecorating the Boston Art Museum. Pierre
La Rose personified the Pre-Raphaelite aestheticism and the
dilettantish Catholicism that flourished at Harvard.

When I think now of the Stylus Club I remember J. M.
Barrie's remark, "People who drink tea are really just as interesting as people who drink whiskey, only Mr. Kipling has
never discovered it." Whiskey flowed in all circles I knew
and there was a potent Stylus punch that also flowed on occasion; but what a good custom was the drinking of tea, then
prevalent at Harvard, to enliven conversation and bring minds
together. It brought together, on our afternoons, Max, Jack
Wheelock and George Foote, Edward Sheldon, George and
Francis Biddle, Hermann Hagedorn, Alfred Kidder, the an-
thropologist of later years, B. A. G. Fuller, already writing on
Plotinus. Among a dozen others was the member who thought
Kipling was the only true successor of Milton and Shakespeare,
and he has recalled to me Barrie's remark, though I do not
remember whether he drank only whiskey. What I do remember is that his uttered observation had at the moment an effect
as of the shattering of glass; for, literary as we all were, the
"Harvard aesthete" was the type to which a majority of the
members were more or less related. Harold Bell represented
this type in its extremest form, a New Yorker, born "with a
gold spoon in his mouth" like an Edgar Saltus character, a
lover of luxury and cats, a gastronome and gourmet. Another
Tancred Ennever, he also dressed with extreme distinction,
travelling as well, on occasion, with a courier and a servant;
and later, invariably true to type, an amateur archæologist, he
joined an expedition to excavate Sardis. He had a rather cruel
face, dead white, with full red lips, that suggested the protrait
of a Borgia, boldly painted, and, aspiring to create "perfect
prose," he wrote sonnets in the manner of Oscar Wilde that

were printed in a splendid quarto bound in white vellum. He liked to quote Baudelaire and Huysmans, Mallarmé and the Marquis de Sade, and he persuaded Bruce Rogers, in those days at the Riverside Press, to design the menu for his twenty-first birthday dinner. What a Neronian feast was that, in a great room at the Somerset Club, with place-cards in the manner of Louis XVI, set in eighteenth-century type, dishes from four or five countries and musicians from New York.

It could not be truly said that this *esprit précieux* was dominant anywhere at Harvard or even at the Stylus; but, except in Copey's circle, the literary note was very far removed from the journalistic. I personally came in the end to share Jacques Maritain's aversion to "the shameless ascendency of the god Æsthetics taken as the ultimate end of human life," as I preferred dogs to cats or the canine to the feline which seemed to me summed up in Santayana. But this did not attract me to Kipling's personality or the school-followers of Kipling in the magazine world. Who could have escaped the charm of Santayana's *style*, which I discovered, like so many, in the library of the Signet, where I was the librarian and where I can still see *The Sense of Beauty* in a shadowy corner of the shelves. It was only later that I found so much that was unsympathetic in the "cynic and Tory in philosophy," his phrase for himself. This was after I had come to feel the magnanimity of William James, at whom Santayana always looked down his nose, as if in the nature of things the post-Catholic reactionary was better than the post-Protestant believer in mankind. Everything Santayana wrote contained an assumption of superiority when he was merely different, in point of fact, thrown on the defensive because he had been hatched from a Spanish duck's egg in a Yankee barn-fowl's nest. So I came almost to feel what the grand old Gaetano Salvemini felt when I asked him years later, on shipboard, if he liked Santayana. "No," he said, *"with enthusiasm!"* throwing up his hands; though I could not deny that, wandering alone, a stranger and exile everywhere, Santayana lived the true life of the sage.

But disliking the feline aestheticism that Santayana stood for did not make Kipling's masculinity more winning for me, his glorification of the "men who do things" and his cult of the efficient of which we had heard too much in our native air. Aestheticism in some form or other really did rule our minds, and if there was any one writer to be found in every bookcase, in my time at Harvard, it was Walter Pater. Edward Sheldon asked his mother, in a letter that I later saw, to send him copies of *Marius* and *The Renaissance* because "the copies at the Library are always out"; and the same taste extended to Yeats, whose vogue was just beginning and whose poems we scribbled all over our lecture notebooks. The Celtic revival was at its height, the Abbey Theatre was on everyone's tongue, with Lady Gregory and Synge's *Riders to the Sea,* and there was a general feeling in literary circles that the best English poetry was Irish now. The Irish seemed to have escaped the hurly-burly of the nineteenth century, the industrial century in which writers were supposed to have made too many concessions to the Philistine taste. I remember with what excitement Ned Sheldon and I heard Florence Farr and called upon her at her hotel in Boston. This was the lady who finally retired to a Buddhist convent in Ceylon and who recited Yeats's poems, to a psaltery that Dolmetsch made for her, and sometimes acted in his plays.

According to Coleridge, the possession in youth of anything like perfect taste is a virtual proof of the absence of genuine talent, and the cultivation of taste at Harvard was not only occasionally mistaken for talent but sometimes went far to stultify it. The atmosphere of Cambridge proved often to be sterilizing, but this was perhaps the necessary price it paid for being literary as no other atmosphere has ever been in this country. No outsider could have failed to observe that in any street-car thereabouts half the passengers were reading magazines or books, a fact that Audubon must have remarked in the early nineteenth century when he called Massachusetts "the reading state." The days of the New England Renaissance were, in 1905, not too remote and living survivors, or epigoni, were still to be seen, Thomas Wentworth Higginson, for one, the frail old man with the legendary past who lectured with a quavering voice now and then. Charles Eliot Norton, the confidant of Emerson, Carlyle, Ruskin and Lowell, still opened his house to students for readings of Dante, and, what was most striking, all the professors, whatever their specialties might be, seemed to be in addition men of letters. That William James was a born writer everybody knew, but Josiah Royce had written a novel as George Herbert Palmer translated the *Odyssey* and produced the definitive edition of George Herbert, the poet. Santayana was a poet himself, and Shaler, the geologist, was the author of an epic poem in no less than five volumes,— *Elizabeth of England* this was called,—while Bliss Perry was a well-known essayist and Barrett Wendell wrote novels and plays and talked as if writing books was a common occupation. I remember Barrett Wendell saying that when you wrote a book you must be sure it opened and ended well, that the parts between did not matter so much, which,—silly as this seemed in a lecture,—comes back to me as a note of the place and the time. For it implied that writing books was something everybody did and that most of us, in turn, would probably do. Just so, in quite elementary classes, it seemed to be assumed that we would naturally wish to look up for ourselves some history of the university of Padua or the Collège de France, that we were instinctively scholars as well as writers; and, when the professors talked with students about their careers and the future, they spoke,—if these were literary,—as men who knew. How true this was I am reminded by another letter of Edward Sheldon who discussed his plans with Dean Briggs, and with Baker and Wendell, all of whom agreed that one could not both write and teach or that, if one taught, one could write anything but textbooks. "If you want to write any-thing else, don't teach at all!" (For I suppose that their own books had been written mostly in their younger days and that they had since felt in some way thwarted.) Ned Sheldon con-tinues, "They all say, 'Have the pluck and courage to face everyone and say, "I am going to write, even at the risk of com-plete failure and humiliation." ' "

Nothing could have been more Emersonian, and in this sense the spirit of Emerson was still alive in his old college. I dare say even that in literary students the sense of the vocation was at that time in Harvard stronger than elsewhere. The poet Edwin Arlington Robinson was the kind of Harvard man of whom I knew numbers then or later, who followed their bent at any cost, committed up to the hilt, whatever the risks might be or the consequences. But Emerson, in another sense, seemed scarcely to be there at all, though the hall of philosophy, just opened, had been named for him,—I mean the Emerson who said, "Make much of your own place," not hankering after the "gilded toy" of Europe. William James kept up this line with what Santayana called his "American way of being just born into a world to be rediscovered," and James had countless fol-lowers of whom I ought to have been one and would have been if I had been maturer. How deeply I came to admire and love this enemy of all despair, of authority, dogma, fatalism, inhumanity, stagnation; but the Harvard that I was prepared to know was much more the college of Charles Eliot Norton whose mind looked backward in time and across the sea. This was the Norton who never set foot in England without feeling that he was at last at home, he said; and when, for the word "England" one substituted "Europe," with the Middle Ages and the history of art, one had the Harvard temper that I knew well. It was the temper of Henry Adams who had lost all hope for the modern world and saw nothing in the American scene but "degradation," while, like Norton, he also preached the gospel of mediævalism as an escape from the vulgarity of the American present. That the world had been steadily going to the dogs since the time of Dante was the complaint also of Barrett Wendell, who deplored the American Revolution that had sundered us from England and the guidance of the British ruling class. Irving Babbitt was all for authority and formalistic discipline as against the Jeffersonian vision he connected with Rousseau, the traditionally American belief that men, freed from unjust social conditions, were sufficiently good to be trusted to rule themselves. Then there was Santayana who described himself as an "American writer," or said he could not be described as anything else, but whom Lee Simonson remembered as always "gazing over our heads as if looking for the sail that was to bear him home." He was repelled by everything that characterized American life, preferring a world "run by cardinals and engineers," rejecting as "all a harvest of leaves" the New England Renaissance and its best essayists, historians, romancers and poets. His smiling contempt for the efforts of men to better the world and humanity was reflected in a host of Harvard minds that were reversing the whole tendency of the great New England epoch, dismissing its faith in progress as "the babble of dreamers." One and all

tended to revert, temperamentally, if not in fact, to the old
European rigidities of the mediæval order, to the cause of "the
altar and the throne," hierarchy and clericalism, against the
fluidities that were bred by American living.

All these influences, brought together, created a special
frame of mind that made "the Harvard graduate," as Henry
Adams put it, "neither American nor European"; and there
were other elements that went to form this anomalous brew in
the twentieth-century decade that I remember. Adams's own
theory that the universe was running down was merely an extreme form of the general feeling that we lived in a uniquely
unlovely and degenerate age in which it would have been far
better not to have been born at all, as Charles Eliot Norton
constantly told his classes. It was no time, in any case, for the
romantic "expansiveness" that Irving Babbitt attacked with
every breath; and the hatred of modern civilization that one
heard expressed on every side predisposed one in favour of anything that was not modern. In reaction against the Puritanism of
the New England forbears an Anglo-Catholic movement throve
in Boston, and there was a semi-serious cult of royalism also,
with a branch of the Jacobite Order of the White Rose. The
members offered expiation on the annual feast of St. Charles
the Martyr, led by Ralph Adams Cram, the prior of the chapter, the architect-disciple of Henry Adams; though this could
not rival the cult of Dante, which Mrs. Jack Gardner also embraced and which had been established at Harvard for two
generations. It had given birth, with the Dante Society, to
Longfellow's and Norton's translations and to Lowell's and
Santayana's important essays; and Dante was an omnipresent
interest like the dramatists of Shakespeare's time, who were
constantly studied and performed as well. Another Harvard
note of the moment was the Sanskrit that Babbitt had studied

with Lanman and that spread the renunciatory attitude which had something in common with Santayana's wisdom of submission, while the urban point of view and the classical stress on order and form had long since supplanted the romantically rural. For the rest, Remy de Gourmont and the French Symbolist poets, steeped in mediæval reverie, were a new mode of the young, some of whom discovered these poets in the library of the Union in *The Symbolist Movement in Literature* of Arthur Symons. There others happened on Flaubert, with his "green ooze of the Norman cathedrals," the Flaubert who said that he laughed when he found the corruption in anything that was supposed to be pure, when, in its fairest parts, he discovered the gangrene. Flaubert contributed his touch to the weary, all-knowing, sophisticated tone, the mocking tone that was sometimes assumed at Harvard, and John Donne provided another note that was to reverberate through the "new criticism" that followed the first world war. John Donne, neglected in England, was an old New England favourite of whom Emerson and Thoreau had written in earlier times,—even Bronson Alcott had written of him,—while James Russell Lowell and Charles Eliot Norton had both brought out in the eighteen-nineties new editions of his poems. Dean Briggs was only one professor who talked of Donne familiarly as a poet about whom everyone went to extremes, whom people inordinately hated or loved and whom he personally cherished as one who preëminently "made the far-fetched worth fetching."

When one added these tastes together, the royalism and the classicism, the Anglo-Catholicism, the cults of Donne and Dante, the Sanskrit, the Elizabethan dramatists and the French Symbolist poets, one arrived at T. S. Eliot, the quintessence of Harvard. Together they shaped his opposition to the "cheerfulness, optimism and hopefulness" that stood for the point of view of the great days of the past, as they shaped also his inevitable vogue in an age prepared to feel with him that poetry can be found in suffering and through suffering only. They shaped the course that led him, quite logically, to England, to which others were drawn temporarily, or only in part, to be drawn back later by powerful elements in their own minds of which at the time perhaps they were unaware. For the "European virus," as Henry James had called it, attacked its American victims in várying degrees, but in some degree or other it attacked most literary minds at Harvard because America there seemed nugatory. What Henry Adams had said of Boston, that it was "up in all things European" but that it was "no place for Americanism" was all the truer at Harvard now where "Americanism" meant Philistinism and by no means what, originally, it had meant for Adams. The special new-world character that all the Adamses had held so dear, seeing it as something elevated and something noble, had become with time there, and elsewhere too for literary minds, associated with William James's "bitch-goddess Success." That New England had a special dispensation was sometimes understood, but what Barrett Wendell called "the wilds of Ohio" were generally identified in these matters with the rest of the country. Henry Adams had somewhere spoken of the "vague look of wondering bewilderment" one always saw on the face of the Boston man who had "discovered America" for the first time; but few at the Harvard I remember wished to discover America or questioned Matthew Arnold's verdict on it. "He who cares," Arnold said, "for the interesting in civilization" will feel that the American sky is "of brass and iron," and many shared the feeling of the most famous of all the expatriates that to live under this meant "brooding exile."

At that time one could discern few signs of the new America that was to dawn, for literary minds, about 1910, when a new culture was being formed, even a new language, the voice of a new spiritual continent and climate. Everyone knew that there had been an American literature of sorts that lay "a generation or more behind us," as the poet Woodberry at Columbia told his classes, but this seemed remote and unrelated to what Woodberry also described as our own "period of dubious fame." But even of that older literature Woodberry was not too proud,—it had produced, he said, not one poet who was even of the rank of Thomas Gray; while the leading critic of the time, Brownell, had obviously found little joy in the writers whom he described in his *American Prose Masters*. For Harvard ears these writers were "of little lasting potence," Barrett Wendell's phrase for all of them, and, as Howells put it, Wendell gave his readers the impression that American literature was "not worth the attention of people meaning to be critical." Henry Adams, who was unaware of Emily Dickinson and Stephen Crane, as of Winslow Homer and Albert Ryder,—though he prided himself on his alertness and his feeling for art,—was typical of the cultivated American public in his belief that in literature and art the country produced nothing "any longer." This recalled the feeling in Germany in Goethe's youth that the literary products of the country were beneath contempt, the conviction that German literature was barbarous which did not change till Lessing established a new epoch for the German mind.

Within four years of leaving college I was to find myself, briefly, teaching American literature on the Western coast, getting up my lectures under a live-oak tree there, on a circular bench on that very Californian campus. Those were the days when English departments were casual and listless and young instructors lectured at their ease, keeping one day ahead of the class and speaking as I spoke with a mind that was full of everything except my subject. What I really cared for then was Italian painting and the mediæval Church, together with the eighteenth century and the European writers round whom Georg Brandes, the Dane, had woven his enchantments, and I had scarcely read "Our Poets" of whom I was to write, in *America's Coming-of-Age*, so cavalierly. In what I both said and wrote I reflected the impressions I had gathered at Harvard,—for, even then, I was still in my early twenties,—where English authors were always cited in preference to Americans, even when these could also be called classics. Invariably one heard of Thackeray, rarely of Hawthorne,—Carlyle, not Emerson,—Charles Lamb rather than Thoreau; and merely to have mentioned this would have been thought chauvinistic, a word that was applied to me when later I did so. I was never tempted to "find salvation" in Longfellow or Whittier, as various unwise critics had a way of saying when I had merely come to feel the relative importance of writers whom I had damned with the faintest of praise. For I had been all too convinced that our literature was wholly "narrow gauge" and that an excess of patriotism was the fault of our critics, as I can see in the reviews which I wrote in college, at a time when, as Santayana said, "We poets at Harvard never read anything written in America except our own compositions." What was there, we might have asked, in America to read? For the Harvard imagination the country was a void, and Joe Husband reflected the general feeling when George Moore asked him in London why he had "hewn coal of his own free will." Joe Husband was one of my classmates who had written a book called *A Year in a Coal-Mine*, relating his experiences there when he left college, and he had replied to George Moore as follows: "If I had been in Europe I might have gone to live in Montmartre as you did, but being in America there was nothing for me to do but go down into a coal-mine."

It was natural that, with this frame of mind, so many then and later went either to George Moore's Montmartre or to George Moore's London, with a feeling like Henry James's Theobald in *The Madonna of the Future* that they were the "disinherited of art." Were they not "excluded from the magic circle . . . condemned to be superficial," since the soil of American perception was so poor and thin, so that they had "ten times as much to learn as a European" and could only "come into their own" as suppliants in Europe? There was Henry James himself to show what they might achieve by this, the James who, in 1905, reappeared in Cambridge and delivered in Sanders Theatre his lecture on Balzac. The return of Halley's comet was a minor sensation beside this prodigious event at Harvard, when the orotund voice of the great panjandrum rolled like an organ through a hall that could scarcely contain the aura of his presence. I always marvelled when later critics supposed that they had "discovered" James and that he had been ignored like the writers in his own stories, the figure in whose carpet no one saw, for *The Golden Bowl* had gone through four editions in its first year and *The Ambassadors* was serialized in a New York monthly. Gertrude Atherton related in a novel how, when he visited San Francisco, society was torn between James and anti-James factions, and innumerable novelists from Edith Wharton to Willa Cather imitated him, while he was the darling of almost all the critics. He was "our one great writer" to Percival Pollard, who liked to connect himself with "the Jacobites drinking to the king over the water," and Huneker remarked that Henry James might be "the discoverer of the fiction of the future." Brownell ruined his own style by following James's, and Edgar Saltus and Edgar Fawcett dedicated novels to James, whose prestige grew more imposing every day. He was the greatest of all the Americans to whom distance lends enchantment, who seem to grow larger than life when they are invisible in Europe, like spectres of the Brocken, those magnified shadows that are cast by observers, when the sun is low,—gigantic misty images,—upon a bank of cloud.

One of my friends spent a summer reading Henry James to prepare for the composition of his own Jamesian novel, while for another, a professional novelist in later years, Henry James was a model in all respects. For, as he wrote, he dwelt himself "in a world of delicately shaded, not too strong emotions and sensations." The old letters of this friend remind me that "all Harvard," all we knew, was in those years "marching on Paris" or marching on London, while a letter from another friend remarks that the American critical world was virtually all "broken meat from the European table." What was the obvious moral then?—"Sit at the first table, not the second." He quotes a saying of George Foot Moore, whom he had heard in the chapel, "Sin is not doing what you are able to do, the best you are able to do, in life," an Emersonian sentiment, surely, but one that, for my friend, plainly meant going to do it in Europe. One had to be careful not to "run off the track at the point of Patriotism," that "open switch to the American train of thought"! This friend had gone in for art-criticism, or the kind of art-historical study that was to flourish presently at the Fogg Museum, an interest that I shared with him and that suggested the mode of life for which Bernard Berenson especially stood at Harvard. Berenson, already a half-mythical figure, seemed to embody in our time a type that Pater described in *The Renaissance*, in the essay on Winckelmann, who had lived in Rome and of whom Hegel said that he had "opened a new sense for the study of art." Berenson, with his all-curious mind, had wandered over Europe with vague hopes of becoming another Goethe, developing himself on many sides before, as he felt later, he had been betrayed into expertizing. In Italy he had explored minutely the Marches and the region of Siena, searching monasteries and churches for works of art, returning again and again to the enchanting adventure.

Long after I had lost the wish for this manner of living, I continued to admire Berenson's philosophy of art, his feeling that its function was to build a house for humanity to live in, to serve civilization by humanizing life. He called this life-enhancement, a notion that was far beyond the kind of aestheticians whom Maritain censured. It was the true humanism that was travestied by others, and Berenson's liberality matched the Goethean breadth of mind that kept him fresh, eager and alert when he was approaching ninety. He was never to lose his confidence in life as well worth while, or, despite its devilish propensities, in humanity either, his faith that liberalism was sure to reawaken, cast as it was, like Brunhild, under a spell of sleep. Meanwhile, the interest in Italian art throve in the Harvard air, and Mrs. Jack Gardner's collection, which Berenson had so largely formed, seemed rather an expression of this than a creator of it. It filled the Harvard mind with images that cropped out in scores of novels and poems,—in Eliot's phrase about Umbrian painters, for instance, and the trumpets and eagles that evoked Mantegna. The characters of the long-dead novelist friend of whom I have just spoken suggested Florentine ladies in brocaded dresses, or ladies of Titian, transposed into modern terms; and in how many other novels Boston girls wore nets of pearls and were pictured as resembling girls by Lombard painters. Occasionally, they had oval Sienese faces. As often as not, when the young men spoke of lives they might have chosen they thought of drifting down Venetian canals in gilt and vermilion barges at carnival time, or floating through Limbo like Paolo with Francesca, or riding into Florence in the time of lilies. They thought of a palazzo exquisitely hung with faded silk brocades and bedrooms with upholstery in old rose and gold, or a villa at Fiesole, smothered in flowers and overlooking russet roofs and Brunelleschi's dome not far away.

To recall this Harvard frame of mind one has only to glance at the novels that John Dos Passos wrote a few years later, *One Man's Initiation* and especially *Streets of Night*, with their constant evocation of the Renaissance and "distant splendid things." The names of Fra Angelico, Lorenzo Monaco, Gozzoli "stream through" the young man Fanshaw's mind, and he says to himself, "Pico della Mirandola would not have been afraid of such an impulse." He thinks how wonderful it would be to have yellow curls like Dürer's in the portrait of himself at twenty-eight, and he remembers the scalloped wavelets, the blown hair and the curves like grey rose petals of Botticelli's wave-born Venus. He tells himself that he will never be able to look Donatello, or the Ghiberti doors, in the face again, and his mind drifts once more to Orvieto and the great Signorelli frescoes in the cathedral there. In *One Man's Initiation*, the ambulancier Martin Howe spends afternoons in France, during the first world war, looking at the Gothic windows of the lantern of the abbey, thinking that if this were the age of monasteries he would, without a moment's hesitation, enter one. He sees himself working in the fields, illuminating manuscripts, calming his feverish desires and drowsing them in the deep-throated passionate chanting of the offices of the Church,— visions that possessed as well many another young Harvard man who wished to escape from the banalities of modern living. Like Dos Passos, in the end, many of these, in reaction, turned towards whatever was "salt in the mouth" and "rough to the hand," to the crass actualities one found in the poems of E. E. Cummings and Conrad Aiken, evoking the slums, the gutter and the "sore of morning." They confronted the world they knew in a drastically questioning frame of mind, whether in fiction, or in poetry, or in criticism.

Meanwhile, at Shady Hill, still dwelt the tutelary sage or saint of these absorbing Harvard prepossessions, Berenson's teacher, Ruskin's friend, the rarely distinguished little old man, the incarnation of "culture," Charles Eliot Norton. Twice I was taken by a friend who had grown up under Norton's wing to Sunday "Dante evenings" in the golden brown study in which Henry James felt he had received his "first consecration to letters" forty years earlier in 1864. There, in the presence of "Dante Meeting Beatrice," the picture that Rossetti had painted for Norton, half a dozen young men, interested, curious or devout, listened with copies of the *Paradiso* open in their hands. They followed the text while Norton read aloud, like a learned, elegant and venerable priest dispensing sacred mysteries to a circle of heretics, perhaps, who were unworthy of them. One felt there was something sacramental even in the sherry and the caraway cakes that a maidservant placed in our hands as we were about to depart.

No doubt these impressions of Harvard are rather too special and personal to convey any adequate sense of the scene as a whole, but in those days the "elective system" permitted a student to follow his bent unconcerned virtually with anything that did not amuse him. So one saw only what one wished to see there. I often wondered if I had learned anything at Harvard that I could not have learned equally well at home, reading, listening to music and looking at pictures, and I think

I was chiefly impressed by the goodness of some of the professors, Dean Briggs, for instance, Bliss Perry and Edward Ken-
nard Rand. It seemed to me later that I had never been
touched by anyone's intellect until I met J. B. Yeats in 1909,—
the old Irish artist in whom I found a master,—no doubt because I was too immature to appreciate the philosophy of
Münsterberg and Royce or the history for which I listened
to Professor Haskins. I learned from Mr. Lowell, in "Government,"—a "science known only to Harvard," as one of my
friends said in a letter of the time,—that our President governs
but does not reign, that the English king reigns but does not
govern and the President of France neither governs nor reigns.
Then, having read in connection with this, Bryce's *American
Commonwealth,* I saw and heard the beguiling James Bryce
in person, the member of Parliament for Aberdeen with his
humorous air of a moulting cock bantam, whom Mr. Lowell
brought to the class one day. From another lecturer I learned
why the poets of Italy, as Dante said, ceasing to write in Latin,
wrote in Italian,—so that the girls could understand their
love-songs; for one otherwise lost these electric sympathies,
quick flashes of response and eyes that changed from line to
line. But little remains in my mind to recall the Harvard of
that time aside from a few phrases that characterize various
professors, or characterize them at least for me,—like Professor
Baker's "after all" or Münsterberg's "wiz uzzer worts" or Mr.
Lowell's "Now what actually happens is this." While my literary interest was counterbalanced by little else, however, there
were many mansions in the house of literature at Harvard, and
Kittredge, Briggs, Baker and Mr. Copeland, Bliss Perry and
Irving Babbitt inhabited not mansions merely but worlds of
their own. If anything brought some of these together it might
have been a feeling for Thackeray in the English novel and

Tennyson as a poet. So great was the stress laid on these that one could already have foretold an anti-Tennysonian and anti-Thackerayan reaction.

Years later, it seemed to me that of all my Harvard teachers I had probably learned most from Irving Babbitt, much as he repelled me and little as I liked his curiously inhuman brand of humanism. With everyone else who aspired to write I had my course with "Copey" but somehow never hit it off with him, unlike Max Perkins, his publisher later and his favourite at the time who was to bring him a wide audience with *The Copeland Reader*. I was "wilful and stubborn," Copey said, and the reason for this was that I did not wish to write in the manner that pleased him, although I could not have said just why, and possibly did not learn why, until I fell in with J. B. Yeats. This true-bred artist and man of letters scarcely saw a line I wrote, but he constantly talked of the writers of the so-called Irish Renaissance so many of whom had grown up in his studio and presence. He had educated some of these in his informal fashion, and he liked least the traits that Copey praised. Not emphasis, or the striking phrase, or Kipling's kind of vividness but the opposite of these, for him, betokened good writing,—Anatole France's *pas d'emphase*, vividness without effect and the phrase that is not striking but that haunts the mind. With these went the virtue of staying at home in one's imagination instead of going out and "seeing life," for he cared for the inner eye as he despised reporting; while Copey, who was an old newspaperman and Boston theatre critic, prepared his pupils for journalism by admiring just this. "I would never have seen what I did see had it not been for your teaching me," said John Reed, dedicating *Insurgent Mexico* to him, and one saw in *The Copeland Reader*, by his omissions and choices alike, what most appealed to Copey in American writ-

ing. He included selections from Heywood Broun, Richard
Harding Davis, Alexander Woollcott, O. Henry and R. C.
Benchley,—entirely omitting Emerson, as he omitted Howells,
—and his idols were the great journalist writers, especially
Defoe. A lover of histrionic effects as well as good reporting,
he had written a life of Edwin Booth, and, an actor himself
as a public reader, he liked young men who were actors too,
particularly when they were also very good-looking. Copey,
in fact, loved every kind of gallantry, the kind above all that
is visible in the figure and the face, the most understandable
of all tastes but one that tends to create a bond with the extro-
vert rather than the introvert mind of the writer.

There were two or three Copeys in the "uncut" state in
every seaport down in Maine, in Calais, for instance, where
he was born and where the old pharmacist said to me once,
"Did I know Mr. Copeland?—I went to school with Charles."
He showed me a photograph of their graduating class with
Copey standing five paces apart from the others, and the old
man said, "Charles was like that always." Having escaped what
he described as the "Ph.D. death rattle," Copey abounded in
his own sense at Harvard, where "Every man in his humour"
was the motto for professors who were actors often and characters all the time. What an actor Kittredge was when, falling
from his dais, he exclaimed, "At last I find myself on the level
of my audience"; and Irving Babbitt, tossing and goring the
writers he disliked, seemed to be acting the part of Boswell's
hero. Babbitt was another Dr. Johnson in his grunts, blowings
and gurgitations, roaring his opponents down, harsh and abrupt
in manner and voice, repeating "There are tastes that deserve
the cudgel." He recalled the tournaments of abuse that flourished in the Renaissance when the *odium theologicum* turned
into an odium of scholars and learned squabblers covered with

insults the "monsters" and "rogues" who said them nay over some question perhaps of the dative case. Did not the elder Scaliger call Erasmus, for opposing the worship of Cicero, a "drunkard" and a "scoundrel," as he called Étienne Dolet the "ulcer of the muses"?—and did not Schoppius in turn prove that the name Scaliger was identical with "jackass" in the Vulgate? He or some other also proved that among Scaliger's forbears there were no less than four hundred and fifty-nine liars. It was from Babbitt, no one else, that I first learned these facts, which in certain ways suggested his own personal temper, for he talked at times like the literary bully-boys who, in the eighteenth century, waylaid Voltaire.

What was the reason for the exasperation that characterized his manner? In part that he was miscast as a professor of French, a "cheap and nasty substitute for Latin," as he called it once, when he had wished to teach the classics. Convinced that French literature lacked, as he put it, "inwardness," he studied it "chiefly to annihilate" it, said Paul Elmer More; while Babbitt, who had some of the masculine virtues, had none of the feminine virtues that he despised in critics and their work. All zeal himself, all partisanship, and without elasticity, he was quite unaware of the irony,—for others,—in his praise of what he called "poised and proportionate living"; and, indifferent to novelists and novel-writing as to painting and to music, he yet laid down the law for artists and art. He challenged, in *The New Laokoön*, comparison with Lessing, who had lived a full artist's life as a playwright and poet, as, at least vicariously, Dr. Johnson also had, surrounded by poets, musicians, painters and actors. In Babbitt's life there had never been a Reynolds or a Garrick, a Goldsmith, a Burney, or a Gibbon, and painful to read were the pages in which he apologized for his own lack of experience in the world of art. He was negative in this realm of thinking and gauche when he adopted the Erasmian name of Humanism for his sect of thought, for he was a born sect-founder whose bias betrayed him when he virtually competed with Dowie for the attention of New York. What a sorry sight was that when, like a baited bear, this scholar contended with the profane New Yorkers, many of whom would not have known the difference if, instead of a Babbitt, he had been a Lessing.

What Dickens's Mr. Jellyby said, "Never have a mission," Babbitt should have said to himself long years before; but, aside from his doctrines, he was a teacher of passionate intensity and a positive personality at a time of indecision. His doctrines, repugnant to me then, grew still more repugnant the more I became aware of my own thought and as I grew in sympathy with "the great wave of radicalism" that was "sweeping over the world," as Babbitt put it. It never seemed to occur to him that this universal movement had sprung from the actualities of modern living, the need of twentieth-century men to shape their society and plan their world, together with the desire of the masses for their place in the sun. And why should there be any opposition between the humanitarian and anything that could rightly be called humanistic?—a question that only arose for me when later I *read* Babbitt to whom, at the moment, as a teacher, I was so indebted. For I owed to him my first initiation into the history and problems of the art I was to practise, and especially into the writings of Renan, Taine and, above all, Sainte-Beuve, who had almost all the qualities I admired so greatly. Sainte-Beuve's wish to "particularize," his love of the specific,—so far from the generalizing tendencies of Brunetière and Taine,—was one I soon identified with the passion for the "concrete" that J. B. Yeats was always praising. How enlightening were Sainte-Beuve's

phrases about the master faculty,—the ruling trait in characters,
—and families of minds, with his "group" method in criticism
and his unfailing literary tact, his erudition subdued by the
imagination. How wonderfully he maintained his poise between the romantic and the classic!—and I sympathized deeply
with the Sainte-Beuve who wrote the life of Proudhon and
believed in the relief of the depressed and the progress of the
world. In many ways Sainte-Beuve influenced me,—even perhaps his weakness in making all his characters "six feet tall,"
the minor ones too nearly on the level of the major,—and I owe
this, and much else, to Babbitt, along with his faith in the
permanent in man and his praise of the *honnête homme qui ne
se pique de rien*. Feeling that I might have been another kind
of man myself and that I might have done a dozen other
things, I was never tempted to pique myself on any special
knowledge of my own or to pass for anything but a "damned
literary person."

CHAPTER VII

# DIASPORA

I HAD scarcely been out of college a month when I found
myself in England. I had crossed in the steerage, sharing a
room with a Frenchman, the chef of a Soho restaurant in
London who spoke little English as I spoke little French,
though we talked about the stars as we roamed the deck. For
those nights in July were calm and bright, and at least I could
say "étoile" and he "Cassiopeia." During the day, for want of
a chair, I sat on a coil of rope, reading *Tom Jones*, full as I
was of England. Other college friends of mine, equally full of
Germany or France, were hastening to Berlin or Paris at the
same moment, for my college experience and my earlier years
had turned me towards the old world as similar prepossessions
also turned them. Like a mysterious music heard from behind
the scenes, "Europe" had always been present in our associations, in our pictures and our memories and in what we
read, and we felt it was the predestined scene of our real
beginnings. We had to "fight out the duel between what was
given to us and what we were driven to prefer," a phrase I
found later in a book by Francis Hackett who, to fight out his
duel, had turned the other way.

As Francis Hackett, who became my friend, was one of the
European literary men who were to be drawn to my country
in accelerating numbers, I was one of the host of Americans

who, in the pre-world war years, were drawn, for both positive
and negative reasons, to Europe. But why in the steerage?—
why did this strike me as so romantic, though I was to find it
dull and flat, a rather tame adventure, for all the smiling good
will of my comrades of the voyage? I was possessed by the
*nostalgie de la boue* of so many writers in those days, and the
steerage for me was related to the slums which Stephen Crane
signalized in his remark that the Bowery was "the only interesting street in New York."

One of the unfathomable mysteries to me has always been
the *zeitgeist* that causes young men of an epoch to act in the
same fashion, to follow the same way of life without knowing
one another or even discussing their tastes or their hopes or
their plans. With a subterranean understanding between con-
temporaries who have never compared notes, who have never
met, they seem to behave as instinctively as birds in a flock,
and many of the young of my time and even the decades that
followed had a "sentimental reverence for sordid things." I
found this phrase later in a study of the time, which said that
they "rejected most of the ways of life of the middle class,"—if
they were artistic or literary, it goes without saying; and one can
see how true this is when one thinks of the "Ash-can" school
in New York, the painters whom presently I was to know so
well. How full the poems of that time were of dingy furnished
rooms, cocktail smells in bars, "putrid windows," sawdust on
floors and disintegrating cigar-stubs in gutters, expressing the
feeling I shared so fully of the attraction of "mean streets" that
Arthur Morrison, for one, described in London. I did not
know Eugene O'Neill when he haunted the New York water-
front and shipped as an ordinary seaman on a British tramp,
nor did I know Wenny in John Dos Passos's *Streets of Night*
who was looking for a job on a railroad section-gang. But, just

as Joe Husband worked in a coal-mine, another of my friends "rode the rails" to see "how the other half lives," a motto of the moment. This was all part of the fascination that outcasts and the so-called lost possessed for the imagination of my moment,—whether for social, spiritual or aesthetic reasons,— and it never surprised me that, as he put it, Stephen Crane had got his "artistic education" on the East Side of New York. The slums were never to lose their charm for me.

For several years, in London first and later in New York, I was to live among the scenes of the "Ash-can" painters, and so did Max Perkins, in Boston, for a while, my only intimate college friend who did not instantly sail away to Europe. Max spent a summer at a settlement-house, "district visiting," more or less, while teaching, reading economics and learning to typewrite, before he decided to go to New York like the Richard Harding Davis young man who took the first train from Yale to become a reporter. Copey, no doubt, the old newspaperman, had worked on Max's imagination; and had not Pendennis been a literary journalist before he became a novelist in London? It had not escaped *me* that Pendennis was a patron of the pawnshops with which at least I was familiar for a number of years, while Max, I am sure, was influenced greatly by Barrie's *When a Man's Single* at the time when he was living at the "Palmetto" in New York. How magnetic was this tale of the "blue-blooded" but "hard up" young man who, on the "Silchester Mirror," hungers for Fleet Street and finally goes to London, becomes a reporter and wins the beautiful girl, of course, in the end. How engaging were those scenes of the young newspapermen at home, in armchairs, with their feet on the hearth and the gas blazing in their lodgings, or in the reporting-room where, being on the press, they could "patronize the Tennysons" if they wrote

reviews. It was understood that young reporters were subsequently destined to "take a high place in literature," as Barrie
expressed it; and certainly, in Max's case, before he went into
the publishing house, reporting resulted in several capital
stories. The buried novelist in his mind had full scope, for
instance, in his much talked of report of the Vanderbilt cup
race.

I know that in going to London I too was partly influenced
by Barrie's picture of Fleet Street journalism, visibly embodied,
for Max and for me, in a common friend at Harvard, the
seasoned correspondent Frederick Moore. Eight years older
than either of us, the author of *The Balkan Trail*, a well-
known book in current-historical circles, Fred Moore had come
to Cambridge to spend a year working with Copey, feeling
that in English composition he had much to learn. Originally
a New Orleans man, quixotically honourable, with an irresistible masculine simplicity and charm, he had proposed that I
should go to London with him, or meet him there, certain that
I could not sink and would learn to swim. Himself a "true
soldier of fortune," a Davis character in actual life, a staff-
correspondent of the *Morning Post* and *Times*, he was admired
and really loved, as I discovered in London soon, by every
editor to whom he introduced me. On his lips the phrase "free
lance" was an incantation and he made "London journalism"
seem pure romance, while the London of writers, in a deeper
sense, meant much to one who had been trained to think that
his own country was a "literary dependency" of England. For
me Boston was not interesting nor was New York magnetic
yet,—or to anything like the degree it soon became,—and the
girl who later became my wife had gone to Paris to spend
three years with her mother and her brother, who was studying
architecture at the Beaux-Arts. At home both my father and

my grandmother had died during my college years and my
mother was happy to forward my interests and plans, while
I had made half-hearted efforts to establish myself in New
York, especially on the *Evening Post,* my El Dorado. For the
weekly essays of Paul Elmer More had some of the magic
for me that Sainte-Beuve's *causeries* once had for young writers
in Paris, and More himself had given me a book to review in
a paragraph, a gesture that led to nothing further. I had even
laid siege to William Dean Howells, asking him to solve for
me the unanswerable question, how to begin as a writer, and
no one could have been more sympathetic than this little
round-shouldered bunch of a man who seemed not so much
to walk as to roll about the floor. With his crepe-like wrinkled
wise old face, he was as kind as a man could be; but what
could he say to a neophyte who wished to write "editorials"
except that one did not begin at the top of the ladder?

Within a few months, or a year at least, my friends had
scattered all over Europe, whether because they were more
drawn there or repelled by their own country or whether they
shared these feelings in equal measure. A few of them felt
that America was uniquely repellent, but these had never
heard the song of Artero de Quental, "What a sad fate, my
boys, to have been born in *Portugal.*" One of my friends com-
plained, "Liberty in America is like the liberty of a man packed
in a crowd. There is no policeman, but he can't move"; and
again, "Every true thought in my mind is repugnant to everyone at home. To be myself is to be impossible there." Another
wrote, "The thing that hangs over me like a gallows at home is
the set and rigid form you are required to force yourself into."
There were some who would always have chosen dead cities
before living wildernesses, and others for whom America was
"detestable . . . barren and sordid," while others again, pre-

pared to go home and embrace the "money shuffle," seized a few months of grace in Sicily or Capri. Resigned to joining their fathers in business until the time came to retire, they basked in Taormina, on balconies, writing sonnets.

One friend, of German origin, returned to spend a year or two in the old house of his family in a village on the Rhine; another went to Lyon to study at the university in what he called that "laborious bourgeois city." A third visited cousins in Ireland "beside the Blackwater," the locale of certain poems that he presently published, while my Henry Jamesian novelist friend settled soon in Florence, not far from another who was writing on Florentine woodcuts. One classmate, who knew Berenson and was deep in the study of Duccio, worked in Italian archives to prepare for his book, and one who was composing literary portraits had gone to stay on the Breton coast at an inn that had once been a château of the Rohans. Then he moved to a sort of peasant hotel, on a beach, beside the ocean, where the chickens and occasionally a pig strolled in at the windows and where he paid eighteen francs a week, less than four dollars in those days, for his room and his meals, together with his washing and his wine. Three musical friends had gone to Berlin, whence one of them wrote from a queer tall building where the odours of chloroform and cabbage mingled on the stairway,—for some of the tenants were dressmakers and the rest were dentists; but he had a huge study with a grand piano that made up for all the reek and a knowledgeable old Pomeranian music-master. With his friends near by he had there "the most delightful part of college . . . in this peculiarly characterless city of Berlin," which resembled London, Paris and New York and every other great city, in fact, in all those qualities that in each were "not distinctive."

Berlin, as he put it, was "metropolitan but characterless" and therefore "the exact reverse of Boston."

Nor, in choosing for a while to live abroad, were these the only friends of mine who were forerunners of the so-called Expatriates later in days before changes in the spiritual climate both in America and abroad sent literary minds in general home to stay. My closest friends,—with Max,—Jack Wheelock (John Hall Wheelock) and Edward Sheldon set out for Europe almost as quickly as I did, although Ned Sheldon was already a success in the theatre in New York with *Salvation Nell,* produced when he was still in college. He was busy following up this "divine comedy of the slums," as Mrs. Fiske called it, working in Italy and France, at Fontainebleau, in Normandy, on Lake Como, "dizzy with labour and drinking nothing but coffee and whiskey," he wrote, "with a copy of Congreve in one hand, Wycherley in the other." Jack Wheelock had gone to Göttingen, where his uncle was a professor, planning to deal in his doctoral thesis with folksongs that had never been collected for which he travelled through Hungary and Montenegro. He wandered as well over Germany, avoiding the fashionable resorts and sights, frequenting beer-gardens, cheap theatres, merry-go-rounds and the river-boats that plied between old red-roofed cities, enchanted by girls with "old-world eyes and Giaconda half-smiles," he wrote, and "a hungry wonder under the high cheek arch." He felt at rather a disadvantage beside the German students who spoke four languages almost as mother-tongues,—and for whom other Americans were often "fish-blooded,"—but he engaged in a duel that left him with gashes eighteen inches long and made him for all time, for me, the prodigy of beaches. Besides Max, almost the only friend who stayed at home was Harold Bell, who had for several years his Europe in Cambridge, where he bought a house built in the Italian style with a tower, a *piano nobile* and a loggia that was already paved with stone. Harold Bell erected a high wall about this villa, which Pierre La Rose redecorated in pink and grey, and, living together in "Grey House," the two friends planned Renaissance banquets with Pico della Mirandolas gathered round the fountain in the garden. I was not there to see how far they were able to carry out these dreams that Walter Pater perhaps had kindled in their minds, but one of their first guests was the Cardinal-Archbishop of Boston.

I did not know, when I went to London, how many aspiring writers had much the same idea at about the same moment, Ezra Pound, Eliot, John Gould Fletcher, Conrad Aiken, "H. D.," and others like John Cournos, all within a lustrum or a decade. Numbers of these, like Elinor Wylie and Robert Frost in 1915, were to publish their first books in England, as I published mine, and most of them arrived with a little of the feeling of the young man Walter Anthon in Robert Herrick's novel *The Gospel of Freedom*. It had been in the air they breathed, in college or at home, that one should not "write for the provinces" but should go to London, in order to begin one's career at the "centre," perhaps to "get in" and get to be known and discussed by the world that counted there. I was too naive myself for this particular shade of thought,—a feeling that was to vanish totally within fifteen years,—and romantic motives governed me, notions of Grub Street and "living in an attic" or, like George Gissing, lodging in cellars. I had delighted in all the stories of penniless assaults on literary fame, the story of Crabbe who sold his clothes to pay for a last meal and of Goldsmith who was caught at home with his trousers at the pawnshop. For I lived in a dream of literature and everything amused me if it brought back the experience of

some great writer,—De Quincey, for instance, in a garret with
rats, sharing his crust in Soho Square with the waif whom he
had picked up in Oxford Street. How eagerly I walked into
4 York Street where De Quincey had written *The Opium
Eater* and infected the clerk whom I found there with my
infatuation, for, previously unaware that the house had a
history, he took me into the upper rooms where the tattered
wall-paper hung loose in the damp half-darkness. Like Barrie's
hero, I was "pleased with poverty" in and for itself, a taste
that J. B. Yeats was to confirm in me,—and a good taste it is,
I am convinced, for writers,—one that led me into some odd
adventures during the eighteen months that I spent in London. I lived in a little street off the Strand, in King's Road,
Chelsea, where I rented an empty studio and slept on the
floor, in Pimlico for a few months and at 16 Old Compton
Street, where I had a room at Beguinot's,—at that time Roche's.
A dingy old copy of a Correggio in a heavy gold frame hung
over the bed, and a mirror flanked the gas-jet in this ten-
shilling chamber.

Meanwhile, I had set about entering "London journalism"
with the letters that Frederick Moore had given me to various
editors who invited me to lunch and tried to discourage me at
first but only succeeded in filling me with great expectations.
I was presently at work in Curtis Brown's agency in the newspaper and magazine department, placed in the charge of Mr.
Snell, who asked my age and if I drank and why the devil I
wanted to go into this business. The benign old growler Mr.
Snell, with his air of an English Mark Twain, had once been
a reporter on the New York *Herald,* and he told me that all
American reporters were cads, thieves and crooks while the
English were all scrupulous, generous and easy-going. After
this we lighted cigarettes and went out to lunch.

My task was to clip stories from English newspapers to be
sent back to America and rewrite European articles in American style,—on pain of "not getting there" I must make them
"breezy"; and Mr. Snell told me that I must also write articles
outside the office and bring in as many as I could write. He
sent me on assignments for an article on the London parks
and another on the trained dogs at the railway stations that
collected contributions for the widows of employees, a third on
the cinema and a fourth on Lord Fairfax, the Virginian who
had returned to England to enter the peerage. I interviewed a
tattooer who professed to have plied his trade not only on the
backs of the Czar and the Prince of Wales but also on the arms
of Lady Randolph Churchill, and I was sent to Canonbury
Tower where Oliver Cromwell, who had visited there, had
left behind a boot that had just been discovered. This boot
had been sold for a hundred and fifty pounds. Then one day
an earl fell into a lake and this little timely incident afforded
a reason for an article on the forbears of the earl, for earls
were supposed to interest Americans, like anything involving the "haunts" of Burns, or of Wordsworth or Sir Walter
Scott or Dickens. For instance, some slight alteration in the
Bull Inn at Rochester, the memorable scene of the ball in
*The Pickwick Papers.* I was asked to return to the railway
stations and characterize their "psychology," or describe them
in terms of persons in history or fiction, and, in fact, at Euston,
Major Pendennis came naturally into my mind as at Fen-
church Street I thought of Fagin.

But it did not take me many months to realize that "journalism," whether in London or New York, was not for me, that
I had not the slightest knack for "stories" or "adventure" or
for articles, indeed, in any form. I was possessed with ideas for
books, which I planned at the rate of a dozen a year, a new

book every night before going to sleep, predestined as I was, however, to do my share of hack-work, at intervals, for many years to come. I was to have a hand in thirty-one translations, while reviewing, rewriting other men's books, editing a volume of Houdini's tricks, ghost-writing the memoirs of Iliodor, the "mad monk" of Russia. How much literary drudgery I was fated to perform, beginning in London where I abridged for the *Wide World Magazine* the autobiography of Geronimo, the Apache chief. I wrote columns for a Manchester paper on American railroads and Tammany Hall, the "Religion of Theodore Roosevelt," Bryan and what not, with an article on "Harvard and American Life" for the *Contemporary Review* and a series of articles on the lives of famous correspondents. I described the outstanding exploits in each man's career, Edward O'Donovan's adventure at Merv, Blowitz's coup with the Berlin treaty, the journey of W. B. Harris to Tafilet. There were others on Sir Donald Mackenzie Wallace, George W. Steevens, Archibald Forbes and the "thousand mile walk across China" of Morrison of the *Times*.

Frederick Moore commissioned these,—for he soon joined me in London,—and showed me how to bring out the drama in the stories, all of which I wrote in the Reading Room of the British Museum, the scene of so many tragedies and comedies of Grub Street. There I was surrounded by earnest students and American genealogists, like the primrose-haired girl in Harold Frederic's novel, and I saw Bertram Dobell there with his battered top hat and grizzled old men in threadbare morning coats. Some of these dozed behind piles of ponderous books and stealthily drew from their pockets papers full of crumbs, and many gave point to the sad implications of the well-known sign in the lavatory, "For casual ablutions only," which I found still there. A few were diving for pearls in the deep waters of learning. They were all Henry Ryecrofts for me, Gissings of a later day who had also perhaps breakfasted on dry bread, carrying with them a crust to serve for dinner, and who settled themselves every morning at their desks with books which "by no possibility could be a source of immediate profit."

In the meantime, Fred Moore came and went, at first to report for three London papers the Casablanca massacres in the fall of 1907; and presently I saw him off for Constantinople. He was the personification of the "nose for news," with an extra sense for events that were about to happen, events that nothing in the papers suggested to others; and, having foreseen that the Sultan was to be deposed on Sunday, he reached Constantinople on Saturday afternoon. Other friends joined me,—half the Harvard I had known turned up sooner or later in Piccadilly Circus; and who should appear at the British Museum but Irving Babbitt, tamed and kind, who walked with me four times round Russell Square. In this neutral atmosphere I saw that I had misapprehended certain Harvard characters who had seemed forbidding, among them the terrible dean with the octagonal glasses who had found so many reasons for upbraiding me in college. Seeing him from afar one day in the Brompton Oratory, I darted behind a pillar to evade his eye, when, caught and cornered, I perceived that his eye was all benevolence and that he actually rejoiced in my immunity in London. Joe Breck arrived, still preaching Berenson, whom he had just seen, and full of the "occult balance" of Duccio's pictures and the "intellectual centre" he discovered in them; and Tinckom-Fernandez, the half-Hindu friend who was to live with me in New York, also spent two or three days with me in Chelsea. Then he sent me a rondeau of his own composition. Lee Simonson followed and another friend with whom I heard Bernard Shaw prove that the world and women could get on very well if men were abolished altogether; and T. H. Thomas later came and stayed two months with me in lodgings in a French house in Pimlico. Our meals were brought up to a large airy sitting-room that was hung with sentimental coloured prints which the land-lady said she had put up especially for us and which we could only remove by slow degrees.

Tommy Thomas was at work on European "letters" for some paper at home, and he had just finished his book on eighteenth-century French portrait-engravers, which made him at once an authority in a fairly large field. I was to see, in connection with this,—and marvel over it all my days,—how swift and sure is the response to authority in England; for Tommy took me to the National Gallery where he told the director,—Sir Charles Holroyd, I think,—that a certain Dutch portrait was attributed to the wrong painter. It was a portrait of Descartes, as I seem to remember, though I do not recall the name of the other artist, but Holroyd was all ears at once and said we must go upstairs and look the portrait over and discuss this question. He listened while Tommy made his case, then, finally convinced, he tore off the label and put it in his pocket; and the name of the other painter soon afterward appeared there. I pictured to myself the pompous protests a provincial director at home would have made if a young stranger from abroad had suddenly appeared and questioned one of his official attributions. Holroyd, candid and direct, recognizing a mind that knew, fell without a moment's hesitation into conformity with it.

Much I liked the English,—and, while there were certain English types that I always found detestable, there are certain American types I have found still more so. I liked their his-

trionism too, their pleasure in bearing and dress, the pageantry
that suggested to me a perpetual ballet, as when, for instance,
responding to a knock at my grimy Soho door one day, I confronted a footman in livery on the landing outside. He was
an emissary from one of my mother's three families of cousins
who lived in England in a splendour I had seldom seen at
home, but, for my imagination, he might have stepped out of
a Sheridan comedy or a Hogarth picture of the contrast of
high life and low life. Amusing to observe, however, this
was the world that Goethe described as "suitable only for
women and people of rank,"—it was a kind of play that I
found rewarding only when I saw it across the footlights; and
at twenty-one, meanwhile, and shy, I was an outsider in my
own world, unlike various friends who made themselves at
home there. Some of these friends were lunching with Shaw
and playing tennis with H. G. Wells, or, like Joe Husband,
spending hours with the "elderly old blackguard" in Ebury
Street,—J. B. Yeats's phrase for George Moore. For Joe's handwriting had seemed to Moore "as beautiful as Mallarmé's," he
wrote, and it had occurred to Moore that Joe might be persuaded to make a transcription on vellum of *The Brook Kerith*.
But I saw these great men also across the footlights,—Shaw,
for one, who reminded me of the Etruscan warrior in the
museum in New York, for he had, with his grey beard, the
muscles of a boy. Many times I heard him speak, an aging
man springing from his chair with youth in every gesture and
sally of the voice. I often saw Chesterton's bushy head, and
one day in St. Martin's Lane I encountered J. M. Barrie, pipe
in mouth, with his deep black eyes and bright red necktie. He
was turning down an alley to the stage-door of the theatre
where *What Every Woman Knows* was about to open. Then
at the British Museum I stood beside a familiar face that said

to the young man at the desk, "Any books for Ellis?"—and I was surprised when the young man asked "What initial?" and the man with the beard was obliged to answer "H." For I had instantly recognized Havelock Ellis.

Many years later AE wrote to me that one should never try to meet celebrated persons, that in the end one inevitably met the persons whom one was intended to meet, the persons whom one had truly a reason for knowing. He said that, for instance, in Donegal, on the shore of a lake, he had observed a man standing as lonely as a seagull and that, falling into conversation with him, this man quoted the Upanishads, the book that he himself was constantly reading. It had always been that way with him,—destiny brought one face to face with those whom it was good for one to know; and I had vaguely felt this too, as I have experienced the truth of it, for in time a writer meets everybody and what does it matter? What is good is that he meets his real comrades of the spirit. But I was fearful in earlier days that my diffidence might be cowardice and that "seeing Shelley plain" was a young writer's duty, as Boswell had sought out Voltaire, Rousseau and Hume before he set his cap at Dr. Johnson. I felt that in failing to follow the example of Boswell I might be missing something of real value, as J. B. Yeats felt when he missed the chance to meet Rossetti, who had seen and liked one of his early pictures. All the young artists of Yeats's time who aspired to a kind of poetic art had been agog about Rossetti, who sent three messengers to him with invitations, and "I did not come," Yeats later wrote. "I think I was afraid of the great man, diffident about myself and my work." Yeats added, in *Early Memories,* "To be afraid of anything is to listen to the counsels of your evil angel," and I dare say it was so with me, for I stood in awe of all the men who were eminent in my craft.

I felt about far lesser men what Flaubert felt about Shake-speare,—that he would have died of awe if he had met him; and I was frightened by the mere sight of Swinburne, whom anyone might have seen on Putney Hill. For every morning at eleven o'clock he passed through the gate of "The Pines" for his walk up the hill over Wimbledon Common. I had felt a slight shiver of awe whenever a bus marked "Putney" passed me anywhere in the London streets, and I could not have expressed the mysterious excitement with which I observed that quiet dwelling. The old bookseller on the corner had often been in the house, he said, where books were piled in thousands on chairs and sofas, and sometimes the poet, for whom he bound books, sent word asking to borrow one which he had somewhere in the house but could not find. I had to light a cigarette to give me an excuse to glance at the little turbaned figure whom I saw emerging.

Diffident as I was, however, I was not unfriended during the numberless hours that I roamed about London, sometimes with "Uncle Nick," who lived at Roche's over me, the old retired barrister who had spent years in New Zealand. There he had known Samuel Butler, who had later lived in Clifford's Inn in the days when he had a "little needlewoman"; and, in fact, the old circle of Butler, or the remnants of it, gathered for dinner at Roche's now and then. Uncle Nick and R. A. Streatfeild, the editor of Butler,—the music critic,—despised the rival circle of Yellow Book survivors, the "rank crowd" that Ernest Dowson had formerly brought there, as much as they despised the placard religion of the tabernacles and almost as much as they loved the music of Handel. Uncle Nick, who had seen the soldiers marching off to the Crimean War, remembered hearing Disraeli in the House of Commons dis-missing as "mere coffee-house babble" the thunders of Glad-

stone who denounced the "Bulgarian atrocities" of 1875: he
had dropped his monocle with a click against one of the
buttons on his coat in the silence that accompanied his smooth-
faced defence of the Turks. The old-fashioned rationalist
Uncle Nick, who strolled through the streets with his arms
behind him, was a great concert-goer in his afternoons, and
he spent mornings in auction-rooms and rummaging the book-
stalls where he made extraordinary finds in the penny boxes.
In one of these later I saw a copy of my own first book which
had been exposed for a while in the sixpenny box, where I
had observed it many times with the rain bespattering it so
that the gilt on the cover grew dimmer and dimmer. When it
sank to this penny box I rescued the book.

Uncle Nick's favourites were seventeenth-century authors,
Fuller of the *Worthies,* for one, Sir Thomas Browne and the
Jeremy Taylor of the exquisite essay on Marriage, while, an
epicure as well as a bibliophile, he was devotedly attached to
all the French people in the house where he had lived so long.
He told me about the little dressmaker whose room was on the
top floor and who had at last despaired of making a living.
Unable to pay her bill, she had confided to Uncle Nick that
she had to go on the streets "like everybody else," and that
evening the chef knocked on her door, asked how large her
bill was and said, "Here's the money. Don't be a bad girl."
The next morning the cellerer came up and gave her ten
pounds more, and before evening every man in the house had
offered her money "to be good on." So much for the French,—
"and in Soho," Uncle Nick added.

Among others who were kind to me was Mrs. John Richard
Green, the widow of "Short History" Green whom I had read
as a boy (and thought of as an early Victorian with his white
neckcloth),—and there was Mrs. Green, still young, the witty

red-haired senator of the still far from conceived of Irish Free
State. When later I told J. B. Yeats that I had met Alice Stop-
ford Green he said that her father had wished to marry his
mother long before either he or she was born,—if they had
married there would never have been a poet Yeats,—and I
could tell him of the evenings when Mrs. Green kept open
house and her Irish officer-nephew held the floor there. His
way of keeping the conversation in his own hands was to say,
"You're right, you're right, you're per-r-r-fectly right,—there
was never a truer word spoken," a device that struck me as
worthy of Benjamin Franklin. For, paying full tribute to the
value of others' ideas, he was able in this way to continue
expressing his own. Kind, too, to me was Spencer Wilkinson,
not yet an Oxford professor, though he had the white beard
of Father Time, who put me through my Harvard Greek,
reciting the passage from Homer that I sometimes spout even
today to the ocean waves. He blew me up for not spending a
guinea on the twenty volumes of Lessing in German which I
had just seen, as I told him, on a neighbouring book-stall, for
perhaps he had never encountered an American who had not
a guinea to spare for books that in any case he could scarcely
read. I would have liked to spend the guinea on the little
portrait of Carlyle that stood for months in the window of a
Chelsea junk-shop, a portrait for which I was told the sage
had sat for the painter,—"W. Greaves,"—an old man who was
still living in a street near by. A year later, when I was in
New York, I read one day that Roger Fry and various other
critics had "discovered" Walter Greaves and said he was almost
the equal of his teacher Whistler, and that his pictures
were selling for two or three hundred pounds and even his
drawings now brought forty or fifty. But the critics soon
changed their minds; and, returning to London in 1913, I

saw some of his drawings in a print-seller's window that were priced at five or ten shillings just as before. His vogue had risen, his vogue had passed, all within a year or two, and the old man was a nobody again, still living.

One friend whom I made at the British Museum was an Anglo-Polish painter who was reading Pater and certain Latin poets,—he was thrilled by Propertius, who suggested to him subjects for pictures,—and with whom I stayed for a week or two in Paris, where I had urgent reasons for spending Christmas. Carol F.-W. was at work on drawings for a Polish translation of the Rubáiyát, and he had exhibited at the autumn Salon that year and was having some success selling his pictures. Lee Simonson was with us there,—he was in the circle of Gertrude Stein, intending at that time to become a painter,—though presently Carol F.-W. wrote to me from Warsaw, in exile for a time from both Paris and London. His family were all away,—it was summer in the empty house, with the housekeeper "safe under lock and key" and everything done up in muslin and brown paper wrappers, and he had nothing to do in Warsaw but gossip with his aunt, walk through the charming parks and read Kipling and Ouida. The acacia trees were loaded with blossoms whose scent came up into the window and gave him romantic thoughts as he lay in bed, and it struck him that I would enjoy this "little Paris," as he said the Varsovians somewhat imprudently termed it. For the whole town might have been packed into the Place de la Concorde. And yet its career was the most tragic in Europe; it was even more tragic than the career of Paris,—and who could have guessed in 1907 how tragic the career of Warsaw was still destined to be?

In that direction my mind never roamed, though I thought often of Italy, of Naples and Florence and the Campo Santo at Pisa with 'the long wild grass and the buttercups that looked up at "The Triumph of Death." Closing my eyes, moreover, I also saw Gibbon's old house at Lausanne where at that time his library was still reposing. I could see the garden and the southward view overlooking the slope to the lake and the mountains of Savoy rising beyond. But the London streets filled my imagination as I measured the cracks in the pavement, feeling that if I stepped on a certain crack I might expect to succeed in my next undertaking, for my mind was very far away from the journalistic work I did and fixed upon what I thought of as my personal writing. Still the Harvard aesthete, I caught myself writing about Tammany and Bryan in the style of Arthur Symons or Yeats's prose.

How little time meant as, at twenty-one, thinking of all I was to do, I walked hour after hour on Hampstead Heath, stopping perhaps for tea at Jack Straw's Castle. Sometimes I sat like Poe's "man of the crowd" in the bay-window of a coffee-house and, catching sight of someone who interested me on the street outside, I put on my hat and followed him until it was dark. The coffee-house was usually a Lyons or an ABC where sardines on toast cost fourpence with a penny for tea, and occasionally I walked at night under the acetylene flares of the stalls when the Soho streets were a nightmarish phantasmagory. I felt myself hallucinated and moving through illusions. Once, in the East End, it struck me that every man I saw was legless or armless or wanting a nose or an eye, as in some Beggars' Opera or Hogarthian hell; and meanwhile at Roche's I read Leopardi, Pascal and *Wilhelm Meister* and planned especially a study of Vernon Lee. I read this sympathetic writer day after day at the British Museum, though my book dwindled into an essay for a magazine at home, while I dreamed of another on the English art-critics from Reynolds to Pater and John Addington Symonds, of which at least I wrote one long chapter on Hazlitt. For I was still thinking of the art-criticism that I had begun in a juvenile way with a paper, at fourteen, on Paolo Uccello, the first composition that I remember writing except for an infantile story called "Mary the Cook." But I was a slow and laborious worker, as I have remained, in fact, for I never write more than a page in the fullest morning, and I envied writers like Hilaire Belloc whose secretary I knew,—it was she who typewrote my first book. He would send Miss B. a wire telling her to go to his country-house for the period of a recess in Parliament, and there, in a fortnight of mornings, prowling in his study, he would dictate the whole of a long novel. It was all impromptu, for he was active politically and had little time to think of writing, although sometimes, reviewing for the *Morning Post,* he would leave a taxi ticking below while he bounded up the stairs with an armful of books. He would take the first book off the pile, run his eye through it and begin to talk, dictating ten reviews in fifty minutes, which seemed to me astonishing because Belloc was almost a great writer at times and could never have been called a common hack. But his review of Frederick Moore's *The Passing of Morocco* set me wondering about this sort of mind, for, in his hasty way, he made only one point about the book and on that small point he was mistaken. As I remember it, he said that the Foreign Legionaries did not wear little red caps in Morocco, and Moore, who was fresh from that country, had seen the red caps. What made it all the stranger was that the half-French Belloc had had as a young man his military training in France and the French army was one of his great subjects.

At the approach of spring, in February, 1908, Fred Moore came to my rescue once again, for my mind had turned back to America, which seemed to be my theme, and I was eager to write a book about it. Full of questions about the country, I felt I might answer some of these if I could find the place to work them out, and Fred suggested a village in Sussex, West Chiltington, near Pulborough, where one of his friends was living, a black and white artist. At that time J. L. C. Booth was on the staff of *Punch,* in which every week he had a drawing,—usually some hunting scene, with horses and hounds,—and he found me a room with casement windows in a farmhouse called "The Friars" where once Queen Anne was supposed to have spent a night. It was also supposed that a monk lay buried in the cellar, for the house was a fragment of an old monastery; and there I was to spend four months writing *The Wine of the Puritans,* which was published in London in the autumn of that year. There was a rambling old attic and my walls were papered over ancient beams and hung with gilded mottos I was glad to put up with, for I was fond of Mrs. Adams who woke me up tinkering at the fire and depositing my breakfast by the bed. I thrashed about in my tin tub, boiled my shaving water, dressed half out of the window watching the starlings, drew my table up to the hearth, glanced at the newspaper and lighted my pipe, a corncob that was called a "Missouri meerchaum." Mark Twain had popularized this even in England. Then, reading my letters first, I set to work. I took my midday meals with Farmer Adams and his wife downstairs in the tinselled dining-room, where we had mutton, hot or cold, seven days in every week, invariably topped off with suet pudding.

In the afternoon, sometimes alone, at other times with Moore or Booth, I went for a ten-mile walk over the Downs, or to Storrington or Arundel, still further away, and occasionally the parson, Mr. Caldecott, who had time on his hands to kill, sent me a little note suggesting a stroll. He addressed me as "U. S. A. Brooks" in the first of these. We passed gypsies camping by the roads and a Tree of Justice that was hung with stoats and with weasels, owls and moles dangling from the branches, as a Christmas tree is hung with coloured balls, while the buds came out on the other trees and the primroses and daffodils blazed in clearings in the woods and over the fields. They filled at Easter the little church with the twelfth-century frescoes so that it looked like a jewel-case lined with yellow velvet,—not an inch of stone showed through the primroses that blanketed the walls; and there Mr. Caldecott preached with his riding boots visible under his cassock and the choir consisted mainly of our friend Booth. It was only a year later that Booth and Moore, returning to Constantinople, were shot, and all but fatally, in a cross-fire in the streets when Booth, shot first, dropped his camera and Moore, stooping to pick it up, felt a ball passing through his shoulder and his neck. He fell like a log and could not twitch a finger,—he was paralyzed for a year from neck to heels; but he recovered to spend a long life of adventure in the Near East, in China and in Washington at last. Booth was not so fortunate. Giving up his work on *Punch*, he farmed for a while in Australia and then he was killed at Gallipoli in the first world war.

I, meanwhile, had been thinking much of Americans and America, which I seemed to see better in perspective, living abroad, and which, for some reason, possessed my mind, supplanting as an interest more and more my interest in the Middle Ages and the history of art. I did not realize at all how much the *zeitgeist* controlled me here, just as it controlled my feeling for living in the slums, or how many other American minds were moving on lines that were like my own with similar dislikes and hopes regarding our country. The authors of

*Babbitt* and *Marco Millions,* like Waldo Frank and many another, felt as I felt about the predominance of business, together with the nervous tension of life at home and its provincial immaturity. It seemed to me later, looking back, that
all the young writers of my time had been asking, What is
wrong with American living?—not realizing that anyone else
had been asking the same question,—seeking for answers in
one form or another and whether they wrote poems or plays
or novels or short stories or criticism. Some shared the typical
Harvard feeling that Americans were born Philistines and
could only become anything else through contact with Europe, and I actually supposed that the only chance an American had to succeed as a writer was to betake himself there
with all possible speed. But could that solve the problem? I
was convinced as well that a man without a country could do
nothing of importance, that writers must draw sustenance
from their own common flesh and blood and that therefore
deracination also meant ruin. For me, at that time, the American writer could neither successfully stay *nor* go,—he had
only two alternatives, the frying-pan and the fire; and the
question was therefore how to change the whole texture of
life at home so that writers and artists might develop there.
For writers and artists were the centre of the universe for me,—
the oyster existed solely to produce the pearl. With whatever
degree of absurdity or sense, these ideas were to fill my mind,
with certain related ideas, for a long time to come, leading
eventually to my studies of Mark Twain and Henry James,
neither of which ever quite satisfied me. The fault of both,
especially the latter, was that in order to make my case,—which
had some truth at least on the plane of types,—I was obliged to
force individuals into general categories, to fit complex persons

into beds of Procrustes. And yet, to a large degree in both
cases, I think, the individual tallied with the type.

One influence that had brought to a head my feeling about
America, shaping as well the first form in which I expressed
it, was the English writer G. Lowes Dickinson,—an amateur
sage, I would call him now, not to disparage him but to mark
a distinction. His book *A Modern Symposium* had greatly impressed me, and my friends and I must have had it in mind
when, in college, we formed a group to discuss various questions once a fortnight. Each member was supposed to represent
some particular point of view, as the poet, the painter, the
musician, the economist and so on. Dickinson became the rage
on his second visit to the United States,—he was almost a national idol for a few years,—and the reason seemed to be that
he so disliked the country, in which he was able to find nothing that was good. One might have found in all this a masochistic element, as if Americans liked whips and scorpions,
and at any rate it showed our appetite for criticism, for the
movement of national self-scrutiny on which we were embarked. We seemed to be hungry for punishment, in the
phrase of the moment, as if the impulse of the "muckrakers"
had spread beyond the political sphere and invaded every corner of American living and thinking. To Dickinson, America
was a barbarous country where no life of the spirit could survive and from which the artist was inevitably driven to Europe, inasmuch as only there could he exist and create, a land
without leisure, religion or beauty whose ideal was an activity
for its own sake that repelled all thought of disinterested con-
templation.

This chimed well with my juvenile fantasy and the questions I was disposed to ask, Where so many were prosperous,
why were so few happy?—Where there was so much humour,

why was life so joyless?—Where there was so much intelligence, why was there so little writing that was good?—and why was I abroad when I believed in living at home? All these questions boiled up and over in the unripe little book that I wrote, in the form of a dialogue, in the Sussex farmhouse,— writing it first as a series of letters and then as a long essay before I followed Dickinson in his conversations. I had in mind a French phrase that I had picked up somewhere, "It is not night but only the absence of day," for, seeing the actual America merely, and not too much of that, I saw nothing of the potential that counted for me later. The book was published before I went back to New York.

## CHAPTER VIII

# NEW YORK

FIVE YEARS later I returned to England to spend another eighteen months writing and teaching a class of working people. But now for three years I lived in New York. "Why waste the best years of your life in a new country?" my Soho friend, Uncle Nick, had written to me, and in fact my reasons were mainly practical, for America to me was negative still, as it was to so many of Henry James's people. I still saw chiefly what it lacked, beside the older civilizations, instead of what they lacked and America possessed, the virgin soil Turgenev saw in his own "great fresh country" where each could feel that he had a role to play. For that I was still far too immature.

I found a room in a lodging-house on West Twenty-third Street in New York, in the old block that was known as London Terrace, built three generations before on the family farm of the bishop who wrote the poem that begins " 'Twas the night before Christmas." There were three big trees in the front yard, with a cast-iron fountain and a bench, and, within, the kind of furnished rooms that O. Henry so often described with half-broken chairs and the odour of mildewed woodwork. It was kept by a brawny Scotswoman with a drunken husband, and there was an ancient libidinous chambermaid, always dressed in rusty black, who might have stepped out of an eighteenth century novel.

There I found already established another Scot, a gentle soul whose foot was also on the first rung of the literary ladder. R. W. Sneddon was a humorist from Glasgow who had had some sort of connection with the theatre there and who longed to live in Paris but feared he was destined to remain under the Stars and Stripes,—"more stripes than stars." He dreamed of the *vie de Bohème* that appeared in his unpretentious tales and the plays that he wrote or adapted from certain French authors, sitting ten or twelve hours a day, concocting jokes for *Judge* and *Puck* or toiling for *The Smart Set* and *Harper's Weekly*. Serenely laborious, pipe in mouth, with his little Parisian coffee-machine, he wore a brown robe that was like a Franciscan habit, and, making each year a hundred dollars more than he had made the year before, he aspired to be out of debt in some measurable future. He was approaching this by a sort of arithmetical progression, outdistancing one or two housemates who had no such hope or even any such ambition. For the house soon became a Grub Street dormitory. Tinckom-Fernandez settled there, joined for a summer by Conrad Aiken, whom I saw briefly then and never knew well, and, among others, two English actors, one of them an ex-naval commander whom I was to meet again in later years. Charles,—to omit his other name,—had two large theatre trunks filled with gaudy clothes that he wore on the stage, including a white flannel suit with purple braiding, and sad was the day when Mrs. Lloyd locked him out with the clothes inside because he had not been able to keep up with the rent. Then Violet,—to omit her other name,—bailed out the theatre trunks and carried Charles himself away to Egypt.

It was a discouraging household, especially in winter, when

the trains on "Death Avenue," at the corner, ploughed through the snow and one had to resort to the free-lunch counter at the saloon across the street that was one of Edwin Arlington Robinson's haunts. For Robinson had lived eight years before in a brownstone house a hundred yards away. But there was much brewing of rum-punch and tea in my big room at the front, with the death-mask of Thackeray and the crucifix over the mantel, and with J. B. Yeats's drawing of himself hailing Sneddon and me on the street only to be left behind in the weary distance. For I had met Yeats soon after my return to New York. I was still at the infantile stage, moreover, when misery seemed to me picturesque, even the groans of poor devils regretting their existence, and I was full of my own histrionics, dramatizing everything I did, sometimes in the manner of Sentimental Tommy. I delighted in holes in my trousers and the bottoms of my shoes, wearing at the same time a flower in my buttonhole or dressing as far as I could in the opposite extreme. I felt I acquired a secret strength by reacting in this way against the popular pattern of the young business man, a type that seemed to me as insipid and banal as the rows of young maple trees on suburban streets. I supposed that by so doing I somehow connected myself with the venerable race of unworldly or vagabond writers who had shared this cult of shabbiness, poverty and failure. Occasionally, wishing to appear old-fashioned, I wore my grandfather's round sleeve-buttons, and, longing for an excuse to wear tortoise-shell glasses, I had my eyes examined, finding that they were all too tire-somely normal. I passed through the mimetic phases that young writers usually undergo, imitating this man's gestures and that man's walk, while, at the same time, I was inept on the actual stage, with neither the talent nor the presence of mind of an actor. In college I had been obliged to act in a German play, in which I appeared as a young baroness with a blonde wig, though I understood so little German that I scarcely knew what the play was about and felt like a shanghaied sailor waking up at sea. Then Sarah Bernhardt appeared in Boston depending on supers from Harvard to fill up the cast when she played in *Fedora,* and Edward Sheldon and I were chosen to act as gendarmes and arrest her and conduct her off the stage to her throne in the wings. Fortunately, on that occasion, I did not have to utter a word, but I could hardly have felt more relieved to escape from the boards and the footlights if I had been arrested myself to be discharged soon after.

Meanwhile, I continued to relish the slums, their colour and variety, the stir in the streets, the craftsmen plying their trades in little shops, and often I spent the whole of a Sunday at a café in East Houston Street, reading and writing at one of the marble-topped tables. I was surrounded there by the real mysteries of the ghetto and by Yiddish actors and newspapermen playing chess and drinking tea like figures from the Russian novels I was greedily absorbing. Among these were some of the East Side characters whom Hutchins Hapgood was writing about, types that had interested Stephen Crane who had lived on Twenty-third Street too, across the way from me, a dozen years before. His housemate Edward Marshall, the crippled correspondent, lived there still, nursing his recollections of the mercurial Crane, a name to me almost as vague then as Edwin Arlington Robinson's name or the name of Theodore Dreiser, who was also in New York. In time these names were to make the town magnetic to an imagination that saw itself in 1909 as lost and astray there. I scarcely knew even the name of Frank Norris, who had read the manuscript of Dreiser's first book in the office in which I presently found myself working.

For, loyal as ever, Max Perkins, already at Scribner's, had discovered a place for me with Doubleday and Page, assisting Walter Hines Page on *The World's Work* magazine, with which for most of a year I was to be connected. Harry Steger, the editor there, shepherded O. Henry, locking him up with a case of whiskey in the hotel bedroom where he had to turn out the stories that Doubleday published. These stories fascinated J. B. Yeats who found them, like Kipling's, all tinsel but quite without Kipling's vulgarity and elaboration, and Yeats said that O. Henry wrote such queer English and was yet so delicious that perhaps one ought to forget Addison and Swift. Meanwhile, Harry Steger introduced me to Francis Hackett, who enabled me to write, for the Chicago *Evening Post,* anything that came into my head, in my own way; and what a relief was that to me, out of my element as I was on Mr. Page's strenuous magazine. It was true I was encouraged to publish in this an interview with Howells, who had been so kind to me two years before and who was living now in West Fifty-seventh Street with a small workroom adjoining a big studio with skylights. The room contained only his table and chair with another chair for me and a bookcase entirely filled with his own publications, four or five shelves, at least, of Howells's books; and this hero of the young realistic novelists was naturally annoyed that I had not read more of his own novels. I doubt if I had read more than one, though I was to read them all in time, drawn almost as deeply to him as to William James, for, in spite of his conventional entanglements, Howells had a beautiful feeling for life and a spacious and generous understanding of it. When the interview was over, he asked me to ride down-town with him on one of the new Fifth Avenue motor-buses, and I remember the alert curiosity with which, from our seat on the top, this old story-teller stud-

ied the crowds on the sidewalks. It was at about this time that
I also saw Mark Twain,—whom I had never seen alive,—lying
in his coffin; for, observing the crowd on Fifth Avenue in front
of a church, I had climbed up to the gallery and looked down
upon him. The funeral was over but the lid of the coffin was
open, and there lay the author of *Huckleberry Finn,* with his
white hair spread loose, dressed for the last time in his white
flannels.

But this chance of a literary interview with Howells was
rare at the Doubleday office, where, among other miscellaneous
tasks, I arranged and edited the humdrum campaign speeches
of President Taft. In this air of advertising schemes and "hit-
ting the women of the country hard," I fostered a little plan
that came to nothing, although one of my friends and I discussed it on a walking trip down the Connecticut valley, starting in the shadow of Ascutney from the Perkins house at
Windsor. This was to set up a small printing-press like Miss
Yeats's Cuala Press to bring out essays and translations of
writers whom we liked, one of the day-dreams that possessed
my mind as I wandered about the New York streets or over
Brooklyn Bridge on a starry night. Or lunched at the Lafayette or at Scheffel Hall, the big dim German beer-cave with
the frescoes under the Gothic roof that was the scene of one of
O. Henry's stories. For, as it comes back to me, there was no
escaping this story-teller whose trail was all over the New
York scene of those days. My Doubleday career, as I ought to
regret, was like Wilkie Collins's business career, characterized
by its "full, vivid, instructive hours of truancy," and even now
I sometimes feel that I should apologize to Mr. Page whom,
in his way, I thought magnificent. I often stretched the lunch
hour to two hours or more reading Balzac's novels at the Lafayette, where one all but lived these novels in the coffee-room at

the front of the house, surrounded by French merchants playing dominoes and chess. The setting recalled the old Franco-
phile New York of the days when ex-President Monroe still
lived in the Egyptian dwelling on the opposite corner.

In Mr. Page's company I found one or two other friends,
Edwin Björkman, for instance, and Tom Mackenzie, the rap-
scallion son of a South African judge,—I am not repeating his
actual name,—who was yet so open-handed and so engaging.
Disowned by his father, he had come to America as a table-
steward on a White Star liner, rolled barrels for a few months
in a Standard Oil yard, tended the door at the Mills Hotel,
driven a taxi and consorted with thieves, while preserving his
innocent air of a well brought up schoolboy. How round and
big were his brown eyes, how charmingly eager his face, how
fresh the flower in his buttonhole, how delightful his voice,
and he lied, took laudanum, stole everything in sight,—his
American grandmother's diamonds at last,—and bragged about
his hair-raising criminal adventures. He had joined our asylum
for incurables on West Twenty-third Street, and there he received a convenient cable summoning him home, along with
his small boy's vanity and a large camera from the office. Seeing him off at the steamer, I also foresaw for him a life-term,
at best, in some foreign prison; and what was my astonishment,
fifteen years later, when I heard from him again,—he was
editor of the principal newspaper in a great dominion. He had
seemed merely an over-ripe fruit that had fallen from the tree
of the dying world which Edwin Björkman's philosophy had
left behind, concerned as this was with the *élan vital* of the
new world that was coming to birth not only in Björkman's
mind but in all our minds also. For which of us did not believe that we were on the verge of the "wonderful era" of
which Jack Wheelock, in Germany, had written to me? Jack

was carried away by *Jörn Uhl*, Gustav Frenssen's novel, as others, then or presently, were carried away by *Jean-Christophe* or *Pelle the Conqueror* or the notion of "creative evolution." That the world had been preparing to take a new step in social advance most of the men I knew agreed in feeling, and Jack Wheelock expressed the general mind when he went on to say, "What a triumphant era we face! The great movement is upon us and the 'muckrakers' in America and the troubles in Russia,—with the upheaval through all the rest of the labouring classes in Europe,—are but signs of the coming day. The labouring men are beginning to realize that it is unnecessary for a hundred men to live a life of agony that one may live a life of unhappy wealth . . . Revolution in Russia is imminent and when it takes place its effect will be as stupendous as that of the French Revolution and followed by as glorious an outburst of song."

This was the general feeling of the pre-world war years, the dawn of the "century of the child," as Ellen Key called it, a child that was going to be fed on H. G. Wells's "food of the gods," as many thought in that expansive time. Edwin Björkman thought so, busy as he was on *The World's Work* reporting projects of social advancement and reform, while he also wrote essays on Francis Grierson, Robert Herrick, William James and various other voices of the "new spirit." He popularized especially the Scandinavian literature that flowered in the American mind so briefly but so fully and, throwing so intense a light on the vital problems of the time, stirred the will that was bent on solving them. I had caught my first glimpse of the socialist movement at Harvard when Jack London, still in his twenties, lectured at the Union, with his open shirt and the shining face of a sailor boy fresh from the sea, vibrant with expectancy, vitality, hope and promise. Even Max

Perkins, the sceptical Yankee, was touched by socialist ideas
and he wrote me a thirty-one page letter from a hospital, after
an operation, deploring the regime of competition. He was
convinced that, freed from the profit motive, man would become an entirely different creature and that a negligible part
of his time would have to be given to material work when
machinery replaced slavery for the masses.

While I cast my first vote for the socialist ticket, I was a
chameleon, mentally, still, turning in any direction that caught
my fancy, with never an average moment or a confident moment as I went through my metamorphoses. Socialism seemed
to me "fairly insipid with veracity," to use Henry James the
elder's phrase, but otherwise I had not found my East and
I was only certain that write I must and wholly on my own
terms. All manner of hopes were held out to me if I would
wait for another ten years and make teaching or office-work
my principal interest, putting my whole heart into this for a
time, but something in me that seemed to me quite as organic
as my lungs obstinately refused to agree to do this. Obliged to
earn my living, I was bent on avoiding at any price the kind
of official entanglements that mortgage one's conscience, and
I clung to mechanical half-menial jobs that I could fulfil con-
scientiously without involving my imagination in them. It cost
me nothing, then or later, to refuse invitations to editorships
and other supposedly important and lucrative positions, of
which, in the end, numbers came my way, as when, for instance, Alfred Harcourt asked me if I would like to be "the
W. C. Brownell of Harcourt, Brace and Co." I was not obliged
to put into words my failure to respond to this, for Harcourt,
the brilliant publisher, was an appreciative reader and always
extremely kind to me, and I did not need to tell him how
often I had seen Brownell himself wandering, during the mid-

day recess, in the neighbourhood of Scribner's. I thought of
Brownell, the personification of his own "democratic distinction," as the finest critical intelligence of his time in New
York; but how little of this had left its deposit in the few small
books he wrote, which seemed to me increasingly anæmic and
sterile. Mistakenly or otherwise, I felt that his vitality had
been drained off in the publishing office; and how fully I
seemed to understand the dying Tolstoy's flight from home
and the kind of responsibilities that I so dreaded. Day after
day, in 1910, I followed in a state of enchanted suspense the
newspaper stories of "Tolstoy wandering on," escaping from
Yasnaya Polyana in his peasant blouse and boots, hoping perhaps to join the Dukhobors. In his last desperate pilgrimage
this greatest of novelists seemed to me an emblem of some deep
necessity of artists and writers.

Meanwhile, my college friends were turning homeward, one
by one, reappearing from Europe and settling in New York,
Joe Breck, for example, who was now at the Metropolitan
Museum and with whom I discussed vague plans for a col-
laboration. I looked on the history of art as a sort of possession
of my own, jealous that anyone else knew anything about it,—
a well-known adolescent feeling,—while at the same time I was
not unwilling to share it with someone who knew ten times
as much as I. Another day-dream begotten by Ruskin was a
plan for a history of the Utopian idea which Lewis Mumford
later carried out,—for he was a disciple of Ruskin also in those
days,—striking with this book the keynote of a high career that
I was to follow with the utmost of respect and wonder. Mitchell
Kennerley had brought out an American edition of the small
book of which I had paid half the costs in England, and he
was to publish within two or three years two other books of
mine, studies of H. G. Wells and John Addington Symonds.

I came to regard these rather coldly, feeling, as Havelock Ellis felt, that publishing books of criticism too early is an error,— unless a writer is prepared to eat his words; but when years later Mitchell Kennerley took his own life in New York I wondered that there had been so few to praise him. What did it matter in the end that he sometimes played a double game? He made little or nothing out of his exasperated authors, and who else would have printed them, who else would have looked at their first little books, which Kennerley delightedly acclaimed and so charmingly published? Like John Lane in England, whose agent he had been, he backed books often at a loss, with a feeling for talents that no one but he distinguished; and he should be remembered as the friend of a whole generation of writers whom, in surprising numbers, he first brought out.

Edward Sheldon was living in New York, though only intermittently, for he was already too popular to do his work there, with half the most famous women of the stage waiting in his anteroom to talk over plays that he was to write for them. He seemed to breathe telegrams and his suitcases bulged with unopened letters, while he remained unspoilable with his high good spirits, passing from triumph to triumph in a world that I knew nothing of but always ready for adventures in any other world. Occasionally at rehearsals he would ask me to take out to lunch some actress who struck me as a formidable creature,—for I always spelled the word Actress with a large A at that time,—thrusting into my hand a purse that was filled with golden ducats, well knowing that in all probability my pockets were empty. But I observed that the more dangerous the ladies looked the surer they were to ask for milk toast and rice pudding. Ned's plays were coming out virtually at the rate of two a year,—the most popular of all, *Romance*, in 1911,—

mingling the glamorously erotic that he so loved in Byron with the bawdy, the macabre and the clownishly funny. Nothing amused him more than a barker expounding the merits of a side-show freak,—"Is she fat? Is she *fat?* Oh, my, my, *my!*"— which presently appeared in his play about Coney Island.

This was one of the notes he struck in the showers of post-cards that came from him when he broke away in order to do his work. He was perhaps in England near J. M. Barrie and Arnold Bennett or staying with the Norman Hapgoods in some quiet village, in a rectory all roses without and dimity within, playing tennis in the afternoon with William Faver-sham, across the green, in the court of an Elizabethan manor-house. He would write about Tetrazzini's singing or Mrs. Campbell's Hedda, or he would quote something that Annie Russell had said to him, or possibly Viola Allen or Margaret Anglin. He was travelling with John Barrymore in Italy again, rewriting scenes and even whole plays for him, "unbinding" this "Prometheus," as Gene Fowler later said, "awakening him to his mission." Or he was on Lake Como, in a big old frescoed farmhouse, surrounded with tuberoses and heliotrope as he worked on a play. He wrote from Urbino, Ravenna, Tivoli, Parma, a town all seventeenth century with a perfumed bro-caded cathedral, Correggios, great candelabra and altar-cloths of gold. He sent me two or three photographs of the theatre in the Farnese palace, a ruinous old barn of a place with seats out of plumb, with battered equestrian statues in it, wooden cupids with broken heads and a vast worm-eaten dusty aban-doned stage. The sunlight that came through chinks in the roof threw spotlights on the floor of this, and, standing in one of these, he looked out at the empty tiers and imagined that he was a Scapin or a Scaramouche. He saw himself with high heels and a small black mask. Then he wandered on to the

picture gallery with the portraits of the old duchesses and
dukes, together with their dwarfs and lapdogs, all alike. They
were very pink and white, with slanting eyes and small full
mouths, secretive and suggestive as the closed shutters of a
house at noon.

Once in England Ned Sheldon went to see Eric Bell, in the
shining new sanitarium with the quiet trained nurses to which
Eric, another of my Doubleday friends, whom Ned, whom
everybody loved, had been condemned for tuberculosis. J. B.
Yeats was especially fond of this nephew of the publisher
George Bell who had come to New York for adventure and
broken down there,—for he "wouldn't follow rules," Yeats said
sadly,—and he had been shipped home again, doomed to spend
his remaining days among minds like "tubercular cabbages," as
he put it in a letter. One of the patients was a medical student
who had just reached the Rider Haggard stage, one was a
rubber planter who quoted Kipling and one was the sort of
Englishman who stares at you for an hour and says, "That's
rather a decent tie you have on." Eric was as much in revolt
against England as I was against America: he laughed at his
unimaginative countrymen who were always seizing colonies
and climbing mountains. Why their mania for "aiguilles" and
"cols," their singular wish in Switzerland "to get to the top of
everything and sit on it"? He had been himself in Switzerland,
at another sanitarium, where he thought the scenery was too
theatrical, with its picture-postcard villages and clear-cut peaks;
and, as for the English, he could not see them as idealistic
altruists whose one real dream was "improving the condition
of the natives." He had fallen in love with what he called my
"genial and to me congenial country" where he had begun to
write articles and impressions of people, free-lancing and even
attempting Casanovian memoirs, while, tall and well-made,

witty and gay, with a wonderful sense of the absurd, he had wildly indulged a natural taste for mischief. At home again, dying at twenty-seven, obliged to eschew the "great indoors," he was, he said, getting to be like one of Hardy's minor characters, "developing into one of those chaps who can tell the hour by looking at the sun and tell the time of year by watching the birds."

Ned Sheldon was always quoting Eric who spoke of the kind of party, for instance, after which all the guests, on the following morning, felt obliged "to write notes of apology to everyone else." He said that "the only trouble with living at home" was that you were "treated as one of the family." Struggling to keep alive while he seemed to be bent on destroying himself, Eric had escaped for one winter, at least, in New Hampshire, living as a hired man on the place of the painter Abbott Thayer, labouring as he had learned to do in Switzerland. He felt like Michael Fairless in *The Roadmender*, as he said, in his little hut covered with snow there, sallying forth at seven in the morning to work in the woods or fields, winning his bread again with two dollars a day. He found the real happiness in manual toil that Tolstoy had discovered, with the white old snow-capped Monadnock looking on as he cleared away fallen timber with his axe, listening in the evening while Abbott Thayer discussed his researches in protective coloration and living with the family, who were all for the simple life. They started going to bed, in relays, at seven.

No one guessed that Ned Sheldon, at almost the same age, was beginning to die, like Eric, on the physical plane, though, the more he was disabled, the more his spirit came to life as in one of the great souls one found in the lives of the saints. The time was not far off when he was to write, "I can walk a little. I go from bed to couch,"—he had walked eight steps

with each foot in less than six minutes,—and when he said that
he was unable to move his legs at all,—"or I should take to-
night's train and burst in on you." It was after this that he
became the "father-confessor of the theatre" in New York and
what Thornton Wilder called the "dispenser of wisdom, courage and gaiety" when he dedicated to Edward Sheldon *The
Ides of March.* Living vicariously in the careers of his friends,
a counsellor and guide for each of them, uncannily perceptive
as well as heroic, he was, in a time when everything overshad-
owed wisdom, the only wise man whom many knew. Con-
fronting day after day the abyss of non-being, he submitted to
find bread in stones and life in the blank mind, and all without self-pity, objective towards himself and, full of pity for
others, always laughing. Blind and unable to turn his head, he
could not see the model of the galleon in full sail on the shelf
behind him, but whoever placed it there perceived the sym-
bolism that no one who ever saw him could have missed.

I had left Doubleday's, meanwhile, feeling that I was out
of place attempting the kind of magazine writing one did
there, and, explaining my case to Mr. Page, I said good-bye to
him, happy enough to escape from a false position. J. B. Yeats
called me the most impulsive man he knew, but I never regretted that I was impulsive then, for I reasoned that if I
acted promptly something would turn up in line with my real
interests, as I saw them. And, as it happened, the Standard
Dictionary had lost a definer of words that day and I was
engaged at once to take his place, thus beginning a two-year
stretch as one of an army of professional hacks, working on a
dictionary and presently on an encyclopædia. Twenty-five dollars a week was the usual reward for taking all knowledge as
one's province, for writing articles on Chinese literature, Ara-
bian poetry and Italian art or re-phrasing definitions from the

rival Webster. At five cents a definition, I could earn this amount in five hours a day, and, finding that if I did more, the rate was reduced proportionately, I kept a margin of time for my own writing. For the encyclopædia I took notes at the Astor Library, the architectural fantasy on Lafayette Street, undergoing what Frank Moore Colby called the "trials of an encyclopædist" when he was himself the editor of a similar work. But I learned something about words and about arranging facts and discriminating among authorities,—most important of all,—and, for the rest, I could not see that the witty Colby, whom I met, had been "badly damaged" by his calling. He described this as "twenty years among the barebones of all subjects and seeing the full rotundity of none." One of the encyclopædias that Colby worked on collapsed at the completion of the letter A. Mine did not collapse until it went through D.

Many times since those days I have wondered about my comrades there, the regiment of "writers for the booksellers" with whom I laboured, a remnant of Grub Street, astray from the eighteenth century, that included R. W. Sneddon along with me. Even Jack Wheelock worked with me on the dictionary of proper names, side by side with an elderly colleague who turned on the gas in his room one night because he could not face his sixty-fifth birthday. "What a pity," the editor said, "when he had got our style so well!"—when, triumphantly fulfilling the law of adaptation to environment, he had been a success, if he had only known it. There were possibly fifty others in this legion of hacks who drifted with the literary tides like a mass of seaweed, settling for a few weeks or months wherever there was work for them to do, then shuffling on their coats and moving on. It might be another encyclopædia or a set of business manuals or a popular world history in a dozen volumes, but when a project had been carried through there was always another to be taken up and they turned on one tap as easily as they turned off another.

It was a foreign legion, mainly, made up of threadbare soldiers of fortune, decayed scholars, illusionists, renegades, misfits, Englishmen who had lost caste and unfrocked Irish priests, together with a handful of young aspirants for the literary life. Most of them were veterans who had been jostled and broken by our metallic American world and who were truly nomads of a twilight of letters, O'Shea, for one, who might have been a scholar-hermit in the Ireland of the saints and Donnelly with Barry Lyndon airs. Another was Morgan, if that was his name, who could relate in seven tongues the exploits of his fifteen years as a soldier in Morocco. I think of them all as generalized in a type that might have been William Maginn, the original of Thackeray's Captain Shandon, the founder of *Fraser's Magazine,* who spent most of his life in debtors' prisons, inerrant as he was, "barring drink and the girls." If not always "bright," like Maginn, they were always "broken."

Among all these comrades there was only one whose secret I ever learned. This was the Nabob, as the others called him, who was different indeed, in appearance at least, from the shaggy-chinned derelicts about him, with his hawk's nose and eye and the grey drooping moustache that fell with such admirable curves from his well-shaven cheeks. His coat had been cut with distinction, his apple-green scarf was of exquisite silk, his spats were never dishonoured by a fleck of mud, and, looking more ducal every day than he had seemed the day before, he inspired a kind of awe in the breasts of the others. For, humbled as they had been by life, they saw him as a creature of the upper air, toiling in their limbo, presumably, for some reason of amusement, in charge of the division of "art" on the encyclopædia with which for a number of months I was connected. It happened that, having completed the articles on Avicenna, Buddhism, the Chinooks and finally Denmark (Literature),—rising in the alphabet from A to our terminal letter,—I found that I was expected to deal with Bernini, Bramante and Brunelleschi, and thus the Nabob's eye fell upon me. "By the way," he added, when we had discussed the preliminaries, "I have a new cap here. If you are going out of town on Sunday, will you take it and break it in for me?" It was a new idea to me that caps were broken in, and this was a cap of many colours that scarcely fitted into my philosophy of costume. But I took it, feeling vaguely that the cap would prove to be a clue, for the Nabob had begun to interest me.

Not long after this I went to see him. It was an icy night, just before Christmas, and I imagined the cosy evening we might have before the fire, chatting about Bernini and Brunelleschi. Expecting to see a well-stocked library, an elderly bachelor's haven, perhaps with an old master or two and a Roman bust, I stopped at No. 13, one of those brick houses in Stuyvesant Square that sometimes already sheltered birds of passage. But I was rather surprised when the Nabob, coming to the door himself, led me up four flights of stairs, and I found myself in a hall bedroom, a servants' room in former days, with an iron bedstead, a bureau, a huge wardrobe and two chairs. There was not a book in the room, or even a picture, save for one photograph representing the well-known face of an elderly eccentric, the garrulous son of a celebrated diplomat father. This man had made a few stabs at fame by writing reminiscences of certain crowned European heads he had encountered as a boy and, oddly enough, there was something in the face that closely resembled the Nabob's hawk-like distinction. A gas-jet, high on the wall, threw a merciless glare

over the room. The Nabob opened one of the drawers, drew
out a stub of a candle, lighted it and set it on the bureau,
though its flame was drowned in the oily flood of the gas.
Then he said abruptly, "Why not call me Jack?"

Our efforts to launch a conversation were not very success-
ful. We tried Brunelleschi, but I could see that the Nabob
had something much on his mind, and it came over me that
I was the first person with whom for years he had had a
chance to talk. I felt that, whatever his secret was, I was about
to hear it when he went over to the bureau and, opening the
drawer again, drew forth an armful of magazines and books.
Turning page after page, he showed me this illustration and
that, and there he was in every one of them. There were the
hawk's nose and eye, the grey moustache with its admirable
curves, there was the Nabob in all his sartorial splendour, as
an old Virginian colonel or a Scottish duke. He was perhaps
descending a palatial stairway or leading down the aisle a
bride divinely fair, holding a levee at some garden fête or be-
nignly saluting his daughter at her moment of betrothal.
Now thirty years old, now seventy or eighty, he was always
the perfect cavalier, for the Nabob's fortune had literally been
his face. Providence had given him the mask and bearing that
dukes should have, and he had shown his gratitude for years
by sitting for the illustrators as a model.

Then he unlocked his wardrobe, and there were the coats
that had so dazzled our dingy Grub Street limbo. There were
the waistcoats, the walking-sticks, the hats on the shelf, the
spats on the floor in a dozen piles exposed to the glare of the
gaslight. One by one he took them out and tried on this cap
or that, turning about the little room,—shabbier still by contrast,—showing me all the trophies of his ruling passion. It was
for this that the Nabob toiled every day as an unexposed au-

thority on the history of art. This was the glory for which he saved and schemed, to which he came home at night and awoke in the morning, his profession, his story, his secret, his destiny, his existence.

As for myself, it seemed to me that I was marking time in these miscellaneous drudgeries of the literary tyro, but time meant little to me then,—there was so much to spend or waste in the long vague stretch that lay before me. Later I found in Chateaubriand's *Mémoires d'Outre-Tombe* a phrase that expressed the feeling of so many in those days: "Let the young generations wait in hope,—there is a long time coming yet before we reach the end." That, at least, was my feeling about myself and about the world; and how sad it was to seem to me forty years later that young people could no longer feel that way.

## CHAPTER IX

# YEATS AT PETITPAS'

FOR A good part of a year John Butler Yeats had been living in New York before Edward Sheldon and I fell in with him in a little room in an old hotel where he sketched portraits of both of us in the pastels that he had just taken up. He had come over in 1908 with his elder daughter Lily, who was exhibiting embroideries in Madison Square Garden, and he had refused to go home again, although he was seventy at the time, saying, "To leave New York is to leave a huge fair ... In Dublin nothing happens except an occasional insolvency," whereas "here anything may happen" and "a sort of gambling excitement keeps me here." A lady who was cunning about the future had said to him many years before that he would not win success until he was old, but that then his success would be universal; and he had found Dublin, where he had painted everybody's portrait, not too sympathetic for an artist. He remarked in a lecture that "malignant criticism" would have been the fate of Watts if this English painter had been obliged to live there, and that if he had been "born in Dublin Watts would have read for the 'Indian Civil' and perhaps—passed," bidding farewell to art. The only thing the Dubliners admired was "mundane success," he said, a preference we others had found also in New York, but Yeats was uncommitted here, with the world all before him and a sense that life for him was "just beginning." Like Swedenborg's angels he felt he was advancing toward the springtime of his youth, putting forth every day new shoots of talent.

So he seemed to his New York friends, the artists and writers who gathered about him when he had settled at Petitpas' in West Twenty-ninth Street, the boarding-house kept by three sisters from Brittany with the restaurant in the back yard where Yeats sat at the head of one of the long tables. If some of these artists and writers were young and not invariably discerning or wise, they gave him all the sympathy he could have wished for, with the companionship that he said artists hungered and thirsted for, proud and solitary as they might affect to be. For, he said, "The artist gives that he may receive," and all these companions understood how rare were his own powers of growth,—he seemed to develop new faculties under their eyes. It was true that his portrait-painting was not as good as it had been in the fine pictures that I was to see in Dublin, pictures that seemed "to come to us," as Yeats observed of his favourite Watts, "out of the mists of memory and romance." From Watts he had first learned the true meaning of painting; and what profundity there was in his treatment of Standish O'Grady and John O'Leary, of George Russell,—AE,—and Katherine Tynan Hinkson, making all the surrounding portraits seem brittle and shallow.

That he was a "born portrait-painter imprisoned in an imperfect technique," Yeats was to write later to his elder son; and this had become more apparent as his life went on. But, at seventy, taking up pastels, he also wrote his first play, and these were only two of his new ventures, for, finding himself "quite an orator," he wrote the essays many of which I carried away for *The Seven Arts* and *The Freeman* later. "I was afraid to return to Dublin, afraid as a child dreads the fire," he remarked in one of the letters that were afterwards published,

"and I may add that New York saved my life . . . a dark saying which I could elucidate"; and there he was like the growing boy that he said an artist should always be,—"who is
never and never will be a grown-up." He continued, "An old
man should think of the past, but I am still interested in the
future,"—except when the death of some old friend brought
back "that long-vanished dream of my youth and marriage";
and saying, "We are happy when we are growing," he was
always looking for "improvement in my work" and what he
called "an immense change in my fortunes." No wonder he
attracted other artists and writers.

This old man eloquent, so "eagerly communicative,"—a
phrase in his *Early Memories* that was self-descriptive,—found
himself therefore surrounded by Robert Henri, John Sloan
and other bright souls, both men and women. They dined
with him at Petitpas', where George Bellows also appeared,
with Glackens, the brothers Prendergast, a number of young
writers,—among these Alan Seeger and Eric Bell,—and our
Twenty-third Street actor friend who spoke of the "perpetual
look of surprise" of Fred King of the *Literary Digest*, another
who was there. Yeats shook his head over Eric Bell's adventures of the flesh, almost condoning the sins, wholly loving
the sinner, admiring also, as poet and man,

> the eager
> Keats-Shelley-Swinburne mediæval Seeger,

whom, in *The Day in Bohemia*, John Reed described.

> Poe's raven bang above Byronic brow
> And Dante's beak,—you have his picture now;

and all he required, to complete the picture, was the long
black Paris student's cape that my brother-in-law-to-be had
worn at the Beaux-Arts. It was like the black military cape that
Poe took with him when he left West Point and that he

wrapped round Virginia when she died on her mattress of straw, hugging the tortoise-shell cat to keep herself warm. I lent Alan Seeger this cape for a winter. Meanwhile his "remote and dignified courtesy" greatly appealed to J. B. Yeats, with the eyebrows and long eyelashes that Yeats liked to sketch, his red lips against the dead white face, and his habit of looking downwards, chin on hand,—"a man to me infinitely more interesting than Rupert Brooke," as Yeats wrote to the son whom he always called "Willie." Occasionally W. G. Blaikie Murdoch also appeared at Petitpas', the Scottish nationalist who had written a book on the "greenery-yallery" Nineties and was full of strange learning especially about Japan. Blaikie Murdoch followed his own personal notions of style, sprinkling commas over his writing as a Parsee sprinkles red pepper over meat so that the substance is invisible under the coating. His writing was packed so tight with commas that it could neither move nor breathe, and I once had to spend half a day removing from one of his articles enough at least to let in light and air. Bald as a tonsured monk, with a mind as ripe as an old Roquefort cheese, Blaikie Murdoch was living in a basement somewhere, cooking his meals on a gas-jet, not far away; and, as he talked, he would stealthily manœuvre stray crusts of bread on the table into the yawning pocket of his old brown jacket. How similarly helpless in the brazen world were many friends of mine who were only at home in the golden world of art.

For me, as for most of us, Yeats himself was invested with the glamour of the literary revival in Ireland, so renowned at the time, and his talk abounded in recollections not only of "Willie" but of AE and Synge, Lady Gregory, the Abbey Theatre, George Moore, Dunsany. We had special reasons for our interest in this, for we felt we were on the verge of a not dis-

similar movement of our own, the first phase of another revival that expressed an American coming-of-age, an escape
from our old colonial dependence on England. Yeats himself
said, "The fiddles are tuning all over America," as in Ireland
they had been playing for a decade or more, and various figures of the Irish movement were living in New York and also
appeared at Petitpas'. By far the best known were the Colums,
Padraic and Mollie, and there was also Frederick Gregg who
had once been regarded as Ireland's hope in poetry by AE and
others. Gregg was a writer on the New York *Evening Sun*.
Another of the friends of "Willie's" youth,—indeed, his most
intimate school friend in Dublin,—who had settled in New
York with his Russian wife was a tall black-bearded Orange-
man, the son of a member of Parliament and the founder of
the Hermetic Society that gave rise to the movement. For that
coming together of a group of young people who were interested in the wisdom of the East and met to discuss the Upanishads and the Vedas had led in turn to an awakening of literary minds, just as their study of the Indian mythology and tra-
ditions had stirred their feeling for the Irish mythology and
past. From the Hindu gods it was only a step to the gods of
ancient Ireland. Charles Johnston had lived in India as a civil
servant, translating the Bhagavad-Gita and other scriptures;
and in Dublin, where he had been a leader of the Theoso-
phists, he had married Madame Blavatsky's niece. This "splendid placid woman, like a summer sea,"—J. B. Yeats's phrase
that perfectly described her,—virtually ran the Russian cathedral in East Ninety-seventh Street, for she was an ardent member of the Orthodox church. Her Presbyterian-Buddhist husband had become a staff-writer on the *New York Times,* a
learned, austere and humourless man who wrote a book called
*Why We Laugh* and who liked to dine with the father of his

old Dublin friend. In their up-town apartment the Johnstons kept open house, and Charles Johnston, as I remember, had a passion for ice cream and used to send out for this at all hours of the night. Like AE and "John Eglinton," who was called the "Irish Emerson," he delighted not only in Emerson but in Whitman and Thoreau, the American sages who were devoted to the wisdom of the East and whom J. B. Yeats admired also. At least, Yeats had been one of the first to acclaim Whitman in earlier days and he had read *Walden* to "Willie" at the breakfast table. The poet Yeats later recorded that this occasioned the writing of his poem *The Lake Isle of Innisfree*.

The younger Yeats came to Petitpas', too, when I was in California, so that I failed to meet this extraordinary man,—although some years before I had heard him lecture,—and I think J. B. Yeats was somewhat afraid of the formidable son who seemed not to overflow with human affection. In every way humane himself, he was at ease with other people who abounded with the milk of human kindness, and a passage in a story of Willa Cather put me later in mind of him and what I supposed was his feeling about William Butler Yeats. "When kindness has left people, even for a few moments, we become afraid of them," Willa Cather says, "as if their reason had left them,"—leaving "a place where we have always found it"; and this notion was confirmed for me when I read J. B. Yeats's *Letters to His Son* whom he chides more than once for being "inhuman." He could not refrain from reproaching the poet for being "laconic and cold" in a letter to his "old and good friend Charlie Johnston"; and he asked, "As you have dropped affection from the circle of your needs, have you also dropped love between man and woman?" Writing again to his son as "a man who has cast away his humanity," he feels that "Willie" is tending toward the Nietzschean line, which belongs to "the clumsy and brutal side of things," proud as he was of this man of genius who had "given a tongue to the sea-cliffs," the first-born of his four gifted children. The two profoundly respected each other,—there was never any doubt of that,—and the son knew how much he owed his father; but the father would have understood Dolly Sloan and made allowances for John Sloan's wife when the son could not understand and could not forgive her. Mrs. Sloan mistakenly supposed that W. B. Yeats had money to spare when, visiting New York, he stayed at a great hotel,—at Lady Gregory's expense,—with the Irish Players; and, feeling that perhaps he did not know how sadly poor his father was, she went and appealed to him to assist his father. It was a blunder, but human, as J. B. Yeats would have seen at once, for all the fierce pride of the gentleman that he shared with his son,—aware as he was that Dolly Sloan, who had "no bravery at all," he said (meaning no bravado, no parade), had "the courage of the devil." For the sake of what lay behind it, he would have pardoned the blunder; he would not have felt merely the cold contempt with which his son bowed Dolly to the door, uttering one phrase only, "Good day, Madam."

No doubt the poet had reasons enough for turning against the human, seeing this perhaps as "all too human," like so many other writers of the post-war years; but the father's humanity bore, nevertheless, the same relation to this frame of mind that the sun bears to the moon as we see them from our planet. It was the fruit of an expansive age, and the culture that reflected this,—a diastole as compared with the systole of the age that followed,—and it had behind it a universality that everybody recognized and that many, like Yeats himself, have found in Shakespeare. If not the fruit of security too, insecure as the person might be, it sprang from a whole-hearted feeling about men and about life; and what strength lay behind the remark in the *Early Memories* of J. B. Yeats, "I am a cheerful and perennially hopeful man." It mortified him, he went on, to be so cheerful, convinced that he "shared this gift with all the villains . . . for it is their unsinkable buoyancy that enables these unfortunates to go on from disaster to disaster and remain impenitent." But, loving the sinner, as Yeats did, he saw the goodness in the sinner too, finding "man's inconsistency always a charm"; so that, worshipping human nature, as he said Shakespeare did, he found himself in a really impregnable position. One could not be too human; one could scarcely, in fact, be human enough; and for Yeats, who had "suddenly amazed" himself, "by coming to the conclusion that revealed religion was a myth and fable," this was all that was left for the law and the prophets. He had been reading Butler's *Analogy* as a student at Trinity College in Dublin when this counter-revelation suddenly surprised him; and it had settled for him the question of becoming what his father was, "a respectable Episcopalian clergyman."

This was the keynote of Yeats's thinking and of his portrait painting too, an art whose genius was "largely a genius for friendship," regarding which he further said that the best portraits were painted when friendship governed the relation of the sitter to the painter. He added that even its technique was "mainly a technique of interpretation," and in order to secure in his work the relation of friendship he seemed positively to shun lucrative commissions. Choosing to be fond of me and having trouble painting me, he would not listen to me, as he worked on my portrait, when I begged him to spend his time on more profitable sitters, although he was in arrears with the rent of his studio in Dublin and kept dreaming of people fishing and catching nothing. No, he knew my face now,—he had got another canvas and was bent on doing me again,—he was

determined to do me to his own satisfaction, with a little bust
of Goethe in the picture, resting on a volume of Bernard Shaw
and W. B. Yeats's *Ideas of Good and Evil*. For he was convinced that his first portrait of me was a failure. He had come
to my office in the rain in despair, so depressed that he could
not sleep; and he sent me sketches of himself facing the canvas
in hope, in exultation, in dejection and at last in triumph. This
was all because I had had the joy of establishing with him a
human relation and because we could talk congenially while
he painted, as he had encouraged his models to talk in Dublin
and in London, especially when the girls talked about "nothing." For he said he was not so much interested in any "interesting things" they told as in their "natural gift as truthful
tellers,"—in short, in themselves, in the human nature that
pleased him as it pleased Charles Lamb, whose note, he said,
was a certain "capricious wildness."

It was by this criterion that he divided the goats from the
sheep, the people of Belfast, for instance, from the other Irish
in a country where "we solved all our doubts in matters of conduct," he said, "by thinking well of our fellow creatures . . .
We prided ourselves upon it," he added in *Early Memories;*
"we considered it a gentlemanly trait," unlike "the puritans
who cling to their creed of the badness of human nature because it helps them in their unnatural war of commercial selfishness." I cannot guess what Yeats would have thought if he
had lived into a later time when "original sin" was the rage
with the literary young and when this had ceased to be identified with "puritanism" and became the mark of a High Church
Anglican line. For him it was the special mark of the "dull
people of Belfast" who were always talking of their commercial
triumphs and a large part of whose religion might be stated in
the phrase, "The man who sells his cow too cheap goes to

hell." Yeats's clergyman father had said, "Nothing can exceed
the vulgar assumption of a Belfast man,"—who liked to think,
Yeats went on, "My sons and my daughters and the men I em-
ploy are bad and naturally faithless, therefore let me coerce
them." Had not Bunyan talked the same way with his "Mr.
Carnality," his "Mr. Facing-Both-Ways" and so on, finding
epithets and names to belittle and degrade the temple of human nature and all its altars? I remember the distaste with
which Yeats repeated a phrase of Kate Douglas Wiggin, the
popular novelist whom he met one afternoon, "Whenever I
hear of human nature, I want to use a whip."

For himself, he would rather have listened to a Mayo man
whistling a tune, or telling a fairy-tale or a ghost story, than to
the greatest man in Liverpool or Belfast, and the Irish were
natural writers of plays, for they were like people sitting at a
play, watching the game of life, enjoying their neighbours. It
was in the nature of things that Ireland had produced in
Farquhar, Congreve and Goldsmith, in Sheridan, Oscar Wilde,
Shaw and Synge, all the ablest dramatists of latter-day England; for the Irish, with their inborn love of dialogue, were
"surrounded by a dialogue," said Yeats, "as lively, gallant and
passionate as in the times of the great Eliza." Would not
Shakespeare have liked to sit "with the courteous peasants
round their turf fires, listening to their musical sentences and
their musical names"? Inevitably plays like Synge's rose out of
their folk-tales and wild philosophy, rich in poetry and humour. They knew no distinction between the natural and the
supernatural, and in this Yeats himself was sometimes like
them.

For, with his love of whatever was human, he lived at moments on the border-line where it passed into the subhuman
or the superhuman, and I remember the perfect good faith

with which he received and passed on the news that the banshee had been heard crying round his brother-in-law's house.
George Pollexfen, the astrologer, a solid man of Sligo, had
died, wrote Yeats's daughter, just before dawn, and one of the
nurses had awakened her when the crying first began because
the other nurse was so alarmed. All three women had heard
the crying, which they supposed was a cat before they fully
realized it was the banshee,—it sounded like an old woman in
distress; and, often as I saw Yeats repel the usual gush about
fairies, there were no doubts in his mind on that occasion. His
voice was all gravity and awe as he read me the letter. It put
me in mind of the stories about AE, for instance, who would
suddenly say, in the woods, in the Dublin mountains, "There
is a figure over by that tree," and, taking out his pastels and
sketch-book, would begin to draw it; and of his Blake-like
visions of ancient gods in forest glades and the spectral maidens
and children whom he had seen. Then there was Mrs. William
Sharp who told me in London once how, in Provence, on the
road, on a blazing day in August, she had felt something
twitching at her dress and, looking down, saw it was a faun,
complete with furry flanks and a boy's face. She and her husband,—"Fiona Macleod,"—had plainly seen this faun, which
scurried across the road into the brush beside it. Once, when
her husband and the poet Yeats were frying eggs on their
kitchen fire and the two were talking about the fairies, Yeats,
seeing the pan was suddenly empty and unaware that he had
spilled the eggs, exclaimed to Sharp, "You see what's happened now!" Was he only half convinced that the fairies had
purloined the eggs,—because fairies do not like to be talked
about? Who knows what goes on in certain imaginative minds?
In the case of J. B. Yeats, I am sure only of one thing, that he
believed in dreams as omens. He was always dreaming and

telling his dreams in one of which his own father appeared and asked "How long I expected him to support me," a sign of the lifelong distress, no doubt, of the man with a family on his hands who has never quite been able to make ends meet. Yeats often consulted Mrs. Beattie, a professional palmist whom he knew in New York, and he always followed her advice if it agreed with his wishes.

All this confirmed his own belief that the Irish were mediæval still, while it showed that he was himself quintessentially Irish, one of a race with "time to enjoy themselves and for the sake of enjoyment to be courteous and witty and pleasant." They were mediæval again, he said, in thinking that "how to live is more important than how to get a living," although, as for himself, he had honestly followed "the chimera of success," and no one with imagination could ever have reproached him. If he liked America in many ways, it was because he found so human the American ideal of "happiness for oneself and others," while he disliked at the same time its doctrine of getting on and its nervous energy and efficiency, both damnable to him. For they killed good manners, conversation, literature and art. His own politics were akin, he said, to those of "American hopefulness," and he liked the "buoyant American full of courage with the key of the future in his pocket," much as he disliked the American habits of emphasis and dogmatism, partly because he felt they were his own faults. He also disliked the "sour-faced socialists" for whom artists and poets were egoists and who dragged down and trampled on the aesthetic sense, saying that he was himself a socialist, meaning that he was for socialism when, and only when, this too was human. Why did he turn against Walt Whitman, drawing mischievous caricatures of the "emotional man" in letters to me, remarking that his poems were not works of art and that he was not a poet but a bard, a judgment that Whitman himself would gladly have accepted? Yeats had, as ever, a very good reason, that Whitman stood for the effort to turn into poetry "the collective mind," but this was another way of saying that Whitman too was imperfectly human, to recall the standard by which Yeats judged all things. He was largely indifferent to AE for a similar reason, saying that he was at once a mystic and a materialist who valued "liberation" only as a "mystical doctrine." England for him was inhuman too,—"your villainous old country," as he described it in a letter to an English friend,—the country "where everyone hates and distrusts his neighbour,"—though his general Irish resentment was always tempered by a special delight in particular English men. And how rapidly his feeling about England changed when the country was menaced in 1914 by those whom he saw as the still more inhuman Germans. "I am enjoying the unexpected in finding myself in agreement with England," he wrote at the outset of the first world war, and he could not say too often that "Ireland must help England" in the lean years he foresaw as following the war.

Human as Yeats was, however, and, above all, companionable, he was in no sense a gregarious man: he was, rather, one of the solitary men who live "in the hermitage of their own minds" and "follow the untrodden way that leads to the surprising." He abounded in these phrases describing the type from which he felt all poetry sprang,—just as prose was the language of the socially-minded,—much as he loved conversation, the forte of the Irish and, from his point of view, their greatest possession. "Whenever any Irish reform is proposed," Yeats said in one of his essays, "I always ask, How will it affect our conversation? France has her art and literature, England her House of Lords, America her initiative. We have our con-

versation." But he combined with this the solitary spirit that
had always sustained itself by reverie and dream, and, going
off every afternoon for long walks alone, he occasionally took
a ticket for some unknown station in New Jersey. Did he hear
there "the bird of poetry singing to itself in the heart of the
wood, coaxing and admonishing its own soul, thinking nothing
of others"? Ever since he had left school he had "lived under
cloudy skies," he wrote, "leaving happiness behind me," ac-
quainted with the solitude that Americans never knew, he said,
for they knew, he added, nothing but movement. They should
have adopted the three legs that represent the Isle of Man, for
these would have suited them better than the eagle,—given as
they were to modes of motion and making war on solitude,
frequenting the highways and the main roads. It was "implic-
itly and even explicitly an offense for them to steal away," as
he put it, "into by-ways and thickets," and what a price
the Americans paid in the "frantic brand-new egotism" that
marked, for one example, the American woman. For she was
no longer a mystery. Behold her pacing Fifth Avenue with her
business-like air, thin-lipped, with eyes bright and hard as
jewels, the embodiment of commanding decision with her
young athlete's figure but as easy to read as an old almanac.
What had become of the lines of allurement? She no longer
undulated with slow grace; she was neither feline nor was she
deerlike. She no longer possessed the three-fold charm of mystery, subtlety and concealment.

Here, as in everything else indeed, Yeats was paradoxical,
perpetually veering between incompatible positions, but always in the spirit of his own remark that what was important
to preserve was not mental consistency but integrity of soul.
"A poet should feel himself quite free to say in the morning
that he believes in marriage and in the evening that he no

longer believes in it," and in this sense—I quote one of his letters,—he was a poet, while his integrity could never have been
open to question. He liked diversity for its own sake, and one
might add mischief too,—"I tried several times to roll in the
apple of discord, but they all looked as if they did not see it,"
he said, for instance, regarding a certain conversation; and he
constantly posed antitheses, contrasting views or types of mind,
all of which corresponded with facets of himself. He would
compare the "solitary" with the "companionable" man or the
"man of temperament" with the "man of soul," or he would explain the difference between "conviction" and "opinion" or
between the "emotion" he distrusted and the "feeling" he admired. He deplored once "this entangling web of grey theory
in which I have spent my life,"—though, in fact, its greyness
was seldom apparent to others,—and it troubled him exceed-
ingly and even drove him to desperation when he was pressed
to define the terms he used. For example, he often praised
"character," and then he would praise "personality," of which
it turned out that "character" was the enemy or the "ash"; but
what did this matter when, in the end, one knew he was
praising something real about which he had important things
to say? When he dispraised character he meant merely that he
disliked petrifaction, when he praised it he meant that he
liked singularity and strength, and because they favoured these
he praised the old-fashioned home and school, brutal as they
had been in many respects. For, along with unhappiness, they
tended to produce the individual differences which followed
from the solitary life they also bred, so that, like trees in a wood
that differ in each case from their fellows, every boy evolved on
a different plan. "Talent is the commonest thing in the world,"
he said on one occasion. "The rare thing is character. It is
character that gives one a point of view,"—a truth that became

apparent to all his friends as they advanced in life and saw scores of brilliant talents wither away.

Because of this wisdom J. B. Yeats was to leave behind him a great and abiding memory in many minds, for, whatever the virtues of Americans may be, wisdom is not one of them and most of his friends had never seen a wise man. So all-pervasive was the cult of youth at the time when he was living in New York that wisdom indeed was all but unrecognized there; and one might say that in America the wise man was an obsolete type,—the species was extinct, the mould was broken. Who had ever heard of an American sage since the days of Emerson and Thoreau?—and I doubt if Yeats would have been recognized either if he had not been so happily endowed with articulate talent, warmth of heart and wit. His sayings delighted artists because of his plastic imagination, because the gates of wisdom for him were the eyes and he knew shapes and surfaces, forms and colours and how the light fell on chairs and walls; and he delighted writers whether he was wise or not, for there was something like wisdom even in his folly. He was not irresponsible when he said that Napoleon and Cromwell and Theodore Roosevelt belonged, as compared with artists, to the "servile class"; and when he remarked, "An indulged facility is the clever man's curse in painting and writing," he won the minds of all his listeners. How frequent these perceptions were!—as when he observed, "The tangible is valuable only for the sake of the intangible"; and he pleased writers as much by what he said of words as by what he said in disparagement of phrases. Dostoievsky avoided these because, as Yeats put it, "he avoided half-thoughts and self-deception,"—and "in avoiding phrases he escaped being literary,"—while words, unlike phrases, were Yeats's delight. In *Early Memories* he recalled that his father had loved strange words: "A new word was to

him, as to me, a pearl of discovery, fished up out of some
strange book he had been reading, and we would enjoy it together"; and his son, the poet, shared this pleasure. Did not
W. B. Yeats so delight in the name of the disease from which
he died that the pleasure almost consoled him for having the
disease? When he heard that he was an "antique cardiac
arterio-sclerotic," he said, "I would rather be called that than
the King of the South of Egypt." With what relish, in his turn,
J. B. Yeats repeated an expression of his father's dearest friend
Isaac Butt, the founder of the first Irish Home Rule party for
whom Yeats himself had devilled as a young law student. The
words were "mimetic, kittenish, ferocious." Yeats loved to quote
the servant girl who was happy when the priest, her employer,
returned because there had been "the colour of loneliness in
the air," and he almost approved of Swinburne because his gift
of language was "like the sea for strength and copiousness."

There were many who delighted in Yeats's reminiscences,
his talk of Samuel Butler and Heatherley's art school, where the
two had been fellow-students in London in the sixties, of York
Powell, the Oxford professor, and the Fenian leader John
O'Leary who had spent nine years in an English prison. Sometimes he talked of his wife and his children when they had
lived in London and he tried to make his way as an illustrator,
and I felt as if I myself had known their faithful old servant
Rose and Mrs. Yeats, tending her window-box, homesick for
Sligo. There still comes back to me a phrase from a letter of
one of his daughters, "There has to be one person in every
house to find lost things and feed the cat," for he constantly
read his letters aloud, drifting off into remarks about painters
and painting, poetry and what not. Once, for instance, at a
midday meal, he expounded Æschylus to me, and once he observed that the northern races are all for big women who are

like plough-horses while the Mediterranean races prefer humming-bird women. On another occasion he talked for an hour about John Stuart Mill's housemaid, who burned up Carlyle's manuscript of the *French Revolution*, deducing her ancestry from this fact and relating how three generations later her great-grandson ended his life on the gallows.

Then I remember an evening at Petitpas' when Robert Henri, outraged, said that he had sent three pictures to an Academy show and that two of the pictures had been sent back while the third, a portrait, had been hung in the worst possible position. Yeats's reply to this was, "Hanging committees are always right," while he glanced round the table defiantly for signs of disagreement. He continued, "If they hang a good picture in a good place, everyone says, What a good picture and how appropriately hung. If in an indifferent place, they say, What an indifferent picture and how appropriately hung. Then, if the picture is hung in a bad place, they say, What a bad picture! However it may be, the committee is always right." One day Yeats related to me a story that R. A. M. Stevenson had told him,—the art-critic who was a cousin of Robert Louis. The two Stevenson cousins with two other Scotsmen, one a grandson of Christopher North and one who drank a bottle of whiskey a day, were out for a walk in Edinburgh, when they were all quite young, for the sole purpose of breaking the Sabbath. On the outskirts of the town they met four clerks who were evidently also bent on breaking the Sabbath and, after they had agreed together to set about converting the clerks, Bob Stevenson got down on his knees and prayed for them. The four clerks, greatly moved, promised that they would go back to town and never attempt again to break the Sabbath, whereupon Stevenson rose to his feet and, bursting out laughing, said, "Why, men, we're making fools of you. We were out to break the Sabbath ourselves." But by this time the four clerks were seriously back in religion again, and they set out in good earnest to convert these pagans.

What did I learn myself from Yeats? He taught me to cherish the concrete, eschewing the abstract and the speculative wherever one could,—for this word concrete was always on his lips, savouring for him of the green bough of life beside which, as he felt, all theories were grey. I had found this preference in Sainte-Beuve already and later I found it expressed again in Blake's phrase "Art and science cannot exist but in minutely organized particulars," words that I was to recall when the time came for me to write my history of the literary life in the United States. Meanwhile, in reaction as most of us were against a commercial world and the puritanism that we somehow identified with it, we were especially happy in all that he said of material success and the waste of life involved in the pursuit of dollars. We had already been attracted to Dublin by Douglas Hyde's characterization of the business world there as the "antique furniture department," an expression that might have been Thoreau's as a philosophy like Thoreau's lay behind Yeats's own remarks about poverty and idleness. When he spoke of the "sacred duty of idleness," he meant "that idleness which is so diligent, idleness, the teeming mother of the arts," the diligent idleness of birds that sing as they build their nests and of old country parsons like White of Selborne. "Only a great and varied culture can instruct us how to traverse the wide expanses of idleness," as he once put it, expanses that will grow wider and wider as the eight, six and four-hour day involve the majority more and more in leisure. Yeats's way of achieving idleness was the way of poverty, freely embraced, a hard way that had always been the way of the wise, like Thoreau, when they were not endowed with this world's

riches. Yeats had not sought this deliberately and he saw the
disadvantages of it. "A man shackled in impecuniosity," he
said once, "is like a bird tied by a string. The bird flies up to
tumble back distractedly." Yet he also said that the "angel of
impecuniosity" had always given him his freedom; and who
could wonder that he did not wish, or only half wished, to
jeopardize the protection of this sensitive angel?

When, many years later, in Dublin, I met the painter Jack
B. Yeats and spoke of his father's courage in crossing the ocean
to start life anew at three score years and ten, he said, "As
you mention courage, how about this? Once my father's eyes
gave out momentarily and he believed that he was going blind.
But, saying nothing about this, he called for my sister Lily and
began dictating a novel to her. If he was no longer to be able
to see to paint, he would turn himself into a writer and the
sooner the better." In fact, without ceasing to paint, he became
a writer, and all in the natural course of things; but what force
of life the story represented, the force that kept him in his
adventurous exile so buoyant and so bountiful and, as he
said, so cheerful and full of hope. This was the man whose
last words, addressed to a friend, in the middle of the night,
were,—as he lay dying in his room in New York,—"Remember,
you have promised me a sitting in the morning."

## CHAPTER X

# CALIFORNIA

O NE DAY in August, 1910, walking along Twenty-third Street, I noticed that the door was open in the dingy building where John Sloan had his studio on the top floor, so I ran all the way up to tell John and Dolly that I was going to be married. There I found J. B. Yeats, who admired Sloan greatly, even to the point of writing to "Willie" that England and America had "produced only two serious painters, Hogarth and Sloan (not including Blake who was more poet than painter and not including landscape painters"). Sloan at that moment was painting a picture of the long table at Petitpas', with Yeats at the head, myself at his right and Alan Seeger at his left, chin on hand, and, having me there as a model, he seized the occasion to work for two hours painting me. He had already painted Yeats in the act of sketching one of the group, with Celestine Petitpas bending over the table.

They were all sympathetic when I gave them my news, although Yeats presently sent me a note to tell my wife-to-be that Darwin called marriage a great waste of time. Nevertheless, it was for this I went to California a few months later, early in 1911, feeling for the West a chilly fear as of something far away, though I could not have answered the question, far from what? I was thinking perhaps of what Ruskin wrote about a scene in Switzerland which he compared with a corner

of the Rocky Mountains, some hypothetical spot that was un-
speakably grand, asking why this latter stirred him but did not
move him deeply, as in the case of the former, with tragic
emotions. For me too, obsessed with history, the West was a
void, though I had only to see California to fall under the
spell of it, beginning with the sunlight over the live-oak trees.
It was February and at first I was puzzled by this light: why
did it seem so magical, why so strange? Then I saw it was a
winter sun shining over a summer scene, an entirely new
combination to unaccustomed eyes. For I was used to so much
greenery only under a summer sky; and, besides, how strange
was this vegetation, the flowering mimosas, the manganita, the
tangles of cactus, the palms, the eucalyptus. The fuchsias grew
like shrubs in the gardens of Berkeley, where there were
streets called "ways" on one of which Arthur Ryder lived, the
friend of my childhood in Italy, now professor of Sanskrit.
Carmel was a wildwood with an operatic setting where life itself also seemed half operatic and where curious dramas were
taking place in the bungalows and cabins, smothered in blos-
soming vines, on the sylvan slope. There were sandy trails for
streets, wandering through canyons carpeted with moss and
with great white pines that caught the wind and shreds of the
grey fog that swept in from the sea. There I was married in
April, and I was to return there, three or four times at least,
for many years.

In Carmel I spent several months before the college term
began and I undertook to teach at Leland Stanford, living in the
alfresco fashion that everybody practised on this quite romantic
peninsula of Monterey. The wild past was still present there
with even the remains of an outlaw's camp, the hut of Joaquin
Murieta in the San José canyon, where Easter lilies grew as
daisies grow elsewhere; and there was the forest scenery that

Robert Louis Stevenson, after his visit, pictured in *Treasure Island*. There were the white-washed Mexican shanties of John Steinbeck's *Tortilla Flat* and the old adobe house where John Steinbeck himself was living when I returned to the peninsula later, one of those dwellings with Castilian roses covering the red-tiled roofs that survived from the old Spanish Mexican colonial times. If, moreover, one no longer saw the caballeros of the eighteen-forties with strings of bells on their embroidered pantaloons, Jaime de Angulo, with his Arab horse and his red sash and El Greco beard, had all the look of a revenant from that earlier time. This was the Spanish ethnologist-doctor who had lived with the Indians in the Southwest, where he collected the Indian tales that he was to put into final form as a dying man forty years later on his mountain-top ranch. There was never a figure more fantastic than Jaime de Angulo came to be in those days when, living alone, looking out at the Pacific, a decayed Don Quixote, ragged and mad, he boxed with a pet stallion and carved his meat with a great knife that hung from his middle. But Carmel at all times abounded in every sort of anomalous type,—for one, the old newspaper-correspondent who conversed every night with the people of Mars and had twelve typewritten volumes of these conversations. George Sterling, the poet, who had precisely the aspect of Dante in hell, a suicide later, like his wife, haunted Point Lobos where the poetess Nora French had leaped from the cliff; while others who had come from the East to write novels in this paradise found themselves there becalmed and supine. They gave themselves over to day-dreams while their minds ran down like clocks, as if they had lost the keys to wind them up with, and they turned into beachcombers, listlessly reading books they had read ten times before and searching the rocks for abalones. For this Arcadia lay, one felt, outside the world in which thought evolves and which came to seem insubstantial in the bland sunny air.

I often felt in Carmel that I was immobilized, living as if in a fresco of Puvis de Chavannes, for there was something Theocritean, something Sicilian or Greek, in this afternoon land of olive trees, honey-bees and shepherds. There was also, down by the Big Sur, or, rather, beyond on the coastal trail, a no man's country as far as San Luis Obispo, a wilderness, sinister and dark, where, supposedly, robbers dwelt, another "Rogues' Harbour," like that of old Kentucky. One heard all manner of ominous tales of mysterious people hiding there, murderers who had escaped there, renegade whites and outcast Indians living in huts and caves, and the evil that seemed to brood over the region was all the stranger and more marked because of the splendid beauty of the mountainous coast. Even the lonely upland ranches that straggled by the road, northward from the Big Sur, overhanging the ocean, seemed somehow accursed or sad as one passed them on foot, as I did that first year on a three days' ramble, stopping at one ranch, for instance, where a tragic-looking woman was living quite alone with her steers and her sheep. At another ranch a burly bruiser with the look of a Mexican Brigham Young was riding with a troop of women, lashing his cattle. Long before Robinson Jeffers had published his poems about that coast one felt there a lurking possibility of monstrous things.

At that time I did not know Robinson Jeffers, nor do I remember on which of my visits to Carmel I began to see him, always at the same time on the ridge between Carmel and Monterey where the old trail through the pines joined the road. At four o'clock in the afternoon, invariably, if one happened to follow this trail, emerging from the woods on the brow of the hill,—where the gulf of Monterey appeared, suddenly, below,—there, overlooking the long slope with live-oaks scattered over it, Jeffers drove by in his old Ford. One could set one's watch by this coming of the poet in his brown tweed coat with his collar thrown back in the manner of Audubon or Byron, driving to Pacific Grove by way of Monterey. Then a few years later I used to see him on my walks around the Carmel point when he was building Tor House on the bluff above the dunes. He seemed to be always toiling up the cliff trail as I passed, with a boulder from the beach on his back, like Sisyphus; for, with only the occasional help of a mason, he set up this massive house himself with the tower that looked like a primitive Norman keep. Later he surrounded it with wild sweet alyssum, and a path of abalone shells led up from the gate. White pigeons circled round the tower, suggested perhaps by the white pigeons over the pueblo near Taos that had for him, no doubt, a special meaning.

For Jeffers, who looked like an Aztec with his slate-grey heavy-lidded eyes that reminded one of the eyes of an old tortoise, lived in the Stone Age, mentally, in a sort of historical vacuum, and seemed to be naturally drawn to the prehistoric. He surrounded himself with mementos of this like the rock-pile resembling a cromlech that he built behind the house. In one of his poems he saw all history as a "rotted floor" sagging under man's foot, and for him humanity was simply "the mould to break away from," while, with no concern for the living world, his mind harked back to primordial times before men were obsessed with the illusions of philanthropy and progress. I remember the pleasure with which he pointed out to me that the stones in the walls of a big house near by were laid as they were in King Arthur's castle of Tintagel. But even that period was late for him; and, wholly removed as his mind was from the modern human world, he would have felt more

at home in the circle at Stonehenge. America did not exist
for him, its towns or people, its literary life, even the best
poets of his own time, and he and his wife on their travels
always went to the British Isles, or, rather, the small islands
surrounding Ireland and Scotland. They knew all of these, the
Arran isles, the Orkneys and the Shetlands, where they found
ruins and where they loved the fog, for they were "angry with
the sun" that overpowered them at home,—to quote another
phrase from Jeffers's poems. There they found old whalebones
too, bleached driftwood and the fossils that took them back
before the time of man, feeding the poet's fantasy of the prehistoric. No humanistic mind could sympathize with Jeffers's
nihilistic point of view, but, for all its bleakness, there was no
doubt of the real grandeur of feeling or of the elevation that
marked his poems.

As a matter of fact, antipathetic as the burden of his work
might be, this poet was destined to survive many changes of
fashion. Pointedly ignored in years to come in the dominant
critical circles, he possessed an integrity that weathered both
attacks and silence, an unmistakable indivisible unity and
wholeness of belief and mood that one finds in very few writers
in any generation. Yet how deadly to the human sense was
this belief in violence, which had been, as he said, "the sire
of all the world's values" and which led him to choose for an
emblem the hawk,—he named his "Hawk Tower" after it,—
that one saw constantly poised over Point Lobos. Accepting
Spengler's eternal recurrence of otherwise meaningless culture-
cycles, he defended primitive barbarity as the fate of mankind,
seeing it as quite good enough for the species he despised with
his own active neo-Calvinism. For he was the true child of
his father, the theological professor who had taught him to
read Greek when he was five, so that Æschylus and Sophocles

were also in his blood along with the predestinationism of
Jonathan Edwards. While his people were "all compelled, all
unhappy, all helpless," a phrase that one found in *Thurso's
Landing*, they were also, on the whole, "vipers" and justly
damned; and this drew Jeffers temperamentally to the leaders
of the Fascists for whom men were inferior animals to be
driven with whips. But I often wondered why he took the
Spanish civil war so hard that after it he seldom wrote again.
He was evidently confused by this, and it struck me that perhaps, admiring the hawk for so many years, he had never
previously watched the hawk really in action. For this defender
of the bird of prey was the most humane of men who had
never himself killed either bird or beast.

What was it in the Carmel atmosphere that so conduced to
violence?—for Jeffers's themes had usually a basis in fact there.
I almost witnessed a murder, for instance, that reappeared in a
poem of his. It was committed at night in a shack in a eucalyptus grove where a Mexican woman with a Cuban husband
stabbed her lover, a Filipino, and thrust the body into an oven
outside. The crime was clumsily gruesome enough and brutally
careless as well, for a passer-by saw the body in the early morning while the murderers were found, asleep and indifferent,
within; and although I had not seen the crime, I saw the
child who witnessed it, the daughter of the Mexican woman
who was present in the shack. With eyes that seemed permanently frightened, she kept the gate for a number of years at
the lodge of a wild park not far away. But nihilism too was
endemic in Carmel, like suicide and murder and along with
the Mediterranean beauty of the scene; and it seemed the right
place for Henry Miller to say that "it doesn't matter a damn
whether the world is going to the dogs or not." For Henry
Miller was to live in time on the ridge near Jaime de Angulo,

adding that it does not matter either "whether the world is right or wrong" or whether it is "good or bad." Who was there to say him nay in the world that Mary Austin called "culturally and spiritually the most impotent society that has yet got itself together in any quarter of the United States"?

The world that Mary Austin meant was the world of the *rentiers*, rich and poor, who had swarmed all over California, not the real California people whom one seldom saw and who had much of the character of the first pioneers. I remember a fruit-raising family whom I encountered at San José and who might have been one of the great clans of a primitive race, and everybody must have been struck by the independence of the San Franciscans, who had none of the provinciality of Middle Western people. They had chosen, for instance, a few decades before, to make a pet of William Keith, the painter of the Barbizon school that was dominant then, who had first painted the high Sierras in the manner of Bierstadt and Thomas Moran when this newly discovered grand scenery had astonished the public. But Keith had presently taken to heart Whistler's remark about Switzerland, saying it had produced no landscape painters because the scenery there was on too vast a scale, while he also pointed out that the great landscape painters had come from countries where the scenery was mild and tame. Of course that was not true, for the Chinese had painted high mountain scenes and the only question was how one saw and did them, but Whistler put an end to the American ten-acre pictures; and Keith went to France, saw the Barbizon painters and began to paint clumps of trees himself, hillsides and pastoral glades on the Berkeley campus. No old drawing-room about the bay would have been complete without a Keith, for the San Franciscans were sure they had a good painter, and it did not interest them that nobody else was aware of this, or ever, so far as I know, discovered it later.

One found this independence elsewhere only among the Bostonians, who cared nothing about others' opinions regarding their pets. As for Carmel, meanwhile, everybody painted there, the new abstractionists along with William M. Chase, who opened a school there before he died and whom I had often seen in New York, with his beard, his high hat and the long black ribbon of his *pince-nez*. Then one day Thomas Moran appeared, bringing back the seventies, the days when my father had known the old Far West. This lifelong friend of my parents-in-law, active as ever at eighty-three,—whom Ruskin had once guaranteed a living if he would return to England where he was born,—still talked about Whistler and the pot of paint he had flung in the face of the public as if he were a bad boy living round the corner. For Moran defended the "honest painting" that Ruskin had praised him for, representing the leaves on a tree as a naturalist sees them, and he spoke of the Grand Canyon as he had known it and painted it when the old geologist Agassiz was living. Honest painting meant for him painting this in such a way that one knew the sandstone from the limestone and the limestone from the slate.

Meanwhile, at Leland Stanford, where I had begun to teach, Hans Zinsser, the bacteriologist, was my next-door neighbour, a young man delightful to look upon and as picturesque on his half-bred horse, a mixture of Arab and broncho, as Jaime de Angulo. He was a real caballero, or I should say a Teutonic knight, mettlesome as a racehorse, both fiery and winning, and really a knight-errant too, for his friends were constantly in distress and he seemed to be always riding to somebody's rescue. I never knew anyone in whom the protective instinct was so strong, who, young as he seemed to the end, was so paternal, while, with his masculine physical charm, he had an opalescent mind and a nature that struck everyone with its variety and fullness. "Reacting," as he wrote, "like an Æolian harp to every wind that blew," he was in active revolt against specialization, for Goethe was always in his Rhineland German mind and his desire was also to live in the "whole." One might have thought it was a matter of chance that he happened to be a scientist instead of an all-round mind of the Renaissance type, for, playing his fiddle, he kept up with three or four other arts while he maintained a great laboratory with a dozen assistants. Turning out sonnets and other poems that were unpretentious but often good, along with his bacteriological books and papers, he upbraided me for the literary narrowness through which I failed to resemble some Frenchman or other. Meanwhile, how expansive and what a companion Hans Zinsser was on an all-day tramp over the hills at Palo Alto with a pouch that was full of gargantuan sandwiches and the bottle of wine that he brought along for lunch in the shade of a moulting eucalyptus.

Hans Zinsser's first wish had been to write before he discovered in biology too the sort of romantic appeal he had found in the arts, and eventually, in his *Rats, Lice and History*, he made the life of a disease more moving than most biographers are able to make men. He cared for his writing, he said to me, intrinsically more than for anything else, and, as he showed in the case of Hart Crane later, he entered the minds of writers by a deep inner line. He told me about his relations with Crane, whom he had met on shipboard when both were on their way to Mexico, and Crane, as I gathered from meeting him once, was a difficult man to approach or touch,—at least I found him thorny on a first encounter. But Hans, talking poetry with him, had bridged the gulf at once, and, seeing how mentally ill he was, gave him the fatherly counsel that Crane himself commemorated in one of his poems. He recorded his "humble fond remembrances of the great bacteriologist" who had besought him to follow the pattern of living in which he might have found a happy fulfilment, and this was emblematic of Hans's relation to writers, to whom he was drawn as one of them. I remember one of my friends, a writer, who, after meeting him casually, said, "Your Dr. Zinsser strikes me as a genius"; and so he was if, as Coleridge remarked, it is a mark of genius to carry into mature life the feelings of a boy. For he lived as a boy lives who is always setting out for adventure; and for him there was no waste of life to be exchanged for a crowded hour, for all his hours were crowded with productive excitement.

Hans Zinsser recorded his first glimpse of David Starr Jordan, the president of Stanford University, in a hotel bedroom, sitting on the bed and trying to pull the largest boot he had ever seen over a still larger refractory white-socked foot. More than once I later witnessed the same scene in hotel rooms when, as Dr. Jordan's secretary, I travelled in England,—after I had left Stanford and was teaching there,—and when he was lecturing at Oxford and Cambridge and dictated letters to me, labouring, while he talked, with his huge congress gaiters. In all respects Dr. Jordan was big, awkward and benign, and the real magnanimity that went with his elephantine bulk evoked a kind of reverence as it evoked affection. It was true that he had a bad name for dismissing professors with unpopular views, Thorstein Veblen, for instance, and Edward Alsworth Ross, for like various others in similar positions he was at the mercy of the donors of the time for whom, as they said at Stanford, professors were "cheap."

As a college president, Dr. Jordan was probably out of his

element, for he was by nature a dreamer and too easily coerced, and I remember the puzzled look with which he said of Veblen, "What can you do with such a man?" For Veblen had had a way of asking his girl students to spend week-ends with him in a cabin in the woods. I had scarcely heard of Veblen then, though I was to read him delightedly soon, marvelling when I met him a few years later that he had played such havoc with the other sex,—for no troll in the forests of Norway could have been more ill-favoured; but in Carmel I often saw Mrs. Veblen and hired her weary old horse for picnics with the children down the coast. Once, moreover, on a moonlight night, a buxom damsel called on me and said, "I was the girl who caused all the trouble," thinking perhaps that since I was at Stanford I might pull wires to get Veblen back, although I was the least important of young instructors. But, to return to Dr. Jordan and the lectures on peace that he delivered abroad when I travelled with him as his secretary, he was one of the many good minds of the time who could not believe how much of the brute, how much that was pre-reasonable survived in civilized man. Nor could Bernard Shaw or Lowes Dickinson believe this either. But I could not understand why later this naivety was so despised, as if it was intrinsically contemptible as well as stupid, considering Swedenborg's belief that the most celestial angels have scarcely any perception of the existence of evil.

That teaching was not my vocation I discovered at Stanford soon, for neither in fact nor by choice was I a scholar, and I was too full of my own thoughts to enter as a teacher should into the minds of students. I had seen great teachers like Gayley at Berkeley,—Professor Gayley of the "Classic Myths," —who, for the sake of their students, threw time to the winds, writing an occasional book as a secondary matter, while, for me, not to be writing a book was not to be alive at all and I wrote parts of three while I was at Stanford. One was the life of John Addington Symonds that Mitchell Kennerley soon brought out, another was *The World of H. G. Wells,* which I was to finish in Brittany a year or two later, and the third was a book on French pensée-writers, *The Malady of the Ideal,* a phrase of my favourite Amiel, who figured in it. Later I worked over a new translation of Amiel's *Journal* that my son made and that was more comprehensive than Mrs. Humphry Ward's, twice as long, in fact, and far more faithful; while the small book in question was beautifully published in London by the idealistic Tolstoyan A. C. Fifield. A tale hung thereby for me, for Fifield, the publisher of Samuel Butler whose lodgings had been near his office in Clifford's Inn, was one of those high-minded souls whom one found in the radical circles that abounded on all sides before the first world war. Fifield, a countryman and a true lover of humankind, was solely concerned as a publisher to produce fine books finely, while he lived, I was told, on the proceeds of his small farm, one of a host of imaginative men who were organizing Fairhopes and Waldens in almost every corner of America and Europe. They were bent on leading men out of the morass of materialism, hoping to save the world from poverty and war and trying to rescue the resources of life from greedy speculators and place them under control for the use of all.

I met at Stanford a few of these types not only among the professors but among the students, occasionally ex-miners and ex-cowboys, some of them at the socialist "local" that flourished in the town, an institution one found all over the West. These locals, as a rule, were led by immigrant "intellectuals,"—a word I heard then, I think, for the first time,—Germans, Jews and Russians with minds that were full of Karl Marx and Freud,

Krafft-Ebing, Nietzsche, Bakunin, Kropotkin. I did not by any means realize then the part which these socialist locals were playing all over the country in the pre-war decade when there was a feeling of revolt in the air that went with what Max Eastman called the "just-before-dawn of a new day." The revolt was largely against the Spoon Rivers, the Gopher Prairies and Tilbury Towns, the Zeniths and Winesburgs that were appearing, or were soon to appear, in the novels and poems of a new generation of writers, but also against the social conditions which the muckrakers had revealed along with the Lawrence strike of 1912. These socialist locals were centres of light for the young people who were growing up with an interest in ideas where ideas were few, in certain cases preparing them for descents on Greenwich Village and for resonant later careers as movers and shakers. There one felt more than anywhere else that this was a renascent time, opening, as one young writer said, a "golden twentieth century" that was going to be very different from the "dark" nineteenth.

A number of motives soon drew me into this circle, or the fringes of it, where Big Bill Haywood appeared on one occasion,—for the I. W. W. had come to the fore at this time,— with a son of the "Chicago anarchist" Schwartz and a picturesque Irishman who had belonged to the Hermetic Society in Dublin. Still a theosophist, Varian, as I think his name was, corresponded with AE and knew Charles Johnston in New York, and in general it seems to me, looking back, that all the liveliest minds I knew were involved in one way or another in radical movements. They attracted sensitive generous young people, the most imaginative, the most humane and those who most enjoyed using their minds, appealing not only to their sense of fair play but to their feeling for adventure and the joy of living. To me at that time the most winning of all types,

historically and actually, were the rebels and revolutionaries
from Mazzini and Kossuth,—and the "romantic exiles" of
Herzen's generation,—to the socialist saints of the present like
"Babuschka" and Tchaikowsky, whom I had met in Copey's
rooms when he visited Harvard in 1906, the hero of the Russian revolution of the previous year. Tchaikowsky, with his
patriarchal beard, was a vivid example for me of those "wan-
derers of the Russian land" of whom I had read, prophets of
a world that had not yet come into being and that might well
have no room for them. One of my friends was a district leader
of the Revolution of 1905 who had been arrested for reading
aloud to peasants the American Declaration of Independence,—
they had met in crowds, by torchlight, in the Russian woods,—
and who had been sent to Siberia and escaped to Stanford,
where he was teaching economics. Merely to affirm that there
were any "unalienable rights" was as much of a crime in
Russia as it later became to differ in belief or opinion from the
communist czar, and my friend Max Lippitt, who called
himself Larkin in those days, was a type of the old Social
Democrat. He stood for the intelligentsia who had joined the
ranks of the working class to become their strategists and their
tacticians,—"going to the people," as they said in Russia,—a
type that vanished in Europe and America in the age of reaction of the world war years only to re-emerge in Africa and
Asia. There was never a man more carelessly brilliant or more
generous towards others, cynical as he was in regard to himself, than this Oblomov that he had become, all but engulfed
in inertia, as if revolutionary activity had broken his main-
spring. Max Lippitt was always an emblem for me of the
mutual attraction that naturally exists between Russians and
Americans whose minds are permitted to meet.

In this circle I encountered another type that was new to

me, the Hindu revolutionist Har Dayal, who was teaching
Indian philosophy at Stanford but mainly in order to conceal
his real life-work as an organizer of Indian rebellion. He carried this mystification so far as to stage at my house a colloquy
with an Indian professor who had come from the Punjab and
who proclaimed his nationalism while Har Dayal boldly
affirmed that the international social revolution was his only
interest. The Punjabi was masquerading as a taxidermist in
San Francisco while Har Dayal, as I discovered later, was
conducting a school for terrorists in Berkeley, living like a
saint or a fakir in a small room near the railroad, with only a
single chair for an occasional guest. He slept on the bare
floor, for he had no bed, disdaining even a rug to cushion him,
as I found when he spent a night sometimes at my house,
living on milk and unbuttered bread with one old brown tweed
suit, detached as he was from the vanities of the world and
the flesh. "I am a revolutionist first and everything else afterwards," Har Dayal remarked in a letter to me, and he perfectly
exemplified the point of view that I presently found in the
*Revolutionist's Catechism* of Bakunin. In this the revolutionist
"has no interests, no affairs, no feelings, no attachments of his
own, no property, not even a name"; for he has broken with
the codes and conventions that govern other people and has
only "one thought, one passion: revolution." Whatever pro-
motes the triumph of this is moral, Bakunin says, whatever
hinders this triumph is immoral, and friendship, love, gratitude,
honour itself must all be sacrificed to "the cold passion for
the revolutionary cause." Everywhere the revolutionist must
insinuate himself, turning everything and everyone to his
purpose, a character one found in some degree in Turgenev's
Bazarov and in Dostoievsky's Verhovensky in *The Possessed*.
That, as I knew him, to the life, was Har Dayal.

For, whether as an Indian nationalist or an anarchist inter-
nationalist, he was a revolutionist at every moment with a
shrewd psychological knowledge of the value of the martyr's
role for attracting and retaining disciples to carry out his work.
I think he was entirely sincere in saying that he would gladly
have been burned alive in front of the post-office at Palo Alto
because this would have raised up a host of ardent apostles,
and he knew the utility of self-mortification in its effect on
others as well as in fanning his own flame. He had studied
the life of Ignatius Loyola, trying to discover the secret of
Loyola's influence over his adherents, and he had the *Spiritual
Exercises* and the history of the Jesuits in mind when he
planned his own "Fraternity of the Red Flag." Novices in this
were obliged for a year to submit to the guidance of one of the
members, accepting the "eight principles of radicalism" that
were listed in the programme and taking the vows of Poverty
and Homelessness, Humility and Purity and the final vows of
Service and Propaganda. The members were to renounce all
wealth, pledge themselves not to earn money or to become
parents at any time, while they were to repudiate every other
social tie and dedicate themselves to "simplicity and hardship."
The object of the order was to establish universal brotherhood
by abolishing private property, patriotism, religion and marriage.

How many disciples Har Dayal won for this cause I do not
know,—he said I would "never make a good propagandist of
the Emma Goldman type"; but I knew he had established
somewhere a "Bakunin Institute," which he called the first
"monastery of anarchism." He hoped to gather recruits for his
order in Italy and France, where he had lived, and open another monastery in Switzerland; and meanwhile India was
always in his mind, which seemed to combine in a curious way

the opposite types of the "yogi" and the "commissar." Nationalism was his ruling passion and had been since the time when
he was so notorious as a student at Oxford, planning with
other Indian students an order of Hindu ascetics to boycott
British institutions in their own country. He was convinced
that the British were undermining the Indian character and
that the Raj was quite as absurd and unjust as a growing body
of Englishmen agreed in feeling, while nothing could stop
the insurrections that were always breaking out there in spite
of all the espionage and all the seizures. They were the result
of what Wells called "the resentment of men held back from
life, with their mouths gagged and their hands bound behind
them," fighting an Empire that George Orwell described as
"simply a device for giving trade monopolies to the English."
As Orwell went on to say, you hated your own people when
you heard your Oriental friends called "greasy little babus,"
and you longed for a rising that would "drown their Empire in
blood," a feeling that Americans like myself seemed to have been
born with. But, while one understood it, Har Dayal's nationalist
propaganda,—which he soon ceased to conceal after I knew
him,—was rather a strain when one perceived that every breath
he drew and every hand-shake had an ulterior purpose. He
sent propaganda chocolates to the children of his friends, be-
stowing on them propaganda kisses, because he thought the
friends might serve his cause, while he regarded lectures as
"a kind of drum to get people together," the "real work" of
"interpenetration" beginning later. I was happy, none the less,
teaching in England the following year, to forward letters and
packages of "literature" for him, though, warning me against
expressing any sympathy for India there, he said, "Never tell
anyone anything about me." I must be "on my guard" against

this one or that one, for Har Dayal was sure that his own friends were shadowed. But he also wrote, "The British government sends spies all the time, which affords a revolutionist much amusement and relaxation in an otherwise intense and strenuous life."

At last Har Dayal was arrested in Berkeley and vanished for a time,—he had left California, forfeiting his bail,—reappearing at Lausanne and presently in Holland, whence he continued to write under various names. One of these was "Würsten," another was "F. Sulzer," a third, more frequent, was "Israel Aaronson." The war was imminent or breaking out, it was a most disheartening time, the intellectuals were cutting a sorry figure and there was no longer any true philosophical class in Europe, he said, to take large views and interpret human interests. Where were the Erasmuses and the Goethes who had once transcended "national cultures"? Even Kropotkin had gone the way of all the rest, the learned and the wise, submerged in partisan blindness. Har Dayal felt personally "cramped and choked in this atmosphere," and he said, "I think that the next half century will be marked by great reaction all round." Finally, when the war was well advanced and I had returned to New York, a letter came from him at Scheveningen, containing mysterious references to journeys to Constantinople, which I was not to mention in writing to *him*. But he wrote mainly to ask me if I would like to go to India as a "lecturer on religion and philosophy" or as a "correspondent," saying that ample financial arrangements would be made for me and for my family in the United States. If so, would I cable to Israel Aaronson in Scheveningen. He ended, "Very busy and sad. Please come without delay." Well knowing that only the Germans could be making these "arrangements," I replied that I was strongly in sympathy with the Western allies.

It was not till 1918 that I heard from Har Dayal again. This time he wrote under his own name from Sweden, where he was lecturing all over the country on India, earning his living so, at the same time studying philosophy and learning Greek. He had been stationed at Constantinople for three years during the war in charge of the German propaganda to detach India from England, and, thrown with influential Germans, he had been disillusioned with them and had come to detest their "absurd country." He had got to the bottom of their junkerdom, seeing them in Turkey, and found them far worse than the English had been, and he was convinced that their greedy ambition and their confidence in force were a menace alike to Europe and to Asia. There must be no Germans east of the Suez Canal! In short, he now believed in "Home Rule within the Empire," the dissolution of which could only result in a change of masters for all the weaker peoples; and this conversion of Har Dayal was presently greeted in the London *Times* as one of the important results of the first world war. It was a conversion that later led to his return to England where he founded a "Modern Culture Institute" and, writing books on Buddhism and rationalism, took up the study of science, zoology, botany and physics. Years later, in 1938, he returned to this country to lecture and came out to Connecticut to spend a day, sitting upright in his chair with a bunch of red roses in his hand for my wife and with the white teeth still gleaming in his dusky face. That week the British government had given him permission to go home again and he murmured, half incredulously, over and over, "The road to India is open." Ten days later, however, he was dead. At that moment he was only fifty-four years old, but his heart stopped in Philadelphia.

Thenceforward, whenever I met an Indian, I was always introduced as "The man who knew Har Dayal"; and his name occurred to me again ten years later, more or less, when I was presented to Jawaharlal Nehru. What could I possibly say that might interest this great man? Casting about for something, I heard myself uttering the phrase, "Do you remember Har Dayal?" and, with a wan smile, the great man said, "We *all* remember Har Dayal," though just how he was remembered I forebore to ask. The overtones of Nehru's reply seemed to speak volumes, and I reflected that some of these volumes I had read in California when Har Dayal and I were still in our twenties.

CHAPTER XI

# IN ENGLAND AGAIN

IT WAS Alfred Zimmern, at that time, or lately, a fellow of
New College, Oxford, who drew me back to England in
1913, arranging for me to teach in the Workers' Educational
Association of which he was one of the two government in-
spectors. The other was Dover Wilson, the Shakespeare
scholar, of whom I saw something during the summer when
the association met for a sort of congress or parley of lecturers
and students. Sir Alfred Zimmern, as he later became, had
fallen in with J. B. Yeats and joined his circle in New York at
Petitpas', where he had made friends with Eric Bell who gave
him a letter to me, and he had come to see me at Leland Stanford. He had published *The Greek Commonwealth* and had
just returned from a visit to Greece; and the green rolling
treeless hills about San Francisco bay had instantly struck him
as resembling the landscape he had known there. I could
never have guessed that forty years later, when he had come
back to this country to stay, we were to meet again as old
friends and neighbours. "It is the dedicated people," he wrote,
"who make the wheels of the world go around"; and he was
an illustration of his own remark.

Thus it happened that once again I lived in England for
eighteen months, this time with my wife and one small son, at
Richmond for six weeks, on the Isle of Wight during the

summer and for a year in Kent, in the suburb of Eltham. My teaching took up little time, for I had only one class,—at South Norwood, near Croydon; and if any students could have softened my stubborn egoism, they would have been these working men and women. Milkmen, shoemakers like old Mr. Baird, who read Greek and came from Lynn, where he had been a district political leader and had once talked with Disraeli fifty years before, carpenters who quoted Horace's odes, they put me on my mettle and made me feel that I was an uneducated man. For they assumed that one could not be educated unless one read Greek and Latin as easily as English. My course was nominally on the English essayists, and it struck me that the class included rudimentary specimens of all the types of mind that came up for discussion. There were embryo Lambs, Carlyles and Macaulays among them, with one actual survivor of pre-Darwinian times. This ancient boatmaker of ninety-six came not so much to listen as to drowse in a friendly atmosphere; and he rose to speak to me at the end of an evening when the theory of evolution had been the subject of debate. He asked me if I had read Dr. Adam Clarke's *Commentary on the Holy Scriptures*, the book which I was to hear of again as Bryan's great authority at the time of the Dayton trial in Tennessee. When I told the old boatmaker that I had not read it, he said, "Ah, but you should read it. For Dr. Clarke proves that the serpent could not have tempted Eve because the serpent has no vocal organs."

With what zest, on the other hand, a young mechanic told me that he was studying Aristotle because "You can't read Aristotle without being a good man," while a young potter named Emery who for six years had attended classes talked about his pottery like a mystical poet. These men cared for literature in and for itself without regard to economic questions, and, while I was expected to relate my subject to their background and experience, they studied for the sole purpose of enriching their minds. They did not seem to be concerned with altering their status in the world, they were interested in Bernard Berenson's "life-enhancement," with all the devoted enthusiasm that characterized many New Englanders in the days of Elihu Burritt, the "learned blacksmith." Har Dayal, who urged me to go and see Kropotkin,—something I failed to do, and much I regret it,—also told me that I must study the "class-psychology" of my worker students and tell him about the new types that I encountered. For "I am always interested," he said, "in variations from the normal. They always indicate new social forces." But one note of this class-psychology that would have disappointed him was a passive acceptance of the caste-system that prevailed in England, the "most class-ridden country under the sun" as George Orwell called it,—or so it struck one outsider who was equally impressed by the personal ardour of so many of these seekers of learning.

That a truly apostolic feeling lay behind this movement I saw at the congress in Oxford, where I spent a week in a huge seventeenth-century study with a cubicle for sleeping in and windows looking over lawns and gardens. New College was locked away from the streets and in these summer vacation days one heard no sound but an occasional tangle of chimes. Zimmern himself personified this apostolic feeling, up to his neck as he was in the cause of education and visiting other congresses in Bangor and Cambridge. Yet not only did he find time to be good to me but he was a master of the art of dealing with people. It was perhaps not easy to reconcile some of the older dons to this irruption of Scythians in their quiet college, swarming about the gardens and lawns at tea-time, or to reconcile the old colonel, for instance, also visiting the college, who was mildly curious about the working class. For him it called up associations of "these little messenger boys one sees running about one's club," regarding whose probable fate he asked various questions. The librarian of the House of Commons and two members of Parliament were there as well, and the conversation recalled to me Lowes Dickinson's *Modern Symposium,* so varied were the points of view, so articulate the speakers. One saw in the evening at dinner, moreover, the pleasure that Englishmen take in ceremony and social histrionics when the company left the table and adjourned to the end of the room where desserts had been set out with decanters of port. The old colonel whose remarks were so inept amused himself all evening long with a little game he played quite by himself, finding occupation of the most engrossing sort in the way he examined his watch and adjusted his glasses. Obviously, what he said meant less to him than the highly distinguished manner in which he said it. For the rest, the company were seated in a semicircle with the two end men about ten feet apart, and the decanters were placed in cups on a small wooden railway, sloping downward and running between these ends. The decanters were supposed to make their way unaided, but they invariably stuck in the middle of the course, whereupon the two men at the ends rose to help them on their way, as they had been doing supposedly for hundreds of years. It would have been far simpler to hand or shove the decanters about; but who would have dispensed with this charming little game? It seemed all the more charming to the players no doubt because Addison or Gibbon had perhaps played it a century or two before.

The talk I heard at Oxford, sometimes adding a word myself, tended to break up any fixed ideas one had, as it broke down in one's mind pet phrases and clichés. Alfred Zimmern took me to see Bishop Gore, who lived as a saint might live in a corner of his palace, the white-bearded patriarch who seemed as wise as J. B. Yeats and who grieved from the bottom of his heart over the trials of the workers. He was especially concerned, I remember, with the horrors of lead poisoning, a risk of the pottery workers who had come there with us. It pleased me to be told that the bishop was a socialist, but I saw in Oxford that one had to know just what one meant by this when so many members of the peerage were socialists also, when others who seemed equally advanced called themselves Tories and even Wells's "new Machiavelli" passed backward through the parties and ended as a conservative rejuvenescent. All this led me to think of the differences between America and England, as it led me to see the good in various conditions of English life that, in one way or another, were different from our own. Its cultural centralization was one of these conditions, the focussing of the general mind so that every English feeling and thought had its instantaneous effect on every other. With statesmen coming down from London to debate in the Union, students could be in close touch with the centre of affairs, and, because society was a coherent organism, new books could have an immediate effect upon it. I asked Walter Lippmann, whom I met in London, if he could imagine a book of his influencing legislation in the United States, if he could conceive of members of Congress reading *A Preface to Politics* and introducing measures that were based upon it. Yet Zimmern told me of a friend of his who had advocated certain acts in a book he had recently published and who saw these acts presently passed through the aid of a friend in the cabinet,—within two years his dreams had become laws. An inner circle ruled, for ill and for good, as I saw when Dr. William Temple became the Archbishop of

Canterbury, fifteen years after I had heard he was going to become so. A devoted schoolmaster with socialist leanings, he too had been at Oxford at this congress of workers in 1913, and I had been locked out with him one evening at New College where his future was already prearranged.

As I recall it, the word "discussion" was the keyword of the moment, in England as in literary circles also in New York; for the general feeling was that all problems could be solved and that the way to solve them was to talk them over. It was supposed that, on the whole, reason governed the general mind and that a fund of good will lay behind it, for few people realized how vast and dark were the irrational forces in men before the first world war so suddenly evoked them. Countless others like myself were full of H. G. Wells's faith that we were "in the dawn of the great age of mankind," and although, like Shaw, as he went on, Wells grew more cautious in his hopes, he felt that the human mind was indefinitely plastic. He did not cease to believe that "education" would win in the race with "catastrophe," and reasonably soon; for he shared William James's faith in the godlike power of the intelligent will to control heredity, instinct and its own planetary setting. He looked with amazement at the confusion and waste of the world, the chaotic indiscipline of men and their ill-adjusted effort, their planlessness and their spasmodic aims, convinced that it was in their power to build another sort of world and a human race that was orderly, happier and finer. He wanted men, he said, to be "intensely alive and awake," with "thought like an edge of steel and desire like a flame," and he believed that all this could be brought about, at least in large measure, by discussion. For this the "new Machiavelli" started the "Blue Weekly," a "centre of force," as he put it, to leaven the press, to get at the universities, to clarify the public mind, to organize research and to foster literature and art. In the novel this weekly was a huge success: it was read by all the people who formed public opinion, maintaining "a stream of suggestion against crude thinking."

Later, the teaching of H. G. Wells lent itself to the saturnine jeers of an age that had lost all belief in the will and in progress, an age for which these ideas were in some way trumpery and in no sense even "great illusions." The mere survival of mankind, of men and the state to which they belong, had become the primary concern of public thinking, and it had always been understood that under these conditions all questions of the "good life" must be deferred. This had been affirmed by Aristotle. For only when survival can be taken for granted can men spend time or thought on organizing what he regarded as the true life for mankind, so that what is impracticable comes to seem futile and, being futile, also inane, a fate that befalls in war-time much that is noble. Wells's vision was essentially noble,—it was totally misconceived when it was called merely a dream of material progress; for are the material and the spiritual unconnected? Countless young men and women felt that mankind was on the march, "entering on a world movement," a "vitalizing epoch," greater than "the Renaissance and the Reformation," as Arnold Bennett remarked in one of his essays, to be fulfilled by coöperation, by knowing how the other half lives, by propagating fresh ideas and by discussion. Alike on both sides of the ocean one constantly encountered groups like the Pentagon circle of Wells or Lowes Dickinson's "Seekers."

Everywhere in London one heard discussions of this question or that, of the "Mental Efficiency Bill," for one example, at a great meeting in Exeter Hall at which, as I remember it, every phase of opinion was represented. The question was the compulsory segregation of the so-called feeble-minded, and, with Cecil Chesterton in the chair, the speakers included a syndicalist, an Irish orator and an old-time democrat. There were two or three Liberal speakers, and a typical Fabian stood out, using all the Fabian phrases, with his back to the wall, for everyone else was against him, as I picture the scene, and especially the chairman's brother, who came lumbering in. With his whale's bulk, with his three chins and a high dull roaring squeal of scornful disagreement, G. K. Chesterton laughed at all the others. One felt as if the whole of England was audibly involved in this debate, something that one could scarcely feel in the vast National Liberal Club, though the air in this seemed fairly to quiver with discussion. It was there in the long hazy smoking-room, with its crowded little tables and its pillars and bays and groups of men sitting in armchairs eagerly talking,—with faces and accents that set the mind adrift across the British Empire from Rangoon to Jamaica,—there I met H. G. Wells himself, introduced by Lippmann, with whom I had been lunching elsewhere in the club. I was almost too excited to speak in the presence of this red-faced man with his shrill asthmatic voice, a half-cockney squeak, pouring forth words like a freshet in spring and looking as if he was on the point of a fatal stroke of apoplexy even as he stood there. I said I was writing a book about him, which evoked from him a benevolent glance, but not till thirty years later did I hear that he had read it. When I then met him in New York he recognized my name. "Yes," he said, "you wrote a book about me when you were young and unwise," and I was ready by that time to accept his verdict.

Although in those later years I saw Walter Lippmann rarely and we had followed paths that were far apart, I had several meetings with him in this pre-war London. Then, early **in**

1914, he wrote to me from New York. We had found that, in our thoughts of America, we had much in common, and he hoped to establish communication with others who were "working on the same puzzles and trying to see into the same fog." He knew a few young men, scattered through the country, who seemed to be arriving at a common understanding, and he told me about a plan for a new "weekly of ideas" that he and a group of his friends were about to start. He felt sure that *The New Republic* was something America needed badly, and it struck me at once as an actualization of Wells's "Blue Weekly" adapted to American conditions and the American mind. It was "to put a critical clinch," as Lippmann said, "into discussion and infuse American emotions with American thought," having "no party axe to grind" and, although "in direction socialistic," not so either in allegiance or in method or phrase. It was to be humanistic, but not in Irving Babbitt's sense; it was to relate the "noble dream" to the "actual limitations of existence"; and Lippmann hoped that in every part the paper would be "vivid with the humours and sights and sounds of American life . . . and yet," he added, "imaginative enough to point through them to a more finely disciplined and what Wells calls a more spacious order of living." (Phrases that bring back Wells himself and the way in which his view of life pervaded the thinking and writing of the young men of that moment.) Herbert Croly was to edit the paper, with Francis Hackett as literary editor and S. K. Ratcliffe as an English correspondent, and with Alfred Zimmern in the picture too and Graham Wallas, who had appeared in a somewhat equivocal light in one of Wells's novels. I had met Ratcliffe at this time, henceforth another lifelong friend who knew every state in America as if he had lived there and who has lived in twenty or thirty states, and Graham Wallas who examined me orally to see if I was qualified to teach in Alfred Zimmern's W.E.A. Later he discussed in his *Art of Thought* my book *The Ordeal of Mark Twain,* regarding which he kindly wrote to me, "I know of no book more fitted than this of yours to reveal to an original-minded young student the obscure and difficult process by which, for those who have courage and patience, the will-to-create becomes the art of creation." This pleased me as much as to hear from a friend who had talked with Freud in Vienna that he too had read and approved of my book.

I might have had later a closer connection with Lippmann and Hackett's *New Republic* if I had been more at ease in magazine writing, but it sometimes cost me a week of laborious effort to turn out a simple book-review. The thought of a dead-line paralyzed me; I entirely lacked the presence of mind that an article-writer must have, like an after-dinner speaker, and my later attempts to earn a living on *The Seven Arts* and *The Freeman* were accompanied by a chronic sense of disaster and defeat. What misery to spend five nights sitting up till three o'clock to find oneself represented in print by a wretched composition that seemed to be still half-baked and wholly inexpressive. But, to return to Walter Lippmann, his words bring back to me some of the excitement of that hour of the literary life, the feeling of intellectual adventure and philosophy in action that filled, before the first world war, so many minds. The mental aura of Randolph Bourne, whom I was to know so well, was altogether composed of this expectant feeling; and *The New Republic,* as one first heard of it, seemed already the symbol of a great coming epoch.

I had first met Lippmann at D. J. Rider's bookshop in a little court just off St. Martin's Lane, the den of a second-hand bookseller who had two small rooms, the shop at the front and an office at the rear. Dan Rider himself, the most lovable of men, with a stubby pipe and a cockney voice, always laughing or chuckling, sold next to nothing,—he seemed to prefer giving his books and pictures away; and he would sigh with annoyance when he heard the little bell announcing that some outsider had opened the door. For him these interruptions were like Gothic invasions, for he seemed to live for conversation, mysteriously active as he also was, with a hand in all manner of pies as an editor and publisher as well as a literary agent. He had bought up at sixpence a copy the whole stock of remainders of Samuel Butler's novel *The Way of All Flesh* before Bernard Shaw had made its author known, and he arranged for the English publication of Mitchell Kennerley's authors in New York. It was this that brought Lippmann and myself together in his office, where he sat surrounded with piles of books, with lithographs and etchings and with various writers and oddities whom he befriended. When I was in the country he wrote to me, "Lippmann is a great boy. He gets more into a day than the whole population of England. His time-table is worked through with the regularity of a railroad." Of course Walter Lippmann's mind was of a rather special type, but he was mature at twenty-three or so when most of us were floundering about in a prolonged adolescence.

It was at Dan Rider's that I also met Jo Davidson, who became from that time forward a part of my life, although twenty-five years were to pass when I scarcely saw him; and several survivors of the Yellow Book circle drifted in and out there with remnants of the circle of William Morris. Rider lived at Hammersmith, where Morris had had his Kelmscott Press, and the aesthetic and the socialistic met in his shop on equal terms as they met in Morris's mind or in the mind of Shaw. Rider had been an active worker in the socialist organizations at which Shaw himself had often spoken, debating on a famous occasion with H. M. Hyndman, the grand old man of English socialism. I spent an afternoon with Hyndman in the Hampstead garden of Rider's friend, the American "millionaire socialist" Gaylord Wilshire, who had made in Los Angeles a fortune in billboard advertising and edited *Wilshire's Magazine*. It was he who had given in New York the notorious party for Maxim Gorky to which Mark Twain refused to go, and, impelled to undo the conditions that had made his fortune, he was directing *The Syndicalist* in England. Hyndman, in appearance Rodin's double with his massive shoulders and chestnut beard, flat-crowned, stocky in build, in all ways robust, still dreamed of waking up some morning to find himself prime minister of the sort of reorganized England for which Morris had longed. The most winning of men, deferential, benign,—calm, rational and keen-witted too,—he burst into furious flood like Old Faithful, the geyser, if someone uttered a remark that struck him as inane.

Another frequenter of Dan Rider's shop was Holbrook Jackson, the historian of the nineties when yellow was the colour of the day, the outrageously modern, and Robert Ross appeared there too, Oscar Wilde's champion and dedicated friend, with a small group that met at the Café Royal. But whom did one not see on the plush-covered sofas or reflected in the mirrors of this long since transfigured rendezvous near Piccadilly Circus, from Lord Alfred Douglas with his rakish air and the old satyr Crosland to the sculptor Jacob Epstein and his wife. These two, sitting side by side, ample in girth, swarthy in hue, looked like a pair of Bedouins just out of their tent. For the rest, who could forget, at Dan's, the latter-day Costigan,—Miss Emily Fotheringay's father in Thackeray's novel,—who also fell downstairs, thanks to a loose carpet, he said, but in all probability propelled by a foot that he had libelled. A well-connected Dubliner, the aging nephew of an earl, Captain Stephens made a furtive living as a gossip-monger writing for a scandal-sheet, while he served also as a spy for the French embassy in London keeping an eye and ear cocked for the Germans there. He was always pulling out of his pocket soiled scraps of paper with shady tales about his cousins and their friends picked up from servants, and with his air of dilapidated elegance he lived on the razor-edge of the British law that punishes defamatory statements. So did Frank Harris who published him in *Modern Society*, as I think it was called, and presently had to leave England to escape from this law, pulling down Dan Rider, financially, with him. For Dan had printed his *Oscar Wilde*, or arranged to have it printed, on the understanding that they were to divide the subscriptions, and all the subscriptions were sent to Frank Harris in France, leaving Dan to pay the bills unaided. The printers turned to him and, unable to pay them, Dan Rider, ruined, was obliged to close the shop.

There I had often seen Frank Harris, who looked like a race-track tout or an old-time stage villain with his handlebar moustaches,—he might have been a Mississippi steamboat gambler,—the legendary Harris who had once been a cowboy and had written stories of the Western plains after he began his career as an editor in England. There too I had seen Strindberg's wife, the second or perhaps the third, the "Scandinavian Duse" who was running a night-club and whose constant motto "Je suis au bout des forces" came into play that very afternoon. For suddenly, at Rider's door, appeared another woman, a milliner with an unpaid bill who had tracked her through the streets and who had cornered her at last, saying, "I've got you this time," while malicious animal magnetism shook the room. There, on how many other occasions, currents of another kind spread from Jo Davidson's presence, all animal glow, for Jo

Davidson had a "special gift for loving" like Willa Cather's old Nebraska farmer's. He was one of those irresistible people, stimulating as the winds of spring, who, as J. B. Yeats said, "go out into the streets, along the roads and gather in their friends by armfuls." But, loving many, he loved a few with a tireless life-long affection; and this man who was sometimes accused of head-hunting was loyal above all to friends who were humble and obscure.

With these first days of my friendship with Jo I associate Georg Brandes, the great Danish critic who had appeared in London and whom I had heard at Exeter Hall lecturing on Nietzsche, the "aristocratic radical," his famous correspondent. I had read Brandes with rapture at Stanford, beginning with *Main Currents*,—in which in a vast panorama one saw all Europe evolving from one epoch into another,—carried away by the picturesqueness of this literary portrait-painter whose supple mind was almost as broad as Goethe's. He had related in his autobiography how Kierkegaard's religious thought had first aroused him when he was a student in Denmark and how he had turned against Kierkegaard because he could not believe that that which was contrary to all reason was the highest truth. It seemed to him, moreover, that his own defects were weaknesses which ought to be combatted and might be cured, not irremediable sins requiring forgiveness; and, meanwhile, feeling in himself, as he said, "the strength of a whole generation," he had ranged from country to country, studying their cultures. He had found in Taine especially a master and deliverer who had freed him from the pedantry of his Dano-German training; and, able to embrace minds as various as Hans Christian Andersen and John Stuart Mill, he had become the model of a good European. I was all the more drawn to him because he loved painters and painting too and because of his watchword, "As flexible as possible when it is a question of understanding, as inflexible as possible when it is a question of speaking."

I had told Jo Davidson about this first lecture at Exeter Hall, at which Bernard Shaw had introduced Georg Brandes, taking command of the audience and, with his usual fiery wit, running away with the occasion, speaking for an hour. The little old goat-bearded critic might well have been vexed by this, but he seemed to be as smilingly pleased as the Cheshire cat whose whiskers, like his, stuck out at random; and Jo, who was determined to make a bust of Brandes, went with me to the second lecture at Caxton Hall. The subject was Shakespeare and the lecture was elementary, for Brandes took no pains to say anything new; but at the end Henry James climbed up to the platform from the front row and the chairman, Edmund Gosse, introduced him to the speaker. Just then I became aware that Jo had vanished. Making his way to the platform, he persuaded Brandes to stop for a moment, on the following morning, at his studio, near Brandes's hotel; and, when Brandes arrived, Jo met him with modelling clay in his hand and quickly sketched his head as he was looking at the sculpture. At the end of five minutes, when Brandes was leaving, Jo showed him the little sketch which pleased the great man so much that he gave him a sitting. The head that followed was one of Jo Davidson's best.

Looking back later, it seemed to me that Brandes and Davidson had something in common as creators of what came to be called the planetary mind, for Brandes, with his art of cross-fertilization, interpreted one to another the notes of at least half a dozen nations. Meeting some of the greatest men of England, France and Germany, he had been struck by their ignorance of the merits of their compeers even in countries

that were closely akin to their own; and he had been equally
at home himself not only in France, Germany, Italy and England but in Denmark, Norway, Sweden, Poland and Russia.
Jo Davidson had a similar protean gift for penetrating minds of
all races and types, so that, as a "plastic historian," he became
in the end a United Nations in himself, representing the generation in which appeared the "global" sense, the sense that
Whitman, his favourite poet, called "orbic." If Davidson's busts
were assembled from the four corners of the earth one would
find half of modern history in them, and no other record of
the sort can duplicate this record of a world that is both one
and pluralistic. Jo Davidson loved its diversity as well as its
oneness.

I had never met, and was never to meet, so naturally happy
a temperament, with malice toward none,—quite literally,—
with charity for all, so buoyant and so free as Jo's, a man who
had taken to the world as he said he took to London, "like a
duck to water." For him it was always a World's Fair, like the
old fair at St. Louis at which, as a boy, he drew portraits and
did sculpture in sand; and, with none of the prejudices or fears
that govern the lives of most people, he passed through life
like a ship under full sail. His was the kind of lordly freedom,
rare in our unhappy time, that characterized so many artists in
more genial ages, and he was an illustration of Franz Kafka's
saying, "I like the Americans because they are healthy and
optimistic." Born before people were conditioned to see mainly
the stupidities and the sins in men, he saw the heroic in high
life as he saw it in low life, drawn as he was especially to those
who have made history in our time, whether they were saints
or poets, soldiers or statesmen. Unmindful, even unaware of
the conventional overtones that reputations have for other people, he approached his subjects with the innocence of an artist

or a child, finding the great irresistible, as he also found door-
men and garage mechanics, helplessly charmed by the human
nature in them. In a way he became the person while doing
the portrait, and his forms more real than living men sprang
from an interest in character that was lost in a later comparatively dehumanized time.

Jo Davidson had all the traits that came to be regarded with
a certain hostility and suspicion when they appeared in artists,
exuberance, fertility, productivity and the inborn vitality
that in certain quarters was even considered vulgar. It was not
till many years after the war that I fell in once more with him
after seeing so much of him for a few months in London, the
"Gomorrah-on-Thames" of Ezra Pound, who had settled there
in 1909 and whom I met for a moment with his friend John
Cournos. I found some of my own impressions in Pound's later
published letters, in his remark, for instance, at about that moment, "You can no more interest London in the state of the
American mind than you could interest Boston in the culture
of Dawson or Butte, Montana." That seemed to me natural
enough in 1914. For we Americans at that time had few literary claims to press and were better employed in quietly learning from others, true as it was that within a few years two
Americans, Eliot and Pound, established themselves in a way
as teachers of the English. I remembered the story about Sainte-
Beuve when he was reproached in an interview for knowing
and saying so little of the interviewer's country,—one of the
Scandinavian countries, I think it was,—"Well, do something.
Then we'll talk about you," which struck me as good for Americans to apply to themselves. For one could not have reproached
the English for lacking curiosity,—there too they were our su-
periors on the literary plane; and they have continued to be so
if by curiosity one means an eager interest in the affairs of

culture. So at least one would suppose comparing the primi-
tivism of many of our writers with the traces of an active culture one finds, for example, in Aldous Huxley's novels and the
poems of Auden,—the "conversational parsley" that Hemingway dismisses and that seldom garnishes the American literary
dish. Dean Inge symbolized for me the kind of curiosity one
found so general in England and so rare at home, for as often
as not, wherever I went in London, there with his apron and
gaiters was the gloomy dean. Three times at public lectures he
sat in the chair in front of me,—one was a lecture on Tibet by
Sir Francis Younghusband,—and whenever I entered a picture-
show there he was wandering about, bent on seeing whatever
there was to be seen. It struck me that Dean Inge must be the
most curious man in the world, for I reflected that if I encountered him eight or nine times in three months I must have
missed him on scores of other occasions. The sight of this
ubiquitous man embarrassed me: it made me feel like a detec-
tive shadowing him.

One friend I met in London, or, rather, one who became my
friend, was the poet from Little Rock, John Gould Fletcher,
whose first remark, as he sat down at the Soho restaurant table,
was that he had published in one month five books of poems.
It was true, moreover, small as these were, each with a different imprint, and he had paid to have them published. I remembered at once that I had seen his queer white skull-like face
peering out through the crimson curtains of the Harvard
Union, a face to which in college I had never attached a name,
and here it was, a poet's face, in London. Fletcher was an old
man's son, and he seemed to have been born old himself, stiff-
jointed, with big angular bones and stooping shoulders; and,
as a stranger from the South, he had been, as he wrote, the
"most forlorn and hopeless individual" at Harvard. He had felt

as lonely and depressed as Maxim Gorky appeared to be when
Fletcher saw him, with his Russian boots, there, looking at Major Higginson's portrait by Sargent, a picture that hung in the
Union where Fletcher himself had spent most of his time and
where, in the library, at nineteen, he had begun to write
verses. Following the lead of Arthur Symons, he had found in
the Union the French Symbolist poets whom later he had introduced to Ezra Pound, for, with means of his own, he had left
Harvard and gone abroad to study, falling in with this other
American poet in London. Pound borrowed armfuls of his
books and presently published the essays that popularized
these French poets in literary circles as part of his campaign to
dislodge the English mind, violently, from its Georgian and
academic rut. This was all again part of the more general
movement of the "new poetry," so called, that put to rout the
established poetic forms. Amy Lowell, arriving in London, was
astonished to find two young Americans there who seemed to
care more for the new poetry than anyone at home.

When I met Fletcher he had passed already out of his Walt
Whitman phase, although he had actually discovered Whitman in London, as a socialist surveying the crowds in Cheap-
side and the Strand, and he was absorbed in imagism, in Rim-
baud's theory of the *alchimie du verbe* and the recently much
talked of Chinese and Japanese forms. Excited by the Russian
ballet, he wrote tributes to Nijinsky, glorifications of colour,
pæans to dancing. It was much later that I knew him well
when he had returned to America and found that essentially
he was a Southern poet, charmed by the old romantic regions
of the South and the Southwest, the heroic saga-lands, as he
called them, of the American past. He went back to the country he had visited earlier with our classmate Alfred Kidder on
an archæological expedition to the New Mexico desert, the

world of the Apaches, the Navajos, the Penitentes and the legendary Seven Cities of Cibola; and he became deeply involved
in the regionalist movement of the South against the spiritual
inroads of the industrial system. But this was just before the
cause of Southern regionalism was abandoned by the rising
generation of Southern poets. After his twenty years abroad,
Fletcher was perhaps too late to have shared fully in the renaissance of American writers, as he was too late to share in the
development of the South,—while he had forfeited meanwhile
his connections in England,—so that with all his stubborn hon-
esty and his great gifts as a poet and critic, he was somehow
lost in the chaos and rush of the time. Amy Lowell too had
been all but forgotten when Fletcher came to his unhappy end,
eclipsed by new writers who are destined in turn for the same
sort of oblivion unless they can endow with a memory their
negligent country. Yet even the English sometimes forget their
good writers. Who speaks any longer of J. D. Beresford, the
author of the trilogy of Jacob Stahl which everyone read with
zest in the first world war years, a lame frail grave man with a
lined ascetic face whom I met in the company of the poet
Walter de la Mare?

How many strange fish, for the rest, one found inhabiting
the depths of the ocean of London, living in clefts of the rocks,
seldom visiting the surface. One was the old essayist Francis
Grierson about whom I had heard so much,—Edwin Björkman
had written a paper on him. He was said to live over a grocer's
shop somewhere in Twickenham, although no one saw him
there or knew his address; but he would emerge in response to
a letter at the Bridge House in Richmond, where he received
admirers and correspondents. These meetings were promptly
written up in the local newspaper, the *Twickenham Times*, the
readers of which were led to suppose that Grierson was a liter-

ary potentate to whom all the great of the earth made pilgrimages. For, humble as the guest might be, he was described as a world-famous professor or some other sort of lion or cock of the walk, the secret of it being that Grierson had a Sancho Panza who not only served as a press-agent but supported him as well. He worked for a small wage, I think, as a tailor's assistant. When Grierson dined with my wife and me and I took him to the door to say good-night, there was a strange man sitting on the steps,—it was Waldemar Tonner, the Polish-American whom Grierson announced as his secretary and who had been waiting there all the evening through. For thirty years already Tonner had spent his time and strength maintaining the romance of Grierson's greatness, a practical soul who worshipped his master and struggled with the world on his behalf, for the high-minded Grierson was as helpless as the hero of Cervantes.

Scotsman that he was by birth, Grierson had grown up in the American West, to which he had been brought when he was six months old, in a log-cabin in the Sangamon country, surrounded by the strange frontier types whom he described in his book *The Valley of Shadows*. He had heard the last Lincoln-Douglas debate and served General Frémont as a page before he had made his way, at nineteen, to Paris where he had become the musical prodigy of whom Mallarmé remarked that he was "the first real poet of the piano." He had lived with the elder Dumas there, playing in the salons that he described in his *Parisian Portraits*, presently starting a second career with a little book written in French of which Maeterlinck said that it influenced him more than any other. Within the last few years he had collected from Orage's weekly the essays that appeared in the small green volumes *The Celtic Temperament* and *Modern Mysticism*, along with the beautiful memoirs of his

Mississippi boyhood, while he gave occasional piano recitals at which he professed to think that ancient Lydian airs flowed through his fingers. There was a touch of the charlatan in him, but there was a curious innocence too in this tall man with his worn old tweeds, his drooping moustache, pink cheeks and crimson necktie. The moustache was evidently dyed and he rouged his cheeks, and that he wore a wig was also apparent from the white hairs that straggled out over his ears; and later when he was caught by the rain and obliged to stay in my house I was sorry that I could not help him in the matter of cosmetics. How without rouge would he be able to appear in the morning, not to speak of wax for his moustache? But only his wig was askew when he came down blithely. In appearance he was evidently living up to an early portrait of himself painted at the court of the czar when he had played there, a portrait that was reproduced in one of his books and showed him as a romantic of the time of Dumas. Still dwelling, with his courtier's air, in this old royalist Europe, he was equally full of the frontier West and Lincoln,—of whom he drew wonderful portraits in his writing and his talk,—and he was to die in America at last, "calm and serene" as he had lived, or so said Waldemar Tonner a few years later. He had settled in Los Angeles, where all the retired prophets go, possessed by dreams of the "invincible alliance" of England and America, between which for so long his own mind had wandered.

CHAPTER XII

# TURNING HOMEWARD

WHEN THE first world war began in August, 1914, I was
in Brittany for the summer at St. Jean du Doigt, living
in a douanier's house facing the inn and the square, finishing
a book I had begun on the shore of the Pacific. Every foreigner
knew at once that only two courses were open to him, either to
get out of the way or to share in the struggle, but, turning
homeward soon myself, I never supposed it would be thirty-five
years, or virtually that, before I again saw Europe. For I do not
count one dark season that I was to spend there. I had always
felt that one lived abroad far more intensely than one lived at
home, that years there were better than cycles in our own
Cathay,—our "Anglo-Saxon China," as Melville had called it;
and this was a common feeling not only with Americans but
with countless South Americans, Africans, Australians, Asi-
atics. For in cultural matters Europe was the sun from which
all the continents drew light and heat; and all from that moment were thrown back on themselves. Things fell apart: the
centre could not hold.

I had known in England a Cingalese, a young art-critic of
ample means, who returned to Ceylon as I was returning to
New York and who, in letters that he wrote to me,—"whistles
from the other side of the wood,"—described his feeling of
exile and desolation in Colombo. He quoted Henry James's

remark, "For those who have been happy in Europe, even Cambridge the brilliant is not an easy place to live in," adding,
"Ceylon is not even brilliant" and "the East is not meant for
anyone to live in but merely to look at and admire from a safe
distance. . . . When you have lived in the West you have irre-
mediably taken the poison of thought into your system and the
East is ever after impossible," although he was planning himself to translate *Gil Blas* and Plato into Cingalese and to paint
because a painter must stand up at his work. "If one sits down
in Ceylon one goes to sleep." In how many other far-away
lands one might have heard similar cries, evoked from young
aspirants who had feasted at the table of Europe and feared
that they were destined, at home, to starve, just as one heard
them in Boston, in New York, in every corner of our own
world, culturally colonial still for all the Walt Whitmans. But
because the European centre could no longer hold,—whether
or not Europe was "dead and stinking," as D. H. Lawrence
said, shaking his beard,—a new Ceylon was eventually to rise
and a new India and China, compelled to make the most of
their own resources. A new America too was to rise, in the literary sense, centered no longer on the East but mainly on the
West, and within a short time the American writer found all
he required in order to exist, in atmosphere and material alike,
within his own country. For these were the years in which
America came of age.

Of this I had had premonitions, especially in England, where
I had written a book that summed them up in a rented house
in the suburb of Eltham that belonged to two old ladies who
were descendants of the voyager Captain Cook. In the little
room in which I worked stood Captain Cook's sea-chest, an
old trunk bound in battered red morocco, and I sometimes used
this as a seat while writing *America's Coming-of-Age* with a

feeling that I too was engaged in adventurous voyages. It happened not only then but earlier and later that my mind turned back to America when I was abroad; for, just as I had written my first book *The Wine of the Puritans* in Europe, so I was to plan *The Writer in America* there. I had gone to Ireland at sixty-five hoping to write a book about it, with notes that I had collected and with questions to ask, feeling that here was my chance to realize a wish of many years by hatching at least one book of travels. But after three weeks I seemed to know less about Ireland than I knew at the start while I was full of thoughts about my own country,—with which I seemed to be locked up mentally for life,—and this was the way it had been in England so many years before when the first world war was on the point of breaking out. To me it seemed clear in 1913 that we were to have a renaissance, that extraordinary forces at home were at work in the silence and that what we required was a critical movement to release these forces, to harrow the ground for the "seed beneath the snow." For there was no doubt about the snow, the cold complacency, the self-satisfaction that accompanied the provincial isolation of the American mind, paralyzing the creative powers which were depressed already by the "cultural humility" that Randolph Bourne deplored. At Petitpas', W. G. Blaikie Murdoch had spoken of the "servile deference" which the European critic met in the United States, saying, "The American people are largely convinced that his verdict is perforce of greater moment than theirs." One had somehow to rectify this feeling of inferiority and the false sense of superiority that coexisted with it, uniting the notes of censure and hope and obliging young writers to question their world while they were finding a world in their natural setting.

These premonitions were sound enough, as the new poetry

presently showed, with Robert Frost, Ezra Pound and Amy
Lowell, with the flowering of the novel in the twenties and the
plays of O'Neill, not to mention American architecture and
American painting. *The New Republic* had come in with the
tide at a moment when, in Europe, the most symptomatic book
was *The Decline of the West*, which scarcely included the
American West that Whitman had called the predestined home
of this country's distinctive realities and ideas. Europe was
Spengler's declining land, and to many Americans, turning
homeward, the shade of Virgil seemed to say what it said to the
young man in *The Cabala* of Thornton Wilder, "Seek out
some city that is young. The secret is to make a city, not to
rest in it." They were prepared to agree at last with Santayana's
observation, "All nationalities are better at home. . . . When
you transplant the species it suffers constraint and becomes
sickly or intrusive or both at once," partly because they had
seen for themselves how true this was or had been in the case
of Americans they knew or of whom they had heard. As time
went on they felt less and less the tension that had been so
marked between their American "duties" and their European
"culture," especially on the Eastern coast and, above all, in the
Harvard men who were "neither American nor European," as
Henry Adams put it. These men had felt overwhelmingly the
beauty of the old world and the charm of life and manners that
went with it, and, born, like myself, with Baedeker as it were
in the cradle, their minds had been Europeanized almost at
the outset. But they were inclined now to see the importance
of solving this tension by cleaving finally either to America or
Europe, attaching themselves to some country that could serve
them as a homeland, for was not the poet Yeats right when he
said, "One can only reach out to the universe with a gloved
hand,—that glove is one's nation"? A few continued to main-

tain the tension, whether they suffered in consequence or not, as it seemed to me that John Gould Fletcher suffered, for he was too old at forty-five, after so many years in England, to remake his life successfully on American terms. The case was less clear with Conrad Aiken and his lifelong liaison with "Ariel's island," for the "instability, restlessness and dissatisfaction" he ascribed to himself may perhaps have resulted in much that was good in his work. But when Eliot embraced, as a nation, England, forswearing the country of his birth, with the social and political philosophy that characterized it, he illustrated the truth of Yeats's remark. I was myself a convert in the other direction, and I was to be accused in time of the convert's zeal.

But I foresaw none of this when I returned in 1914 at a time of arctic loneliness for American writers when no one felt the common purpose that later writers, looking back, attributed to these years of the tuning of the fiddles. It is always the other time that is the time of "purpose." I only felt, as I remember, that my own curtain was about to rise, that my real life as a writer was about to begin, while I was scarcely aware how naturally most of the writers who were soon to appear took and retained the Americanism they had been born with. Oak Park, Illinois, gave Hemingway, as it gave Frank Lloyd Wright, something that New Jersey, New York and Harvard had failed to give many of my friends along with me, the instinctive feeling about their country that enabled them to live anywhere without even a momentary second thought about it. This was the frame of mind which the world-war epoch established on all sides within a decade or two, while, for good and ill,—for much of both,—the word "European" virtually ceased to ring bells in the American breast. The rise of Mussolini, of Hitler, of Stalin alienated many who had loved the old liberal

Europe and felt at home there, and the decline of romantic
feeling and the feeling for classical culture destroyed in others
the tie between the new world and the old. On the other hand,
the rapid growth of American biography and history created a
general interest in the American scene, by so much no doubt
reducing the interest in Europe. Did not the Europeans, moreover, wish Americans to be "American," and had they not
always wished this in literary matters since Goethe regretted
that Washington Irving wrote on European themes instead of
the themes that made Cooper so excitingly new? No American
poet had ever been the nine days' wonder in England that
Vachel Lindsay was in 1920 when he was described as the
only American who "mattered" in poetry because he was "totally and exclusively" transatlantic. The great reproach had
always been that our writers were "not American enough," that
America, as Shaw said, returned to Europe its exports at second
hand instead of "at last producing an art of its own."

I returned with my wife for a winter to our native Wall
Street suburb,—our Yasnaya Polyana in New Jersey,—where
we had lived at the Seminary, off and on, in earlier days, under the sign of Miss Kenyon, in the aura of the Brownings.
My mother and my brother were still living in the town, and
Max Perkins also lived there still, while J. B. Yeats often came
out from New York for portrait-painting visits and to lecture in
the houses of our friends. Thrown back upon myself there, I
thought of my own childhood and the state of introversion
into which I had passed, silently withdrawing myself, at about
fourteen, a state that was unconsciously designed perhaps to
guard me against influences with which I already felt at war.
I had never been at home there or anywhere but in my own
mind where I lived in a fantasy-world remote from "business,"
—the business that was never talked about but that somehow

pervaded this native scene where I wondered if even my father had ever been at home. It struck me that my father's friends had been bankers and stock-brokers by default, for I saw them in retirement apparently happier as amateur photographers and what not than they had seemed in their feverish gambling years. One was an almost first-rate classical scholar, another carved walnut chests that were beautifully wrought. Had my father's practical failure in life over-affected my own mind, as his European associations had affected it also, so that perhaps his inability to adjust himself to existence at home had started my own European-American conflict? Undoubtedly in certain ways I identified myself with him, while I belonged to a generation that had turned away from the business life, like Windy McPherson's son in Sherwood Anderson's novel. I realized, for the rest, in my native town the truth of the Chinese proverb, "A man is more the child of the age he lives in than he is of his own father and mother."

In any case, I had broken away effectively from this childhood world, following a line that had its inner logic, erratic as it seemed to others,—or so I felt,—the sort of line my brother could not establish for himself, so that indecision and doubt were to rule his existence. Unwillingly a lawyer, by nature a scholar,—more than I was or wished to be,—with a passion for historical studies and for languages and travel, he should have been, it seemed to me, a professor of history at Princeton, where he had been the poet of his day. The university press there published his verses with the Tahitian title *Mauna Roa*, for Tahiti, the "Land of Let-It-Alone," was one of the many ports of call that he visited in his restless haunted life. His panacea, as he wrote once, was "packing up and leaving in the morning" for Normandy, Newfoundland, the West Indies, Italy or Oxford, or "going back to Princeton" where he might

revive perhaps his "old buried life of the poet and dreamer."
He had run down to Georgia, when General Longstreet was
still living on his farm, to interrogate this ancient about
Chickamauga, and he camped out in the Rockies where so
many lost their minds, he said, from the "mountain gloom of
Ruskin's *Modern Painters*." Buying a horse and an outfit, he
visited deserted mines that recalled to him our father's mining
ventures, and he was struck by the "sad far-away look" in the
eyes of our father's old friend in Wyoming,—in the eyes of all
the veteran ranchmen there. Translating Greek, German and
Anglo-Saxon poems, he wrote a novel that was more or less
modelled on Pater, and he had known hours of fulfilment as
an ambulancier in France and as head of a Negro industrial
school in Alabama. But more and more he came to resemble
those Hamlets of the French Symbolist poets who turn away
from their loves, preferring their dreams; and at last, when his
life was an afternoon without any mornings, he was prepared
to "embrace the doom assigned."

How had I escaped, if escape I did and only partially at best,
from so much of the sadness and wreckage that surround a
life? The earliest dream I remember was a dream of flight, and
as this recurred in my childhood constantly, and even in my
later years, I invested it with a complex meaning as time went
on. I must have been very small when I experienced this
dream first, one evening, as it comes back to me, after my
mother, still young and gay, leaving for a dinner-party, had
kissed me good-night. I presently fancied I was on the lawn
when a Hindu, suddenly appearing, in a coat of many colours,
chased me with a knife,—a glittering knife that he held in his
outstretched hand,—and, just as he approached me, running, I
soared into the air and floated away, free, aloft and safe. On
other occasions the fiend was not an Oriental, he was merely

a nondescript minatory figure that pursued me, and I was not even anxious when I saw him approaching, for I knew I possessed the power to float away. The Freudian idea of this dream I revised with my own. It is an old notion that writing provides for the writer a vicarious existence in which he can take refuge from the menace of life, its miseries and mishaps and often insoluble problems, together with his own ineptitudes, his disabilities as a man, his weaknesses, fatuities, inadequacies, gaucheries and blunders. It was always to be so with me, my sanctuary, my retreat in a world in which, without it, I would have foundered, and I was seldom to lose my trust in the power that quite obviously saved me, on two or three critical occasions, from the Hindu with the knife.

What struck me, finally, in my native town, which I had left after my college years and was to leave for good at the end of one winter,—when my wife and I settled in Connecticut, near many of our friends,—was the almost pure "Anglo-Saxonism" of the world I had grown up in as contrasted with the world I had come to know. The first title of *America's Coming-of-Age* had been *A Fable for Yankees,* for out of sheer habit I had felt that our countrypeople were "old American," in the anthropologists' phrase,—and my publisher pointed out to me what I knew perfectly well, that Americans were no longer Yankees, even of the South. They were as multi-racial as the crew of the "Pequod" in *Moby-Dick,* and only "society," in the narrower sense, maintained the old American base, whether in my birthplace or in the country at large. It is true, in that ancestral world there was something reassuring, a cosy homogeneity that one lost with regret, as there was a charm in the literary world that accompanied the social world and that I sometimes saw during these years. Occasionally on Sunday afternoons I went to the Century Club in New York where one of my un-

cles by marriage was the oldest living member and where, as
we mounted the stairs and entered the great gloomy upper
rooms, Rip van Winkles rose from all the sofas. They were ancient New York editors, architects and authors who had acted
in some cases as diplomats and consuls abroad and who, at the
sound of our footsteps, roused themselves from their afternoon
naps, plucking their beards, like the old men of Homer.
Then, presently gathering in a circle, they began to talk, ex-
changing recollections of the acting of Macready and Walter
Savage Landor's style and the days when they had served as
attachés with Lowell and Motley. My venerable uncle by marriage remembered hearing a speech that Lamartine delivered in
the Paris of Louis Philippe. To me it was delightful, but
Homer himself was scarcely more remote from the Greenwich
Village I knew and my friends who were writers, Russians,
East Indians, Japanese and as often Italians and Swedes as
men of my own nationality from Iowa and Kansas. I had always assumed that one had to be outside society, in the narrower sense, in order to be inside the world I cared for; and
this was no longer an "old American" world.

I realized that I had grown up in a crowded little corner of
the country, with windows opening towards Europe and closed
towards the West—of which, as my writing showed, I knew
next to nothing; but, presently repatriated, I was a convert to
a state of mind, not in any important sense to a mere visible
country. As an actual nation the United States was nothing
greatly to boast about, for its virtue was largely the result of
fortunate conditions; and for this I felt only the affection that
people usually feel,—whether Welshmen or Indo-Chinese,—
for the lands of their birth. I detested the giant Business and
its more and more veiled will-to-power, and what I came to
cherish was a certain philosophy or point of view that one

found expressed, quite clearly, in the American scriptures, the great books of the eighteen-fifties, by Melville and Whitman especially, that had much in common with Lincoln and with Jefferson and Paine. These books conveyed the uniqueness of the American tradition, a line that was paralleled by other lines that ran through other American writers but that ran also through writers of other countries, while *this* line had no parallel in Europe or elsewhere, for it sprang from the nature of the republic, its essence and aim. It expressed a country that was settled "by the people of all nations," as Melville said, and that "all nations" might therefore "claim for their own,"— in short, the cradle or the germ of the world state of the future in which all men were "children of an equal brood."

That to foster this germ was the mission of the country the greatest American writers had thought, and Whitman went on to say that America, the "inheritor of the past," was in consequence the "custodian of the future" of mankind. Melville's deduction from this larger premise was that American writers should forthwith take "the practical lead in the world," although neither Melville nor Whitman foresaw the world wars that were coming or the cultural retreat and decline that were inevitably to follow. They could not have foreseen the reactionary notions that American critics were to adopt, while the most influential literary circles denounced as outmoded and vulgar the great beliefs that were basic in the history of the country. But if they had foreseen all this, would not these writers have said with Blake that "without contraries is no progression" and that without periodical returns to the irrational forces of myth and sleep humanity cannot maintain its intelligence and will? That, for the rest, their ideas were not of their own time alone but had a long future before them, and a long past behind, these writers would have been more convinced than ever. They spoke for a democratic socialized world with a humanist philosophy based on the positive elements of all religions; and this was the world that I too hoped to see.